The Costs of Poor Health Habits

THE COSTS OF
POOR HEALTH HABITS

Willard G. Manning

Emmett B. Keeler

Joseph P. Newhouse

Elizabeth M. Sloss

Jeffrey Wasserman

A RAND Study

Harvard University Press
Cambridge, Massachusetts
London, England

Library of Congress Cataloging-in-Publication Data

The Costs of poor health habits / Willard G.
Manning . . . [et al.].
    p.   cm.
  Includes bibliographical references and index.
  ISBN 0-674-17485-2 (alk. paper)
  1. Health behavior—Economic aspects.
  I. Manning, Willard G.
  [DNLM: 1. Alcohol Drinking—economics.
2. Costs and Cost Analysis.   3. Health Behavior.
4. Health Services—economics.   5. Life Style.
6. Smoking—economics.
W 74 C8425]
RA776.9.C69   1991
338.4′33621—dc20
DNLM/DLC
for Library of Congress   91-7043
                                                   CIP

Contents

Preface

In 1988 the five of us completed a study on the external costs of three poor health habits: smoking, drinking heavily, and not exercising. By external costs we mean the costs imposed on others by people who have these habits. Such costs arise from various sources. The ones we considered were collectively financed programs; for example, health insurance, group life insurance, retirement pensions, and lifetime taxes on earnings. We also considered the value of property damaged and lives lost in traffic accidents as the result of excessive drinking. What we found is that smoking, heavy drinking, and lack of exercise have high costs. And although some of this cost falls on the individuals who have these habits, a major portion is paid by others.

In 1989 we presented our results in two articles: "The Taxes of Sin: Do Smokers and Drinkers Pay Their Way?" in the *Journal of the American Medical Association*, 261 (March 17, 1989) and "The External Costs of a Sedentary Lifestyle" in the *American Journal of Public Health*, 79 (June 1989). These articles and subsequent reports in the media have created considerable interest in our results and the analyses that generated them—in part because they have implications for taxes on tobacco and alcoholic beverages, the so-called sin taxes.

The purpose of this book is to present our analyses of the costs of all three habits in greater detail, describing the results and our approach, data, and methods more fully than was possible in the journal articles. Inquiries about the study indicate that the book may have interest for a very diverse readership: for example, federal, state, and local policymakers; researchers in health sciences, health policy, and other academic disciplines; insurance companies; corporate benefits managers; health and consumer advocates; the producers of tobacco and alcohol products; and taxpayers.

To serve the various interests and purposes these audiences would bring to the book, we have adopted the following strategy.

Chapter 1 provides a nontechnical summary of the issues, our estimates of the external costs, what determines those costs, and what can be done about them. It is intended for those who are primarily interested in the magnitude of the problem and its implications for policies and programs aimed at improving people's health habits, lowering the external costs, and/or making people with poor habits pay at least the equivalent of those costs.

The rest of the book is intended for researchers in health sciences, health policy, and other fields, who are interested in our concepts, assumptions, data, and methods, as well as results that are not reported in Chapter 1. We assume throughout this portion that readers are familiar with economic concepts, terms, and analytic techniques. We have tried, however, insofar as possible, to make the discussion comprehensible to other readers who might be concerned about the nature and rigor of our analyses and, thus, the scientific credibility of our results. At the end we include several technical appendixes.

We would like to acknowledge the help, advice, and support that we received in our study of health habits and in producing this book. Our work was conducted at the RAND Corporation, supported by a grant from the National Center for Health Services Research and Health Care Technology Assessment (NCHSR/HCTA), now the Agency for Health Care Policy and Research (AHCPR). We are particularly indebted to Jean Carmody, Stephen Marcus, and Selwyn Waingrow, project officers for NCHSR/HCTA, for comments and advice. We are also indebted to Erik Farag of the same organization, and to RAND for its support in producing the book.

We greatly appreciate the assistance of many colleagues: Thomas Vogt (Kaiser Health Services Research Center of Portland, Oregon) provided suggestions and guidance throughout the work. We benefited from discussions with Bernard Friedman, George Keeler, and Robert Leu. Robert Amler helped with the Health Risk Appraisal model. Jerry Green, Lester Lave, Charles Phelps, and Kenneth Warner, as well as our RAND colleagues James Kahan, Bridger Mitchell, and James P. Smith, gave careful reviews that markedly improved our report. Bernadette Benjamin and Janet Hanley provided meticulous programming and data management, and Martha Cooper cheerfully converted our various inputs into typed, legible English. Joyce

Peterson deserves our special thanks for revising the material to make it accessible to a wider readership.

Finally, the opinions and conclusions expressed in this book are ours alone and should not be construed as representing the policies or opinions of the Agency for Health Care Policy and Research or its predecessor, the RAND Corporation, or any of the people acknowledged above.

The Costs of Poor Health Habits

An Overview

Many signs suggest that the nation's health consciousness has increased phenomenally over the last two decades. "Health-help" is a major category of the self-help books that pour out of publishing houses. Many news programs and newspapers regularly feature health segments. And a veritable industry of health newsletters and magazines has sprung up, spreading the latest word on the nature and benefits of good nutrition and other health habits.

Health news has become big news, and people seem to be responding. Consider just a few indicators. Most neighborhoods are now served by far more health clubs than hospitals. That fact and the strong sales of exercise gear indicate that exercise has become a major leisure-time activity. People evidently are also taking nutritional advice to heart, to judge by the advertising dollars the beef and pork industries are spending to counter claims that fish and chicken are "better for you." As for smoking, health consciousness has obviously disturbed the market: Philip Morris now publishes, and widely distributes, a free magazine extolling the "smoking lifestyle" and championing "smokers' rights."

Despite all these signals that health awareness has improved, statistics indicate that we are not yet on the high road to health. In 1986, the national tab was $24 billion for tobacco products and $18 billion for alcoholic drinks.[1] Between 1977 and 1983, the proportion of the population who smoked dropped by 10 percent, but the fraction of people who were "less active than their contemporaries" and the fraction of heavy drinkers rose by 12 percent and 28 percent, respectively (Schoenborn and Cohen, 1986).[2]

Given these statistics, it is little wonder that improving health habits has become a significant concern. The prevalence of unhealthy habits has prompted large-scale efforts to promote healthy habits, and has raised questions of how government can influence behavior that ultimately impairs health and shortens life. Indeed, health promotion has been a major element of the Surgeon General's agenda for two and a half decades.

Belief in the efficacy of good health habits prompted Joseph Califano, at the time Secretary of Health and Human Services, to say in the 1979 Surgeon General's report: "A wealth of scientific research reveals that the key to whether a person will be healthy or sick, live a long life or die prematurely, can be found in several simple personal habits . . . One study found that people who practiced seven of these simple habits lived, on the average, eleven years longer than those who practiced none of them." These seven habits are not smoking; limiting consumption of alcohol; keeping weight within normal limits; reducing intake of fats, salt, and sugar; exercising regularly; having periodic medical checkups that screen for high blood pressure and certain cancers; and observing speed laws and using seat belts.

Social concern thus far has focused on how health habits affect the health and well-being of individuals, their families, and the social fabric. There is another compelling concern, however, that is not often considered—the economic costs that people who have these habits impose on others. These "external costs," their magnitude, and what can be done to lower them are the subjects of this book. The habits we focus on are smoking, drinking, and lack of exercise.

Why Do External Costs Matter?

People with poor health habits can impose costs on others in various ways, not all of them financial. But the financial costs of health care are among the most obvious and significant—and the rise in those costs has been a critical public concern for the last two decades. In 1950, spending on health care accounted for 4.4 percent of gross national product (GNP). By 1988, the percentage was 11.1; and projections are for still higher costs in the future.

It is true that there is little empirical evidence that people with bad health habits use more health care, or that their increased use of such care is the prime mover behind escalating health expenditures. Indeed, health care costs have risen while smoking has fallen sharply. Nevertheless, poor health habits, including smoking, heavy drinking, and lack of exercise, are considered to be among the primary causes of illness and death in the United States. It seems plausible that a healthier nation (or corporation or union) might have to spend less on health care.

The increase in medical costs has certainly provided an impetus for government, public and private health insurers, and the employers who pay the premiums, to support programs that encourage better health habits. According to the Office of Technology Assessment (1985), cigarette smoking may account annually for 5.3 million person-years of life lost, $22 billion of medical care costs, and $43 billion in lost productivity. Alcohol abuse may account annually for 22,400 traffic deaths, 15,400 other deaths, $11.9 billion of medical care costs, and $20.6 billion in lost productivity (U.S. Department of Transportation, 1986; Luce and Schweitzer, 1978). To date there has been no similar research on the costs of sedentary living, but a reasonable estimate is that they are about one-tenth of the costs of smoking.[3]

People with these unhealthy habits, and their families, certainly bear some of the costs directly. They lose wages, pay a portion of their medical costs, and suffer from disability and premature death. These are what we define as internal costs. The costs we emphasize in this book are "external costs": that is, what smokers cost nonsmokers, what heavy drinkers cost abstainers or moderate drinkers, and what voluntarily inactive people cost those who exercise regularly. As we shall see, the existence of external costs is a major reason for government concern about health habits. Moreover, the magnitude of these external costs can be used to gauge the appropriate level of excise taxes on cigarettes and alcohol.

Collectively financed programs are a leading source of external cost. Such programs may cover some or all of medical care costs, sick leave, life insurance, nursing home care, and retirement pensions. Typically, the premiums or taxes for these benefits do not vary according to a person's health habits (this situation is especially likely in employer group health and retirement plans and public programs). That is, if John Doe and Jane Roe both have health insurance coverage through their employer, their premiums will be the same even though John is, say, a heavy drinker and Jane has only an occasional drink. If John uses more medical care than Jane—because of drinking-related health problems—Jane is in effect subsidizing his heavy drinking through the insurance program. The same is true for other collectively financed costs.

At the same time, if his drinking makes John work less and retire earlier, he will pay fewer taxes for collectively financed nursing home care, Medicare, and Social Security. In other words, he will pay lower "taxes on earnings" that support nursing home care and retirement pensions.[4] Yet he may benefit as much as, or more than, Jane from those programs. If John kills himself in an automobile accident, however, he may have paid into Social Security and not collected any benefits. Then, indirectly, Jane gains financially from his premature death.

Collectively financed programs and taxes on earnings are not the only sources of external costs for smoking and heavy drinking. Although there is considerable debate about the magnitude of effects for "passive smoking," the Surgeon General has estimated that 2,400 deaths per year result from breathing air filled with tobacco smoke (USDHHS, 1986). These lost lives are another source of external costs. To the extent that passive smoking generates health care and other collectively financed costs, a portion of those costs is also paid by nonsmokers.

For heavy drinking, other sources of external costs are loss of innocent lives and property damage caused by drunk-driving accidents, and other crimes committed "under the influence." Some of the property damage is the drinker's, and many drunk drivers are their own victims. We do not consider those costs (or the costs of passive smoking within families) as external.[5] Although they are part of the total costs to society, by our definition they are internal costs to the drinker.

To return to our example, if John's accident claims lives other than his own, it imposes very high external costs.[6] No one knows exactly how many auto fatalities are caused by drunk drivers, but research suggests the percentage is large. A study of 44,000 fatal accidents indicates that 42 percent of the drivers involved were intoxicated (USDHHS, 1987, pp. 8–9).

Drinking is implicated in many other crimes that generate high external costs from property loss and damage, as well as from injuries and death of victims. There is some controversy about the drinking-crime nexus, but statistics show that many crimes other than drunk driving are committed under the influence of alcohol (ibid.). These crimes too impose costs on the criminal justice system.

Regardless of what is known or not known about how smoking, heavy drinking, and lack of exercise affect health and well-being, it is possible to measure external costs. The nature and dimensions of these costs provide a strong economic justification and political rationale for government (and private) efforts to curb these habits. The costs also, indirectly, provide evidence about how these poor health habits affect health and longevity.

Estimating the External Costs of Poor Health Habits

An enormous amount of research has been done on the (variously defined) costs of smoking, less on the costs of drinking, and much less on the costs of exercise, which is a relatively new area of interest. Widely varying estimates of these costs have emerged. In the case of smoking, the estimated annual costs have ranged from $50 billion to $66 billion (in 1986 dollars).[7] Apart from case studies on the costs of alcohol abuse to individual corporations and industries, only two comprehensive studies of drinking costs have appeared so far. One (Berry and Boland, 1977) estimated that costs in 1971 were just over $85 billion [(1986 dollars)]; the other (Harwood et al., 1984) estimated that in 1983 costs were $129 billion [(1986 dollars)]. No comparable figures are available for lack of exercise.

Some differences in cost estimates arise because different studies use different data and make different assumptions. Other differences result from the fact that studies ask different questions. (These factors are discussed at length in Appendix A.) We address two questions here: (1) When an individual decides to smoke, drink heavily, or not exercise, what are the lifetime external costs—that is, by how much does society subsidize these habits?[8] (2) What drives these costs?

To estimate the lifetime external costs of these bad habits, we considered how they affect life expectancy, use of collectively financed programs, and taxes on earnings. For smoking, we also included costs of fires caused by smokers, and for drinking, the costs of drunk driving—lost lives and property damage—and crime. Table 1–1 shows the components of the external costs.

Our study utilized a number of data sources, primarily the RAND Health Insurance Experiment (HIE) and the National Health Interview Survey (NHIS). The HIE, a randomized trial of alternative health insurance arrangements, was our primary data source for people younger than 60. Families at six sites participated in the study from 1974 to 1982. The HIE data contain a wealth of information on habits and medical reasons for use of care for 5,800 people. The HIE did not enroll anyone aged 62 or older. For information on people over 60, we used data from the 1983 NHIS supplement, which was admin-

TABLE 1-1.   Components of external costs

Collectively financed costs
    Medical care
    Sick leave
    Group life insurance
    Nursing home care
    Retirement pension
    Insurance to cover direct costs

Direct costs
    Motor vehicle accidents (lost lives, property damage, other)
    Criminal justice
    Fires

Taxes on earnings

istered to 22,148 people (20 percent of the NHIS sample) by the National Center for Health Statistics. The Current Population Survey, the Centers for Disease Control, and other sources provided supplementary information.

Our analysis differed from previous studies in several ways that should improve on their estimates.

(1) To estimate costs of medical care, most previous work has relied on imputed differences in use by people with and without poor health habits. These imputed differences are often judged from differences in mortality for the two groups. Being sick, using medical services, and dying are correlated, but not perfectly. For example, if John Doe is a smoker and has a quick and deadly heart attack, he will have little medical expense from heart disease. Prorating medical expenses by death rates would give the opposite impression. In contrast, we based our estimates on observed differences in the actual use of medical care among people with varying health habits.

(2) For people with a specific bad habit, previous work has tended to attribute all the differential costs of medical care, sick leave, and the like to the adverse effects of that habit. There are two problems with this attribution. First, a host of other factors can affect general health and use of medical care. People who have bad health habits may differ in those other factors. (For example, smokers tend to be less well educated.) In addition, bad health habits are often themselves positively correlated—for example, people who smoke are likely to drink as well. When studies attribute all the differences to

one habit, they probably overestimate its costs. In other words, when they examine each habit in isolation, they effectively double count. To overcome these problems, we controlled for the other characteristics of smokers, heavy drinkers, and sedentary people, including their other bad health habits. We could do this because our two main data sources contained details on all three habits.

(3) Previous studies have focused primarily on medical costs and sick leave to estimate the costs of habits. They have failed to consider the potential effects that bad health habits have on early retirement and disability, which can be considerable.[9] Our analysis examined all collectively financed costs.

(4) Studies that look at use of all medical services may incorrectly estimate costs. It seems unlikely, for example, that smoking explains why a smoker is treated for food poisoning and a nonsmoker is not.[10] To allow for this problem, we tested the sensitivity of our results to alternative assumptions about what categories of treatment are related to each habit. We analyzed differences in use for all care (excluding maternity and well-care), as well as use for diagnoses that have been linked to the habits.

(5) Much of the previous research looks only at current costs. It is true that some costs are immediate, for example, costs of smoking-caused fires and of drunk-driving accidents. For these costs we divided the estimated national annual costs by the annual packs of cigarettes or excess ounces of liquor consumed. Smoking, heavy drinking, and lack of exercise also have long-term effects that may result in savings as well as costs. For example, both smokers and nonsmokers are covered by collectively financed programs. Smoking causes or aggravates a number of health problems, and it reduces life expectancy. The practical effect is that although current and former smokers may need more medical care while they are alive, they will collect less in pension benefits than nonsmokers will. If we consider only current costs, former and current smokers will seem to be subsidized by nonsmokers. If we factor in the long-term costs, the subsidy drops because smokers in effect subsidize the pensions and nursing home care of people who have never smoked. They do so by paying premiums and taxes to finance pensions and nursing home care, but collecting fewer benefits.

(6) If we consider long-term effects, we have to discount future costs, such as pensions, in order to make comparable costs that occur at different times. A dollar paid into a pension plan today, for instance, is worth more than a dollar received fifteen years from now

(even without inflation). A person can invest today's dollar and earn interest; when fifteen years are over, that dollar will be worth more than two dollars (at 5 percent interest). If we fail to take this effect into account by discounting, we overestimate long-term costs.

Discounting is especially important when we look at policies with long-term effects. If we consider only the economic costs of smoking, a program that costs x dollars today to reduce the effects of smoking should be considered practical only if it saves more than x dollars in the future. If it does not, we would be better off investing the x dollars to pay for the future costs when they arise.

The "correct" discount rate is always a matter of controversy. The cost estimates in this part of the book reflect a 5 percent (real) discount rate. In Chapters 4 through 7 we show the sensitivity of our estimates to this figure.

Table 1–2 summarizes both the external and internal costs of smoking, heavy drinking, and lack of exercise and indicates the major components of those costs. Our estimates represent the differences between costs for people who have these habits and costs for people who do not. It is important to understand who we mean by "people who do not." We do not mean actual people who have never smoked, people who have never had a drink, or people who exercise. Instead, the figures in Table 1–2 result from comparisons between people with the bad habits and people who are like them in other characteristics and habits, except for the habit in question. Our preferred comparison group for smokers is a group of "nonsmoking smokers" who are like the smokers in all respects except that they have never smoked. We can thereby derive a more realistic estimate of the costs that can be attributed to the particular habit.

Smoking

Because smoking shortens life expectancy, the internal costs to smokers and their families are high. Smoking reduces the (undiscounted) life expectancy of a 20-year-old by 4.3 years, or, as Table 1–2 shows, 137 minutes per pack of cigarettes. Smokers also pay 7 cents per pack more on out-of-pocket medical costs, and lose 86 cents in wages and salaries. Finally, the retail price of a pack of cigarettes is about $1 per pack.

But what are the external costs? We have said that our estimates are based on the difference in costs if a smoker retained all his or her other characteristcs and habits but had never smoked. In other

TABLE 1-2. Analysis of the costs of poor health habits

Source	Cost Per Unit[a]			
	Pack of Cigarettes	Excess Ounce of Ethanol	Any Ounce of Ethanol	Mile-Not-Walked
External (dollars)				
Collectively financed	+0.05	+0.20	+0.08	+0.23
Immediate costs[b]	+0.02	+0.93[c]	+0.37[d]	0
Taxes on earnings	−0.09	−0.06	−0.02	−0.01
Total external costs	+0.15	+1.19	+0.48	+0.24
Internal				
Loss of life (minutes)				
Own[e]	−137	−20	[f]	−21
Other family[e]	−5	−6	−2	0
Medical out of pocket (dollars)	+0.07	+0.06	+0.02	+0.10
Lost wages and salaries[g] (dollars)	+0.86	+0.66	+0.24	+0.19
Cost of product (dollars)	1.00	1.00	1.00	0

NOTE: One ounce = 2.2 drinks. External costs = (sum of costs) minus taxes on earnings. All dollar amounts are in 1986 dollars. To convert to June 1990 dollars, multiply by 1.185.

a. Costs and packs/ounces/miles discounted at 5 percent.

b. Fires, neonatal care, innocent lives and property lost in drunk driving, and costs of criminal justice.

c. Assumes all costs due to drinks in excess of five per day by heavy drinkers.

d. Assumes ethanol costs proportional to amount drunk.

e. Not discounted.

f. Because health effects of moderate drinking are controversial, loss of life expectancy was not computed for "any drink."

g. Work loss, early retirement, and early death.

words, we are asking how much more or less would have been consumed in specific services and benefits, how much more would have been paid in premiums and taxes that finance such services and benefits, and how much less fire damage would have been caused. *The difference amounts to $1,000 in lifetime external costs per smoker. Divided by the number of packs smoked over a lifetime, this difference costs other people about 15 cents per pack.*

Heavy Drinking

Estimating the costs of heavy drinking is complicated by having to distinguish not only between drinkers and nondrinkers, but also among drinkers by how much they consume. The rationale is that any smoking is considered harmful, but the results of drinking are more ambiguous. Little evidence has been put forward that light-to-moderate drinking is harmful, and some studies have found benefits from it. Consequently, our analyses distinguished between moderate and heavy drinkers.

Following the practice of the National Center for Health Statistics, we defined moderate and heavy drinking based on people's prorated daily consumption of ethanol. Ethanol is the component of alcoholic beverages that intoxicates. An ounce of pure ethanol is contained in approximately 2.2 mixed drinks, 2.2 (4-ounce) glasses of wine, or 2.2 (12-ounce) cans of beer. We defined heavy drinking as the equivalent of two or more reported drinks a day. That may not sound like a great deal, but a comparison of what people say they drink with tax reports on alcohol sold indicates that people substantially under-report their actual drinking. Estimates of underreporting vary. For our purposes we assumed that people reported 40 percent of their consumption; in other words, they underreported by 60 percent. Thus, we assumed that two reported drinks equal five actual drinks.

Heavy drinking exacts a serious toll on drinkers and their families. At age 20, drinkers reduce their life expectancy by 1.55 years or 20 minutes per excess ounce of ethanol consumed per day. They pay 6 cents per excess ounce in higher out-of-pocket medical costs, and lose 66 cents per excess ounce in wages and salaries. An "excess" ounce is the ethanol contained in the third drink and any additional reported drinks per day.

As for the external costs, we based our estimates on the differences between costs for a heavy drinker and for a "controlled" heavy drinker, that is, a heavy drinker who retained all his other characteristics and habits but whose average daily consumption was *just under* two reported (five actual) drinks. In other words, he consumed no "excess" ounces of ethanol. *The lifetime external costs of excess drinking amount to $19,000 per heavy drinker. This translates to $1.19 per excess ounce of ethanol consumed, or 54 cents per excess drink.*

In thinking about the adverse effects of drinking, especially property damage and loss of innocent lives, it is impractical to base our estimate of the external costs on excess ounces only. By definition, excess ounces must be preceded by "nonexcess" ounces consumed. Further, it may be simple to draw the line of excess analytically, but not behaviorally: for some people, the first ounce may be "excessive."[11] *When we average the external costs over all alcohol consumption, every ounce of ethanol has an external cost of 48 cents.* This translates to about 22 cents per mixed drink, per 4-ounce glass of wine, and per 12-ounce can of beer.

Lack of Exercise

The costs *to* and *for* sedentary people are quite high. Such people pay 10 cents more per mile-not-traveled in higher out-of-pocket costs and lose 19 cents of wages and salaries. Our analysis indicates that not exercising reduces the life expectancy of a 20-year-old by about ten months.

One study (Paffenbarger and Hyde, 1984) estimates that time spent in brisk walking is just returned (undiscounted) in later life and that the life-saving benefits of exercise are roughly proportional to the number of miles traveled in walking, jogging, or running. Thus, joggers can get back double their exercise time in life expectancy if they go twice as far as walkers in the same elapsed time. Over a lifetime, ten months spent in walking is consistent with a moderate exercise program that averages a mile a day.

Surprisingly, the lifetime *external costs* of a sedentary life-style are actually higher than the external costs of smoking. We estimate that each extra mile a sedentary person travels gives him or her 21 (undiscounted) extra minutes of life and saves the rest of society 24 cents in discounted external costs.[12] *Conversely, the external cost to society is 24 cents for each mile-not-traveled, which translates to $1,650 in lifetime external costs per sedentary person.*

What Drives These Costs?

Our estimates of external costs are based on analysis of the components listed in Table 1–1.

For Smoking

The external costs of smoking are largely driven by medical costs, pensions, and taxes on earnings. Smokers and former smokers generate more in medical costs than they would if they had never smoked. When we compared their use of services with that of nonsmokers, we found that whereas former smokers had 12 percent more episodes of outpatient care, curiously enough, current smokers were no more likely than never smokers to visit a doctor. We included former smokers because their heavier use of medical care may be caused by the effects of their previous smoking. The picture was different for hospital care. Smokers and former smokers were hospitalized much more: current smokers had 38 percent, and former smokers 13 percent, more hospitalizations.

Smokers also had lower taxes on earnings. Some of these external costs were offset by the reduction in life expectancy, which lowered retirement and disability costs for these individuals.

For Heavy Drinking

Considering only the same cost components used in the smoking and exercise analyses, we found that the lifetime external cost for a heavy drinker is only $4,600. This value is driven largely by the differences in medical care, sick leave, and taxes on earnings. Most of the costs for medical care and sick leave result from differences for former drinkers. Just as we regarded former cigarette smokers as "ever" smokers in estimating the costs of smoking, we regarded former drinkers as though they were heavy or problem drinkers.

Current drinking has little effect on outpatient care. In fact, "abstainers" had 13 to 17 percent more outpatient episodes than light drinkers. But former drinkers had 22 percent more outpatient episodes than light drinkers. Former drinkers also had 110 percent more hospital admissions than light drinkers, and significantly more sick leave. Among current drinkers we found no significant difference for light and heavy drinkers on any of these counts. While drinking does not have the drastic effect on life expectancy that smoking has, heavy drinkers tend to retire earlier and thus have even greater reductions in taxes on earnings than smokers do.

What accounts for the difference between the $4,600 in external costs for these components and the $42,000 estimate we presented above? By far, the largest external costs of drinking are imposed by loss of innocent lives, property damage, and their concomitant effects on public systems and programs. We estimate that innocent lives lost in alcohol-related traffic accidents alone cost society $24,000 per heavy drinker. Loss of property, strain on the criminal justice system, and social programs add another $14,000 per heavy drinker. These costs account for a large part of the difference between the external costs of drinking and those of smoking and lack of exercise.

For Lack of Exercise

The primary external cost factors for sedentary people are higher use of medical care, work loss, and taxes on earnings. We found that lack of exercise had relatively little effect on outpatient medical costs. Moderate exercisers had 12 percent fewer outpatient episodes, but heavy exercisers had only 8 percent fewer, than light exercisers. The story for inpatient care was different, but only for strenuous exercisers and diagnoses related to poor health habits. These individuals had about 30 percent lower use rates than people who did not exercise. If work loss is any indication of general health, however, exercisers clearly benefit (and have lower external costs): moderate exercisers had 18 percent, and strenuous exercisers 32 percent, less work loss than did light exercisers.

In examining the costs of a sedentary life-style, we contrasted moderate and heavy exercisers only with those inactive people who had no constraints on their role or physical activity. Our purpose was to avoid attributing to exercise the adverse effects of health problems that simultaneously raise costs and limit the individual's ability to exercise.

How Reasonable Are Our Estimates?

We believe they are reasonable, even conservative. The study does have some limitations, which are discussed later and summarized in Chapter 7. When we tested our estimates in analyses that used different assumptions and different data, they fell about midway in the range of estimates generated by these assumptions. The tests support our belief that the estimates presented above are approximately correct.

Table 1–3 summarizes the results of our sensitivity analyses, in which we used different data or made different assumptions than we did in the base-case analyses. For each habit we conducted a separate cost analysis (1) using data from the NHIS for all age groups; (2) comparing costs of people who had the habits with costs of people who actually did not (rather than our constructed group of, for example, nonsmoking smokers); and (3) limiting medical costs to care only for diagnoses possibly related to poor health habits.[13] The second type of analysis should give an upper bound on costs because it

TABLE 1-3.   Estimates of external costs with different data or assumptions

| | Cost Per Unit[a] (dollars) | | |
| | | Excess Ounce of | |
Case	Pack of Cigarettes	Ethanol[b]	Mile-Not-Walked
Base case	0.15	1.19	0.24
NHIS data	0.20	1.16	0.54
Good habits group[c]	0.28	1.13	−0.09
Lower bound[d]	−0.15	1.08	0.10

a. Costs and packs/ounces discounted at 5 percent.

b. Results include constant cost of 93 cents for drunk driving and other drinking-related crimes.

c. Comparison group is people in samples who did not have the poor habit in question.

d. Medical care costs limited to diagnoses possibly related to habits; also, habit has no effect on time of retirement.

attributes all the differences in the two groups to the habit. The third should give a lower bound because it assumes that the habit has such limited health effects. We also conducted analyses (reported later) that considered total costs and included different assumptions about value of life lost, and so on.

Differences in Smoking Costs

The analysis using only the NHIS data produced an estimated external cost of 20 cents per pack of cigarettes, because of differences in work loss in that sample. Comparing smokers with people in the sample who have actually never smoked gave a high estimate of 28 cents per pack. Limiting the analysis to medical costs for habit-related diagnoses gave a lower bound that actually went into negative numbers: every pack smoked represented a 15-cent subsidy for non-smokers.

If we were to expand our external cost definition to include the costs of passive smoking, neonatal complications caused by mothers' smoking, and other costs to individuals other than the smoker, the external costs would range up to 52 cents per pack. We have considered most of those costs "internal" because they are borne largely by the smoker's family.

If we were to add the internal costs of disability and premature death to our estimate, the costs could range from 78 cents to $5 per pack, depending on how we valued the lost years of life. In contrast, if we did not discount costs, smoking would actually have negative external costs. In effect, each pack smoked would save society 91 cents: because smokers die younger, they do not cost society as much in pensions and nursing home care.[14]

Differences in Drinking Costs

Our results for heavy drinking were not sensitive to data or to assumptions other than those used to estimate the costs of drunk driving. This outcome reflects the overwhelming effects on costs of damages caused by drunk driving. The external costs would have been even higher than our estimated $1.19 per excess ounce if (1) we had based our estimates of lives lost in drunk-driving accidents on figures only from states that test accident victims more thoroughly than others for evidence of alcohol abuse; (2) we had included external costs generated by families of alcohol abusers (insured costs of care for fetal alcohol syndrome, sick leave, disability, and so on); and (3) we had used a less conservative estimate of the value of a lost life (say $3 million instead of our $1.67 million per life). Together these changes would add 62 cents to our estimate, for a total of $1.81 per excess ounce.

Internal costs are much higher because of the value of the drinker's own life. We show later that such costs could amount to up to $2 per ounce. Another internal cost is the price of the drinks themselves, about $1 per ounce.

Differences in Lack of Exercise Costs

Our results for lack of exercise were sensitive to different data sets and assumptions. Using the NHIS data for all age groups more than doubled the estimated external costs for the base case. The primary reason is that the medical costs for young people in that sample who do not exercise were much larger than for those in the HIE sample.

When we used actual moderate and heavy exercisers as the comparison group, in order to derive an upper bound on external costs, we found that the effect was in the opposite direction. The negative cost of 9 cents indicated that exercisers actually have higher external costs than sedentary people. This difference reflects two factors. First, actual exercisers are healthier in other ways than inactive people, so they have a greater life expectancy than the "active inactive" comparison group used in the base case. This means that they collect more old-age benefits. Second, sedentary people spend less than exercisers on medical services because they have other characteristics associated with lower medical use (less education, for example). They pay the same premiums as exercisers but use less medical care and get fewer old-age benefits. Actual sedentary people, in fact, subsidize exercisers. But if they exercised, they would do so even more.

Limiting medical costs to diagnoses related to exercise had the expected effect of lowering net external costs. The difference was much greater than we found in the case of heavy drinking.

In all, the results of the sensitivity analyses suggest that our estimates of external costs are well within the range of possible estimates, and somewhat on the conservative side. Thus, they provide a sound basis for considering what might be done to lower the magnitude of the costs.

We must point out that there is a chicken-and-egg issue about exercise and health status. The links between exercise, fitness, and health are well established, and we controlled for as many other differences between exercisers and nonexercisers as we could. Nevertheless, we cannot be sure that inactivity causes poor health, or vice versa. The issue might be settled by a randomized experiment on the effects of exercise promotion, but such an experiment has not been run. We believe, and epidemiological evidence suggests, that exercise is advantageous to one's health; but we cannot be certain that this is so.

What Can Be Done about the External Costs of These Habits?

Our cost estimates demonstrate that smoking, heavy drinking, and sedentary life-styles rack up impressive external costs. Clearly, society has a big stake in lowering such costs, but how can we go about it? Is there some overall solution, or does each problem require its own "package" of solutions?

Education and Other Alternatives

One obvious mechanism is education, and it looks promising. By education we mean more than formal education programs, offered through schools or other agencies. These might provide a mechanism to prevent young people from developing bad health habits, but their potential is still unclear. We are talking instead about the spread of public information concerning health habits.

It can hardly be coincidental that the level of smoking in the United States has dropped so dramatically since the Surgeon General's first official statement, in 1964, linking lung cancer and smoking. Since that time the public has been inundated with information about the detrimental effects of smoking, and per capita consumption fell by 23 percent between 1965 and 1986. It is no longer considered sophisticated to smoke. One writer wryly compared smoking's downward slide in public acceptance to the fate of public spitting—and speculated that ashtrays might soon be as rare as spittoons.

The growth of the exercise "industry" also suggests how powerful informal education can be. Articles and public discussions abound on, for example, how exercise lowers cholesterol, high blood pressure, risk of heart attack, and how it increases life expectancy and works more effectively than dieting to reduce weight. As this kind of information has increased, joggers have become an increasingly familiar sight, in and out of season.

In short, the public seems receptive to information about health habits, and education presents an attractive option. To judge from the case of smoking, however, it may take considerable time to affect poor health habits and thus their external costs. Furthermore, educational efforts may have to be tailored and delivered differently for different audiences. Finally, public attitudes will have to be considered.

Public attitudes figured in recommendations made by Surgeon General C. Everett Koop in May 1989, when he was inaugurating a national campaign against drunk driving. The power of advertising and association was implicit in several of his recommendations: (1) banning the appearance of athletes and other celebrities in alcohol commercials, (2) prohibiting alcohol manufacturers from sponsoring athletic events, and (3) matching the level of alcohol advertising with "equivalent exposure" for health messages about the risk from alcohol.

These recommendations raise constitutional and other legal issues, as did the proposal to ban tobacco advertising on television. That ban was imposed, and one can speculate that the absence of advertising contributed to the drop in smoking: because advertising was not continually reinforcing positive images of smoking, public attitudes were more open to change.

The Arguments for Taxation

For alcohol and tobacco, there is another frequently considered option—raising taxes on cigarettes and beverages. As the health consequences of smoking and heavy drinking have become apparent, taxes have been viewed as a potential vehicle for limiting consumption and improving public health. That aim underlies the Surgeon General's recommendation (USDHHS, 1989) to substantially increase federal and state excise taxes on beer, wine, and distilled spirits, and index those taxes to the rate of inflation.

This argument for taxation has sometimes collided with the principle of consumer sovereignty—that is, people should be free to drink or smoke as long as they are willing to pay the costs. But those costs should include external costs as well as internal. So the principle implicitly supports setting excise taxes at a level that covers external social costs.[15]

Even if people disagree about the appropriate incentives for making choices about healthy life-styles, we suspect there would be little dissent that, at a minimum, individuals should bear the costs of their actions. In other words, we can think of little or no reason to let people who have poor health habits impose costs and risks on those who do not share those habits.

Taxing tobacco products and alcohol is an economically efficient, fair means of discouraging consumption—if excise taxes cover at least the external costs we have been discussing. We have estimated those costs at 15 cents per pack of cigarettes and 48 cents per ounce of alcohol consumed. How do these costs relate to existing excise taxes? *Our estimate of the external cost of smoking, 15 cents per pack, is well below the average (state plus federal) excise and sales taxes of 37 cents per pack.*[16] If, however, we were to treat all lives lost from passive smoking and fires as external costs, the 37 cent tax rate would approximately equal the estimated external cost of 38 cents. *In contrast, our estimate of the external cost of alcohol, 48 cents per ounce, is well above the average (state plus federal) excise and sales taxes of 20 cents per ounce.*[17]

The data on taxes for our earlier articles (Keeler et al., 1989; Manning et al., 1989) are from the mid-1980s. Since then the federal government and several of the states have increased their excise taxes on alcohol and tobacco products. By 1989 cigarette taxes averaged 39 cents per pack (1986 dollars), and the Omnibus Budget Reconciliation Act (OBRA) of 1990 added 8 cents per pack (about 7 cents in 1986 dollars) in two increments of 4 cents each. Taxes on alcohol have risen to about 25 cents per ounce of ethanol (1986 dollars) from the combined effects of changes in state taxes and OBRA 1990.

By our calculations, raising taxes on alcohol can be firmly justified on the grounds of economic efficiency—that is, the taxes now imposed do not equal the external costs of drinking. Smokers are already paying their way, if we judge solely on grounds of economic efficiency.

Two other arguments against taxing cigarettes—and alcohol as well—are based on equity. First, the taxes are regressive.[18] In other words, alcohol and tobacco taxes constitute a higher percentage of income for poor people than for the affluent. Second; light drinkers could argue that heavy drinkers, not they, impose the high external costs. Therefore, raising taxes on their "nonexcess" ounces would be inequitable.

These arguments are easily countered. Consider first the argument that such taxes are regressive. Because alcohol and tobacco taxes each supply only 1 percent of federal revenues, rather small changes in the individual income tax structure can readily compensate for the effect that increased taxes have on income distribution—if such a change were deemed desirable.[19]

To the argument of light drinkers that raising alcohol taxes would affect them unfairly, there are two responses. First, suppose that the government must raise a given amount of revenue to finance expenditures that benefit society at large, such as basic research. This revenue can be raised from a variety of taxes, including excise taxes on alcohol. In this situation people who pay an average amount of other taxes and who consume less than the national population average of 1.7 reported drinks (more than 4 actual drinks) per day will benefit from shifting more of the tax burden to alcohol taxes and away from other taxes (for example, payroll taxes). In fact, three-quarters of adults drink less than this amount. Although 40 percent of the ounces drunk are "excess ounces," the 10 percent who are heavy drinkers consume two-thirds of the alcohol. They will pay the bulk of any increase in alcohol taxes.[20] In other words, greater reliance on alcohol taxes actually lowers the tax burden of light and moderate drinkers if total tax revenues are the same. Second, to the degree that higher taxes deter alcohol abuse (Cook, 1981; Cook and Tauchen, 1982; Grossman et al., 1987), external costs will decrease, and that decrease will offset the increased alcohol-tax burden of light and moderate drinkers. For a discussion of related issues, see Appendix H.

A different argument about taxing moderate drinking is that such drinking may have beneficial health effects; hence we should not discourage it. This thesis does not withstand scrutiny. First, the risk of a fatal traffic accident among youths aged 16–21 (data are not available for other age groups) rises with any consumption of alcohol. Because traffic accidents generate more than half of all external costs, it is dubious that there are any overall external benefits from moderate drinking. Second, based on our later analyses, there are very small or no effects on medical costs from moderate drinking.[21] Third, the bulk of any beneficial effects would accrue to the drinker and hence not be external costs.

Theoretically, excise taxes that charge a fixed rate per ounce are not as good as individualized taxes that impose the marginal external costs of their last ounce of consumption on each individual. The person who has a glass of wine with dinner every night and does not drive afterward is much less costly to others than the person who consumes seven drinks on Friday night and then drives home. Each of these drinkers consumes the same amount of alcohol per week, and so pays the same alcohol tax. Even if excise taxes are set to cover external costs on average, problem drinkers pay less than the full costs of their actions; some of their external costs are paid by non-problem drinkers. Unfortunately, it is difficult to distinguish problem drinkers from nonproblem drinkers at the point of sale; so tax rates are the same for everyone. Even though a flat tax that covers full external costs is imperfect, it is preferable to no tax or to the existing tax, which covers only part of the external cost of drinking. The increased tax will shift some of the burden of drinking back onto those who have caused the cost (see Appendix H for further discussion).

If the primary concern in taxing cigarettes and alcohol is the revenue-raising effect, then there is a strong economic argument for such taxes: there is less induced inefficiency than for some other kinds of taxes (Ramsey, 1927). For efficiency reasons, economists prefer taxes that raise money with a minimum of distortion to normal incentives from a free market. To put it cold-bloodedly, taxing addictive substances will have only modest effects on the behavior of those already addicted, an argument that could justify higher taxes on both alcohol and cigarettes.

Less cold-blooded are arguments that have supported other government and private efforts to prevent (or lower) consumption of these products. The first argument recognizes the regret expressed by most smokers, and their attempts to quit. Smoking tends to start in adolescence or early adulthood: about four of five smokers begin smoking before age 20 (Warner, 1986). At that age, people are usually not well informed and have not matured to the point where future ill health or mortality have much compelling reality for them. Because cigarettes and alcohol are addictive, it is more difficult to stop than to avoid starting the habit. There is some evidence that the proportion of those who smoke before they are 20 can be influenced by the level of taxes (Lewit and Coate, 1982). Thus, taxing cigarettes may lower the percentage who become addicted.[22]

Some may see this argument as paternalistic, but that is from the perspective of experimenting adolescents, not from the perspective of addicted adults who are trying to quit. The latter arguably determines the economically efficient tax. If the loss in life expectancy of 28 (discounted) minutes per pack is relevant to economic efficiency because of later regret, an economically efficient tax would be on the order of $5 per pack, the estimated value of the 28 minutes.

Irrespective of the merits of these other arguments, the difference between the actual tax and the external costs of alcohol is so large that, in our view, federal alcohol taxes should be increased. This is especially true for taxes on beer and wine, which are much lower (per ounce of ethanol) than taxes on distilled spirits.

To the degree that the external costs of alcohol abuse are caused by people who drink in bars and restaurants and then drive home intoxicated, there is a case for an additional tax on alcohol sold by the drink.[23] Ideally, society would tax drunk drivers to force them to pay the external costs of drunk driving. To some extent, fines, suspension of driving licenses, jail sentences, and civil liability attempt to do so. Still, the present legal system does not make, nor could it reasonably expect to make, drunk drivers fully bear the external costs of their actions, especially in cases where innocent lives are lost. Liability insurance, for example, partially shields drunk drivers from the consequences of their actions, and the likelihood of apprehension for driving under the influence is far from certain.

Differences in Tax Rates

Excise taxes on alcoholic beverages and cigarettes are imposed at the federal, state, and (in some cases) local levels. A look at the history and current diversity of tax rates gives no indication that the legislators who imposed them had any particular economic rationale in mind—beyond the exigencies of their respective budgets and a tendency of states that produce these items to tax their products at very low rates (see Appendix F).

At the turn of the century, excise taxes were the federal government's principal source of revenue. In 1902, 36 percent of federal tax revenue came from alcohol taxes and another 10 percent from tobacco taxes.[24] With the advent of income tax, the emphasis on progressive taxation, and the increase in social insurance payroll taxes, excise taxes have become much less important (Clark, 1984). Tobacco and alcohol taxes in 1984 each generated about 1 percent of overall tax revenues.

Taxes on both substances have effectively declined, despite the mounting evidence that their consumption causes adverse health effects and imposes considerable external costs. Between 1951 and 1985, the Consumer Price Index quadrupled but the nominal rates of cigarette and alcohol taxes changed much less. From 1951 to 1983, the federal excise tax on cigarettes stood at 8 cents a pack. In 1983, it was raised to 16 cents, and we have seen that as a result of OBRA 1990 federal taxes have increased another 8 cents per pack. In 1951, the tax represented 42 percent of the purchase price; by 1982, only 11 percent. It increased to 18 percent in 1983, when the rate doubled, and has fallen off somewhat since then.

The story for alcohol taxes is similar. Between 1951 and 1985, the federal excise tax remained at $10.50 per proof gallon of spirits but increased to $12.50 in 1985.[25] Since 1951, federal excise taxes on wine and beer have remained constant at 17 cents for a gallon of wine with an alcohol content of 14 percent or less, and 29 cents for a gallon of beer (Distilled Spirits Council of the United States, 1985).

Given these declines in real taxes, it seems evident that taxation has not been applied in any consistent way to the problem of limiting consumption, much less to the issue of external costs. Because nominal external costs rise with the rate of inflation, we recommend that so-called sin taxes (on tobacco and alcohol) be indexed by inflation to prevent future erosion.

When we look across states, the impression of inconsistency is even more pronounced. If taxes did reflect concern about either health or external costs, we would have to conclude that some states worry a lot more than others about the health habits of their citizens and the consequent external costs. In 1987, state excise taxes ranged from a low of 2 cents per pack in the tobacco-producing state of North Carolina to a high of 38 cents in Minnesota. (Table F–2 in Appendix

F shows taxes per pack by state.) Looking at state taxes on alcohol requires breaking them down by kind of beverage.[26] In 1985, tax rates on distilled spirits ranged from $1.50 per gallon in Maryland to $6.50 in Florida. Taxes on wine varied from 1 cent in the wine-producing state of California to $2.25 in Florida. For beer, the tax variation was from 4 cents a gallon in Arkansas to 77 cents in South Carolina.

If it were decided to increase cigarette and alcohol taxes to discourage consumption and/or reflect external costs, the tax increases should be made at the federal, not the state, level. Minimal variation among states is desirable to prevent bootlegging across state lines and, in the case of alcohol, driving to another state to drink and then driving home.

If taxes were raised, how much would be passed on to consumers, and how would they respond? Theory and history suggest that producers will pass all or most of the increase along to consumers. The exact degree of consumer response is uncertain, but the preponderance of the literature suggests that consumers, even those addicted, will reduce their frequency of smoking and drinking.[27]

What About Lack of Exercise?

The difficulty with exercise is that there is no obvious way to make people who do not exercise pay their way. Lack of exercise differs from smoking and drinking as sins of omission differ from sins of commission. From the standpoint of taxes, society can tax people for "wrongful consumption"—per unit of the substance consumed. It is hard to imagine how they can be taxed for not doing the "right" thing. They could, however, be "rewarded" for doing it.

Thus, the way to lower the external costs of sedentary life-styles is by encouraging and rewarding exercise. Options here are educational efforts (including advertising), benefits to people who exercise, and subsidies to facilities and programs that promote exercise. These might include wellness programs in public and private institutions and corporations, public parks and other facilities that charge no fees or have fees below cost, or rebates on life and group insurance premiums for those who demonstrate that they are fit. Southern California Edison provides an example of the last alternative. The company gives a rebate to cover a portion of employee health insurance premiums to those with good health—as measured by nonsmoking, low body mass index, low cholesterol, and low blood pressure (Mark Kailin, personal communication).

About a sixth of the population is sedentary but not physically limited. Whether educational efforts would warrant the expense, whether subsidies to encourage exercise would make enough nonexercisers more active to justify the subsidy, are issues we must leave to others. If our estimate of $1,650 in lifetime external costs per sedentary person is correct, a relatively small additional percentage of individuals exercising could justify some subsidy.

Taxes and Life-Styles

The costs of smoking, heavy drinking, and lack of exercise are high for individuals, their families, and others. Health promotion programs attempt to reduce these costs by publicizing them and by giving individuals who wish to lead a healthier life-style information on how to do so. Even with active health promotion programs, however, some individuals will choose to indulge in poor health habits.[28] These individuals, for whatever reason, find the satisfactions from smoking, drinking, and avoiding exercise sufficient to offset the risks. Some may be tempted to say, "So be it; that is their own business." Such a position assumes that there are no consequences for others. But there are. Some are financial (for example, higher health costs paid by taxes) and some are nonfinancial (an innocent bystander killed by a drunk driver).

Indulgence in these habits would be closer to the individual's "own business" if sin taxes approximated the costs imposed on others.[29] Such an approach implies that the nonfinancial costs are converted to some kind of dollar equivalent in aggregating costs. For exercise, the analogy to taxes would be subsidies of public recreation facilities such as swimming pools.

We have estimated the costs that smoking, drinking, and lack of exercise impose on others and compared these costs with current tax levels. Although our estimates are necessarily uncertain, they are not too uncertain to preclude useful conclusions.

Taxes on cigarettes are at a level such that smokers pay approximately the costs they impose on others. This situation does not mean that cigarette taxes should not be increased, but it does mean that other grounds for increases must be found. Here are two such rationales: higher taxes will discourage some adolescents from starting to smoke, a benefit they will later appreciate; and cigarette taxes cause relatively less distortion and tax evasion behavior than other taxes.

In contrast, the costs on others imposed by excess drinking greatly exceed current taxes on alcoholic beverages, especially those on beer and wine. Our analyses strongly support the recommendations of former Surgeon General Koop to increase alcohol taxes.

The costs imposed on others by a sedentary life-style are also high. We need to discover cost-effective methods to induce individuals to exercise some minimal amount, because one cannot tax inactivity.

Our analysis supports a considerable increase in alcohol taxes, but changing any tax leads to changes in inefficiencies and inequities. Decisions on the right level of the tax and the associated inequities and inefficiencies is a task that falls to our political institutions. We hope that our work will contribute to more informed decisions.

2

Conceptual Framework

This chapter lays out the conceptual framework of our study, including the assumptions underlying the cost analysis. To make the concepts and assumptions more accessible, we couch the discussion in terms of smoking. The same principles apply to the external costs of heavy drinking and lack of exercise.

Basic Concepts of the Cost Analysis

The principles of our analysis closely follow Leu's (1984) conceptual framework for analyzing the social costs of smoking, which focuses on economic efficiency. This framework involves (1) the concept of external costs, (2) "nonsmoking smokers" as the proper comparison group (that is, *ceteris paribus* comparisons), and (3) lifetime costs.

External Costs

In standard economic theory, smoking behavior is *economically efficient* if each smoker's net satisfaction from smoking the last cigarette equals its social costs.[1] Total social costs of smoking are the sum of internal and external costs. Internal costs are the costs smokers pay, including their share of medical bills, their lost earnings, and their out-of-pocket expense for cigarettes. External costs are the costs they impose on others.

To clarify the distinction, take a simple example for medical costs alone. Suppose a worker has a group health insurance policy that pays 75 percent of his medical bills, and he pays the other 25 percent. Suppose, further, that smoking a pack of cigarettes every day raises his medical bills by $6,000 over his lifetime (the total social cost). The amount the worker pays, $1,500 (0.25 × 6,000 = 1,500), is a component of internal costs. The external cost, $4,500, is the difference between the total social cost and the internal cost. The external cost is the cost our study has tried to estimate.[2]

It is not easy to estimate the total external costs of smoking because of the numerous collectively financed arrangements and the long-term effects of smoking. Nevertheless, the concept of externality is usually clear: a portion of the costs is generally external if costs are financed by a large pool of insured individuals, and premiums (or taxes) do not depend on smoking status.

We have seen that because smokers have shorter life expectancies and thus shorter working lives, they will pay less of the taxes and premiums that finance health care, sick leave, and similar benefits. This differential adds to the lifetime costs that nonsmokers bear and must be taken into account. To simplify the calculation of how much smokers and nonsmokers pay annually to finance these programs, we assume that each pays a given proportion of earnings, and that proportion is just enough to finance these programs.

External costs include premiums and the taxes necessary to finance pensions, even though pensions may be considered transfer payments in some contexts. The customary arguments for ignoring transfer payments in assessing economic efficiency do not apply here (see Arnott and Stiglitz, 1986). In the usual case, transfer payments do not depend on the behavior of the consumer. Thus, they do not alter behavior unless the payment is large enough so that income effects are considerable. In the case of smoking, however, receiving the transfer depends on choices made by the consumer—that is, because smokers have shorter life expectancies, smoking affects the amount of pension payments they will realize (if any) and the amount of taxes they will pay. Those who remain skeptical that effects on pensions should count may consider the following hypothetical example. Suppose the government were to promise that everyone who reached age 70 would receive a million-dollar payment (transfer). It seems likely that many people would stop smoking (or never start) and engage in other less risky activities so that they might receive the "transfer." The ability to change one's activities to get the million-dollar bonus implies that it is not a pure transfer.

Another approach is to consider the consequences of smoking from the perspective of the rest of society. There is an externality due to smoking if there is a smoking-caused change in the total resources available to the rest of society. For example, smoking may draw resources away from the rest of society because of higher medical use

TABLE 2-1. Costs of smoking

Type of Cost	Internal Cost	External Cost
Premature death	Smoker and family	Co-workers and others
Pain and suffering	Smoker and family	Co-workers and others
Medical costs	Copayments	Insurance reimbursements
Sick leave	Uncovered sick loss	Covered sick loss
Disability	Forgone income not replaced by disability insurance	Disability insurance payments
Group life insurance	Negligible	Death benefit
Pension	Defined contribution plans	Social Security and defined benefit plans
Wages	Forgone disposable income	Taxes on earnings
Other costs	Property loss due to fires, paid by person	Insured property loss due to fires
Tobacco products	Cigarette purchases Cigarette excise taxes	—

by smokers—higher use that they did not in fact pay for through higher insurance premiums.

A similar argument can be made for pensions, and other so-called transfers.[3] An individual works in return for wages or salary, and fringe benefits. He or she may elect to consume some of these now and defer some until a later date, such as after retirement. If smoking decreases the likelihood of receiving retirement benefits, then a claim on future earnings is forgone. That is, smoking leads to a shift in future claims or benefits from smokers to nonsmokers, thereby yielding a positive externality to nonsmokers. If smokers are less productive but retain and collect the same benefits, then smoking has created a negative externality.

Table 2–1 illustrates how social costs are divided into internal and external costs. Some terms in the table need clarification. The principal costs, *premature death* and *pain and suffering,* are borne by the smoker and thus are not a part of our analyses. We have not adjusted for altruistic feelings about death, pain, and suffering caused by smoking. We have treated such feelings as internal, since they are more likely to be felt by family than by outsiders. Premature death and suffering among family members and co-workers are also caused by passive smoking. In general, we classify costs borne by other family members as internal because the family constitutes an economic unit (it pools income), but we show below certain ways in which our results would change if we consider these costs as external to the smoker.

As for group- or employer-covered arrangements, *covered sick loss* is sick leave that is subject to some kind of insurance or income-replacement plan. *Defined benefit pension plans* pay an amount upon retirement equal to some function of an employee's wages, often a fraction of the *n* highest-earning years. The estate of an employee who dies before retirement generally receives no benefit from a defined benefit plan. By contrast, *defined contribution pension plans* are like employer-enhanced private savings plans. The accrued payments belong to the employee or his or her estate until retirement, when they may be converted to an annuity. In the analysis of external costs, we have ignored defined contribution plans and treated all retirement plans as part of external costs. Our rationale was twofold: (1) defined contribution plans are a minority of private pension plans, and (2) even in defined contribution plans, the amount of the annuity is usually not a function of habit status.

Cigarette excise taxes could be considered negative external costs. If we defined them thus, the object would be to determine whether the external costs are zero, rather than equal to the current excise tax. Some studies have so defined them. We preferred to keep them separate so that we could compare cigarette taxes to the external costs.

Nonsmoking Smokers

Smokers differ from nonsmokers in many ways besides their smoking habit (Farrell and Fuchs, 1982). For example, they are less future oriented. Therefore, an estimate of external costs should not simply contrast smokers' medical and other costs with nonsmokers' costs. That would attribute all the differences between the two groups to smoking and probably overstate the costs of smoking. The preferable way is to compare smokers with a hypothetical group of "nonsmoking smokers" (Leu, 1984), who are like smokers in every way except that they do not smoke. To accomplish this goal we controlled for age, sex, race, education, drinking habits, exercise habits, family size, income, self-assessed measures of physical, mental, and general health, and seat-belt use. Thus, we can calculate the external costs of smokers *if they had never smoked* but had retained all their other characteristics.

We may still be overstating the costs of smoking—because there may be other significant differences between the two groups. The omitted differences (for example, bad dietary habits or an affinity for high-risk activities) may be correlated with smoking but not (perfectly) with the habits we controlled for. If so, our methods will attribute part of the adverse effects of the omitted habits to smoking. To test the sensitivity of our results, we also compared costs for smokers and never smokers, attributing all of the differences between them to smoking. We use this calculation, which should overstate external costs, as an upper bound.

Lifetime Costs and Discounting

Because bad health habits have long-term effects, our study estimated lifetime costs for smokers. We tracked costs for two hypothetical cohorts of men and women from age 20 to death.[4] One cohort smoked; the other did not. We developed life tables for each cohort showing the probability of surviving to each age after 20.

In looking at the costs of smoking, we were concerned with the costs of *ever smoking versus never smoking*. Therefore, we did not focus on current smokers versus never smokers. Former smokers must be considered with current smokers rather than with nonsmokers because they may still be suffering from the adverse side effects of past smoking. For example, a smoker may develop emphysema from smoking. Even if he or she quits, the external costs of that emphysema are smoking related. Without including those extra costs, we would generate too low an estimate of the external costs of smoking.[5]

In judging long-term effects, we must discount future costs to make comparable costs that occur at different times.[6] Because the proper rate of discount is controversial, we have computed results for rates that span the range between 0 and 10 percent.

We also discounted number of cigarettes consumed and life expectancy. We discount cigarettes for the same reason that we discount costs. A cigarette smoked thirty years from now has different implications for revenues than one consumed today—in terms of both dollars and health.

Consider a world where we make smokers pay the external costs of their actions by paying an excise tax, t, per pack of cigarettes. Over the lifetime of the ever smoker, he has to pay enough into the tax fund to cover his costs. His total tax payments are t times the number of packs ever smoked. But early payments into the system can be invested and earn interest. Thus, a pack smoked today yields more taxes than one smoked thirty years from now, because of the thirty years of interest on the tax receipts. Because the tax rate is constant, discounting cigarettes is equivalent to discounting the revenue stream from the tax for the purpose of calculating the tax per pack that will cover lifetime external costs.[7]

Calculating Net External Costs

We construct an abridged life table to compute the differences in expected costs that are due to each habit. The net external costs are the sum of *immediate costs* per pack and *cumulating lifetime costs* per pack. We assume that the costs of fires caused by smoking are immediate: each cigarette has a certain probability of causing a fire immediately after it is purchased, but once it is smoked the probability drops to zero.[8] For such costs, we divide the estimated national annual costs by annual packs (or excess ounces).

The cumulative net lifetime costs are given by the following formula:

$$\sum_{t=20}^{95} \delta^{t-20} \times P(A|H)_t \times C(H)_t - \sum_{t=20}^{95} \delta^{t-20} \times P(A|NH)_t \times C(NH)_t,$$

where δ indicates the annual discount factor ($1/[1+r]$) if r is the discount rate; $P(A|H)$, the probability of surviving from age 20 years to at least age t years, conditional on having the habit H (smoking); $C(H)$, the annual costs minus taxes and premiums for smokers of age t; $P(A|NH)$, the probability of surviving from age 20 years to at least age t years, conditional on not smoking; and $C(NH)$, the annual costs minus taxes and premiums for smokers of t years if they had never smoked.

The lifetime external costs of smoking included in our analysis are the following:

Covered medical costs[9]
Covered work loss and disability
Group life insurance
Widow's Social Security bonus
Covered nursing home costs
Pensions
Taxes needed to cover lifetime external costs
Fires

For heavy drinking we also include the costs of accidents and criminal activity.

Assumptions Made in Lifetime Cost Analysis

Cross-Section Used as Cohort

Although the cost analyses follow a hypothetical cohort over time, the information on what happens at each age is based on recent (cross-sectional) experience for that age, and not on projections of what life will be like, say, in the year 2050 when those 20 years old in 1990 turn 80. Thus, we did not estimate the effects of secular and biomedical trends on smoking and its health effects. Instead, we used current estimates for parameters such as retirement, medical and nursing home costs, education, and life insurance arrangements. This simplifying assumption is commonly made (for instance, by the National Center for Health Statistics in computing life expectancy) because the alternative is too difficult and conjectural.

Costs for Others in Smoker's Household

Costs imposed on other family members are difficult to classify as either internal or external to the smoker. It is not clear whether these costs are taken into account by the smoker in decisions about where and how often to smoke. If they are, then they should be treated as internal. Although our base-case estimates classify such costs as internal, we show the effect of treating certain costs borne by other family members as external.[10]

Bounding the Effects of Smoking

Poor general and mental health, physical limitations, and chronic disease significantly increase medical and other health costs. Smoking also affects these costs directly. It may affect them indirectly as well, through its effects on those other risk factors. Because we do not know how much of the difference between smokers and nonsmokers should be attributed to smoking and how much to other risk factors, we tried to bound the true effects of smoking.

Lower bound. If smoking has little effect on intermediate risk factors such as high blood pressure and weight, then we should control for any differences between smokers and "nonsmoking smokers" in such factors. The result is a lower bound on the effects of smoking because we assume that smoking does not affect these other risk factors.

We computed a lower bound in two different ways. In the first method, for mortality, we used the Health Risk Appraisal (HRA) program (described later in this chapter) to calculate survival rates for nonsmoking smokers, without altering the values for other factors (such as blood pressure and weight) that smoking might affect. That is, we assumed that nonsmoking smokers would have the same actual values of blood pressure, weight, and the like that the smokers did. For covered medical and work-loss costs, we made a similar assumption, including other habits and health measures in the regression. In the second method, we estimated effects on medical costs only for those diseases probably related to smoking and other poor health habits.[11]

Upper bound. If smoking has strong effects on intermediate risk factors, then the hypothetical nonsmoking smokers may exhibit the characteristics of actual never smokers. For example, they may have lower blood pressure. In our cost estimation we obtained an upper bound on the effects of smoking by simply comparing actual smokers with actual nonsmokers, without controlling for other habits and risk factors. In the HRA model we used nonsmokers' mortality as the estimate of smokers' mortality if they had never smoked. The bound is an upper bound because people with one poor habit tend to have others, but the comparison attributes all the health and mortality costs to smoking.

These two extreme assumptions should bound the true effects of smoking.

Underreporting

Various studies comparing self-reported consumption with national sales have shown that people tend to underreport bad health habits, smoking among them (Warner, 1978). Our study used self-reported data on the amount of smoking to estimate external costs per pack of cigarettes. Consequently, we multiplied reported packs per day in the data by 1.5 to correct for the difference between reported and actual consumption.

People also underreport consumption of alcohol. Pernanen (1974) noted that self-reported consumption of alcoholic beverages accounts for only 40 to 60 percent of alcohol sales. Our comparison of NHIS

1983 estimates with alcohol sales (USDHHS, 1983a) also yielded a 40 percent figure. Therefore, we multiplied reported alcohol consumption by 2.5.

We assumed that underreporting of both smoking and drinking was proportional to consumption, because we had no information that underreporting varies at different consumption levels.

We also corrected pension and transfer income figures, because there is evidence that they too are underreported. Respondents to the Current Population Survey underreport pension and transfer income by 21 percent (U.S. Department of Commerce, 1986, pp. 165–170), but negligibly misreport other income.

Inflation

Inflation can cause problems in combining cost estimates from different years. All components of costs should be expressed in dollars of a common year, so that they can be added together. All estimates in the rest of this book are given in 1986 dollars. When an estimate for a particular cost component was available only for a different year, we assumed costs grew at the rate of inflation and simply multiplied the estimates by the ratio of the 1986 CPI to the CPI in the year the costs were estimated. All our estimates of costs and taxes are stated in 1986 dollars, as they were in Keeler et al. (1989) and Manning et al. (1989). To convert to June 1990 dollars, multiply by 1.185.

The Components of the Model

Mortality

The death rates for our abridged life table came from applying estimates of the relative risk of smoking to the 1980 National Center for Health Statistics (USDHHS, 1984b) abridged life table of the U.S. population. Our two goals were to make the computed mortality for our sample match the national data for each five-year age group, and to correctly estimate the mortality ratio between smokers (both current and former) and nonsmokers. The relative risk of dying for smokers and nonsmokers was derived from the 1984 Centers for Disease Control version of the HRA program.

Robbins and Hall (1970) developed the HRA as a health promotion technique for use in a doctor's office as part of a physical examination. Originally designed for manual calculation, the program has been updated several times by the Centers for Disease Control and is now available in numerous computerized versions. In the clinical setting, the patient usually completes a questionnaire on personal characteristics, family history, behaviors, and certain physiologic measurements. The individual's risk of dying in the next ten years is calculated, from this information in conjunction with national mortality statistics and data from epidemiologic studies. The next step is estimating how much the individual could reduce that risk by modifying his or her behavior. The results are summarized and presented to the patient, accompanied by a list of suggested life-style changes that could improve the chances of a longer life.

We have adapted this procedure for use in calculating the ten-year probability of dying for each individual in our two data sources (described in Chapter 3). We modified the input and output sections of the 1984 Centers for Disease Control version of HRA to accommodate our need to process data on thousands of people rather than a small group. Data from the two sources were fed into the HRA program, after translation into the format required by the program. Table B-1, in Appendix B, lists the 33 major variables incorporated in the HRA calculations and summarizes the program's response to a missing value for each variable.[12]

The most important components of the risk calculation were the mortality probabilities for each of the leading causes of death by sex, race, and five-year age group. These probabilities were based on mortality data for the United States for 1975, 1976, and 1977, obtained from the National Center for Health Statistics. The risk of dying was adjusted up or down from the average by applying "risk multipliers" formulated for the person's characteristics, health-related behavior, and physiologic measurements. The magnitude of the risk multiplier was based on information from major prospective epidemiologic studies, actuarial experience, and expert opinion regarding the relationship between the risk factor and mortality rate due to a specific cause.

The risk multipliers were combined to form a composite risk multiplier for each major cause of death. (See Appendix B for an example of the method used.) The average probability for that cause of death was multiplied by the risk multiplier to produce a risk projection for each individual. The sum of the cause-specific risk projections together with the risk for "other causes" yielded the risk of death for all causes.

Numerous researchers have criticized the methods employed by the HRA. Schoenbach et al. (1983) reviewed these articles and summarized the objections. One is that the HRA does not acknowledge the uncertainties in extrapolating results from population studies to the changes expected when a particular person changes habits. This comment is not particularly relevant to our application, because we are trying to compute *population-wide* effects of changed habits.

Another criticism is that the methods used to calculate the composite risk factor are ad hoc. Although the statement is formally correct, its force is blunted in practice: empirical assessments based on the major longitudinal population studies show that HRA-predicted probabilities of dying are roughly consistent with observed future mortality (Brown and Nabert, 1977; Wiley, 1981). Moreover, the mathematically more sophisticated models developed recently are not substantially more accurate (Breslow et al., 1985; Spasoff and McDowell, 1987). For our purposes, we believe the well-known HRA programs to be adequate.

Medical Costs

We constructed the external medical and covered work-loss costs of smokers and of the hypothetical nonsmoking smokers from the data in two steps. To estimate the "pure" effects of smoking on use of medical services, we used multiple regression methods to control for differences between smokers and nonsmokers not causally related to smoking (see Chapter 4). Next, we took the former and current smokers in our data and used the estimated equations to predict their costs in two situations: once with their actual (former or current) smoking status, and once with their smoking status altered (counterfactually) to never smoked (thereby converting them to our nonsmoking smokers). We computed the difference in predicted use for each former or current smoker, multiplied by the percentage of the bill paid by private insurance or government programs (Medicaid and Medicare, for instance), and averaged the difference over five-year age and sex groups. These average differences became the estimated external medical costs.

As later discussion shows, the corrections for medical costs of secondary or passive smoking by nonsmoking members of households with smokers were so small that we did not include them in our estimates.[13] We had no estimate of passive smoking effects outside the household (say, at work), but if effects in the home are negligible, effects at the workplace are likely to be as well.

A separate issue arises from the retrospective nature of the NHIS, namely, their data do not include the expenses of the aged or of others who died in the past year. Hence, the expenses we estimated from the NHIS were lower than would come from a prospective study of next-year expenses of those who are alive at a particular time. According to Waldo and Lazenby (1984), decedents spend on average seven times as much on hospital care in their last year of life as survivors do. Thus, for each person in the NHIS who died, we multiplied the annual inpatient costs in the life table by seven. (We made no correction to NHIS outpatient expenses for decedents.) We used data on medical services from the NHIS only for those aged 65 and over. For those under 65, we used data from the HIE. No correction was necessary for decedents because of the HIE's prospective design.

We based our cost estimates on a judgment that about 85 percent of hospital and physician costs are collectively financed and approximately half of long-term care costs are collectively financed (Levit et al., 1985).

Covered Work Loss

We predicted costs using multiple regression models fitted to workers only; nonworkers do not have collectively financed sick leave. We assumed that health habits do not cause an individual to begin working, although we allowed for their effects on stopping work through disability and early retirement.

Our estimates of the annual external costs of work loss are the differences in the product, for smokers and nonsmokers, of an indicator for employment, the predicted number of work-loss days (with and without poor health habits), the hourly wage or salary rate times eight (hours per day), and 0.38 the proportion of sick leave costs borne by the employer.[14] For men, we used two alternative work-loss predictions, one based on the HIE sample and the other on the NHIS, but for women we used only predictions based on the NHIS.[15] For the HIE, we used actual wage or (hourly) salary rates for each individual. For the NHIS, we imputed wage rates using age, sex, and education level from the Current Population Survey (CPS).

Life Insurance

Our calculations included only group life insurance, because most individual life insurance policies adjust premiums for habits (especially smoking status). Group life insurance provided by employers usually does not. In addition, most group life benefits after retirement fall to a nominal amount or do not continue at all; hence we assume group life insurance goes to zero at retirement (that is, we assume term life insurance).

Using the Bureau of Labor Statistics (BLS) survey of employee benefits, we estimated that the average life insurance benefit per male worker is $21,000 and per female worker is $15,600. Our estimates were derived as follows. For the 60 percent of workers with earnings-related insurance benefits, we multiplied the annual salary by 1.5; we used an average salary of $20,000 for males and $14,000 for females. For the 30 percent of employees with benefits not based on earnings, we assumed a $10,000 benefit. Additionally, we multiplied by 0.95 for men aged 20–64, and by 0.65 for women of the same ages, to reflect labor force participation. Our estimates were in good agreement with national data, which indicate that group coverage per worker is about $19,300.[16]

Widow's Bonus

When an aged male pensioner dies, his wife's Social Security pension will be increased if she never worked. From the incidence and prevalence of Social Security widow's benefits, we estimated that the average widowed beneficiary stays in that status for nine years. The death of the husband will alter a surviving wife's payments only if she is not eligible for Social Security through her own work experience. In that case the award is raised from that for a "wife" to that for a "widow," which is an increase from 50 to 100 percent of the man's benefit. In 1986 this increase averaged about $2,400 a year.[17] Thus, the estimated bonus is the probability of a never-working wife × $2,400 × 9 years.

Because of secular changes, we assumed that today the probability of a never-working wife is about 0.25, although historically it has been somewhat higher. Discounting reduces the effect of the bonus somewhat, but not as much as if the wife lived exactly nine years. We estimated $5,400 for a 0 percent discount rate, falling to $5,000 for a 5 percent discount rate, and $4,500 for a 10 percent discount rate. (If all wives lived exactly nine years, the figures would be $4,800 and $4,050, respectively.) If a man dies when young, his wife will probably work or remarry. If a man dies when very old, his wife will

TABLE 2-2. Nursing home and other costs for the aged

		Per Capita Annual Cost (dollars)		
Age Group	Percent in Nursing Homes 1977	Home Health Care 1984	Other Care 1984	Total 1986[a]
65–69	1.0	10	200	326
70–74	2.0	20	200	437
75–79	4.6	30	200	707
80–84	10.9	40	200	1,348
85+	22.0	50	200	2,467

a. Total = 1.088 (% in homes • $9,247 + other costs).

probably not survive him for long. We therefore included this cost only for men dying between 60 and 79 years of age.

Nursing Homes

Owing to lack of data on how habits affect dependency, we assumed that nursing home costs depend only on age and not on habit status. Diagnoses considered to be caused by habits are rare among nursing home residents; for example, emphysema occurs among only 0.6 percent of residents and alcoholism among 0.5 percent of residents (Van Nostrand et al., 1979). The average annual insurance-plus-government payment per resident is estimated to be $9,247 (1984 dollars).[18] Combining information on the numbers of nursing home residents with 1978 population data, we obtained percentages at given ages living in nursing homes (Table 2–2). The other medical costs of the elderly covered by insurance were assumed not to vary with age—they are mainly dental and eye care, and pharmaceuticals. We inflated 1984 costs by 1.088 to get the third-party costs in 1986 dollars shown in Table 2–2. The amount of covered nursing home use for people younger than 65 was small enough to ignore.

Pensions

Average pension benefits and other social welfare program amounts received (including Social Security payments, Supplemental Security Income or SSI, public assistance, veterans' compensation, and pen-

TABLE 2-3. Effects of disability retirement

Age	Cigarette Smoking		Heavy Drinking	
	Extra Disability Pension for Smokers (1986 \$)	Adjustment Factor for Earnings Taxes[a]	Extra Disability Pension for Heavy Drinkers (1985 \$)	Adjustment Factor for Earnings Taxes[a]
Males				
45–49	117	1.014	271	1.037
50–54	280	1.033	271	1.037
55–59	397	1.052	271	1.042
60–64	1,091	1.202	812	1.231
Females				
45–49	0	1.000	184	1.080
50–54	50	1.017	184	1.089
55–59	60	1.030	184	1.089
60–64	92	1.067	184	1.143

a. Computed from 1979 National Health Interview Survey as nonsmokers' nonretirement rate/smokers' nonretirement rate. For a description of earnings taxes, see text.

sion income) were taken from the March 1985 Current Population Survey (CPS). They were summed and averaged for each five-year age-sex group. Pension amounts on the CPS are not classified by habit status. Therefore, we examined data from the 1979 NHIS on reasons for retirement. The health retirements were consistently associated with smoking status, but the other retirements were not. In the case of disability pensions, therefore, we adjusted for the greater tendency of current and former smokers to retire for health reasons before reaching age 65 and hence to receive a disability pension; see Table 2–3. Because we assumed smoking is causally related to disability retirement, nonsmoking smokers receive less in disability pensions than do former or current smokers (the amount shown in the Extra Disability column of Table 2–3).

Taxes on Earnings

The medical, sick leave, disability, group life insurance, and retirement benefits considered here are largely financed with premiums paid by the employee, taxes on wages and salaries, and other taxes. We use the term "taxes on earnings" (or "earnings taxes") to represent all the payments into the system that cover these costs. For simplicity, we assume that these costs are financed solely by a constant percentage tax on earnings.[19] To compute the necessary rate, we took wages, salaries, and earnings from self-employment as reported in the March 1985 CPS and averaged them for each five-year age, sex, and education category. Because information on habits such as smoking is not available in the CPS, we used education differences between smokers and never smokers to estimate the difference in their earnings. We computed earnings for smokers and nonsmokers for each five-year age, sex, and education group. Based on results from the HIE data, we assumed there is no difference in wage rates by habit once education, age, and sex are taken into account.

Using the resulting average wages by category and a 5 percent discount rate, we calculated that a tax on earnings of about 10 percent would pay the premiums for the health insurance, sick leave, group life, disability, and pension benefits that we are examining. Because most of the expenses for benefits come later in life than the earnings and hence the taxes, the discount rate has a large effect on the tax rate needed to fund the programs. Therefore, at each discount rate, we calculated the tax necessary to make benefit payments just equal tax revenues.

Differences in mortality and early retirement act to reduce the amount smokers pay in taxes below what nonsmoking smokers would pay. We adjusted for the mortality differences through the life table, but we accounted for the difference in tax revenues that results from varying ages of retirement by multiplying earnings of nonsmoking smokers by the following factor: (1 + percentage point difference between smokers and nonsmokers opting for early retirement)/(percentage of smokers working); see Table 2–3.[20] We then applied our flat tax to these higher earnings.

We did not otherwise account for differential taxes. In the case of pure public goods (national defense, for instance), this omission may have caused us to underestimate the external costs of smoking or drinking. For any given level of national defense, the earlier mortality of smokers raises the tax burden to nonsmokers. We assumed that these effects were offset by nonsmokers' enjoyment of less pollution and less-crowded roads. In the case of government services that are excludable (such as solid waste disposal), we assumed that the consumption of services by those who die is offset by the taxes they pay. These assumptions may, of course, be wrong. Yet it seems likely that any such error would probably understate the external costs of poor health habits.

In sum, we consider taxes only insofar as those taxes are used to finance the costs we account for, such as medical care and pensions. If a smoker dies early and ceases to pay taxes, we account for the consequence that nonsmokers will thereby pay a greater share of taxes for Social Security. We do not account for nonsmokers paying a greater share of garbage collection costs, for example, because there will be less garbage to collect.

Fires and Cleaning of Damaged Goods

We made no independent estimate of these costs. However, we show the effects of including estimates of these costs by others (Harwood et al., 1984; Luce and Schweitzer, 1978).

Secondary Effects of Taxes on Costs

Our working assumption is that an increase in cigarette or alcohol taxes will be fully passed on to consumers in the form of higher prices per pack or per drink. Some economists may be concerned about the secondary effect of taxes on costs. This discussion is intended primarily for them and for others who share their concerns that a major change in taxes might itself alter the external costs of smoking.

Except for the external effects we are examining, our estimates of economically efficient taxes rely on two simplifying assumptions: (1) any change in taxes will not cause a change in the unit costs of producing cigarettes, alcohol, or medical care; (2) there are no other serious problems or distortions in the cigarette, alcohol, or medical markets. In other words, the price of these goods and services reflects both the value of a unit of each to the consumer and society's opportunity cost in diverting resources from elsewhere to produce that unit.

On the first point, we assume that any tax-related changes in the prevalence of the poor health habits will not affect the incremental costs of providing those goods and services. Increased excise taxes, by reducing the demand for cigarettes and alcohol, could lead to improved health. That change, in turn, could reduce demand for medical services. If so, the marginal cost of medical services could fall. In that case our cost estimates would overstate the external costs of smoking in a world with fewer smokers. This seems unlikely: our analysis shows that smoking raises medical costs, but the effect is small relative to total use of medical care. Thus, a drop in smoking and concomitant decrease in medical demand should not cause medical care costs to fall.[21]

In the same vein, we assume that a change in taxes would not have any spillover effect on the underlying cost of cigarettes and alcohol. In principle, an increase in the cigarette tax could reduce the demand for cigarettes, which could reduce the demand for the production factors of raising tobacco or making cigarettes. That reduction, in turn, could cause a fall in the price of tobacco and of those production factors. These changes would then encourage smoking because the cost of cigarettes would fall.

On the second point, we assume that the prices correspond to society's incremental cost of providing these goods and services. This assumption would not be valid if any of the following circumstances held:[22]

(1) If the government artificially restricts production (or subsidizes it), then the market price is already too high (or too low). Our taxes have to be adjusted downward (or upward) so that the price per pack to the smoker is the opportunity cost of producing a cigarette plus the external cost per pack.

(2) If the incremental costs of producing a pack of cigarettes fall as the level of production increases (increasing returns to scale), then a change in demand could alter the price of cigarettes and our tax would have to be adjusted accordingly.

(3) If the market for cigarettes is not perfectly competitive, then we would expect that the firms in the industry are charging prices higher than cost. If so, as for point (1), we need to increase the tax by a smaller amount because we want the price to equal the incremental costs of production plus external costs.

If any of these factors apply or if changes in demand lead to changes in the price per pack of cigarettes, then our calculations are biased. The direction and magnitude of the bias will depend on the particular circumstances. Let us look in detail at cigarettes and alcohol with regard to these concerns.

Cigarettes

It is our opinion that none of these three conditions is an important problem for cigarettes. Although there are government restrictions on tobacco acreage and subsidies to tobacco farmers, we do not believe that they affect the price of cigarettes. Because tobacco is traded in world markets, its price is set there, not domestically.

We were initially concerned that tobacco prices might be artificially high in the United States, because tobacco allotments in this country restrict the acreage allowed for growing tobacco. With all other things equal, the lower the allowed acreage, the less domestic production there will be. In the absence of an international market, the lower the production, the higher the price of tobacco, and hence cigarettes, would be. Because there is an international market that sets the price for tobacco, the allotment program affects only farmers' incomes. For a particular farmer, the size of the allotment is small enough so that his marginal crop is not tobacco. The market for allotments merely capitalizes the value of the allotment.

Given the technology for growing and harvesting tobacco, there is no reason to expect economies of scale at the farm level. At the level of the intermediate market for tobacco, or the factor markets for labor, land, and related supplies, we do not expect to see any spillover effect on prices because of shifts in world demand that might be caused by changes in the American excise tax rates.

Our estimates could be too high if lack of competition in the domestic cigarette market allows cigarette producers to charge prices higher than the incremental cost of producing cigarettes. Not much of the domestic demand for cigarettes is met from abroad, except for some specialty items. To whatever extent domestic cigarette prices are too high because of imperfect competition, the corrective tax should be smaller. The tax should equal the incremental cost of production, plus the external costs, minus the price per pack. If the market is competitive, the price and incremental production costs are equal and cancel out, leaving the tax equal to the external cost. If the market is not perfectly competitive, then the price exceeds the incremental production costs. In that case the tax should be reduced by the difference, and it will be less than the external costs.[23]

This concern about imperfect competition for cigarettes does not appear to be a practical concern. Although there are only a few sellers, the studies discussed in the next paragraph suggest that we can rule out monopolistic pricing. If pricing is not monopolistic for cigarettes, then an increase in the excise tax will be fully passed on in higher prices to the smoker.[24]

Estimates by Barzel (1976) and Johnson (1978) show that cigarette prices increase by 107 and 110 percent of the tax increase, respectively.[25] Sumner and Ward (1981) found a 93 percent increase, with a standard error of 3.6 percent; however, their results were somewhat sensitive to data and methods. Thus, empirical estimates support full shifting and implicitly rule out the three reasons for concern.

Alcohol

The case of alcohol is more ambiguous. Many of the inputs into brewing and distilling are traded internationally. It seems highly unlikely that shifts in U.S. demand for alcohol will have an appreciable effect on the world price of grains, potatoes, and so on, or on the international demand for labor. It also seems unlikely that shifts in American demand for wine caused by an increase in excise tax will have much effect on the world wine market.

We do not expect the price of alcohol to be artificially high because of monopolistic behavior. Beer, wine, and liquor are traded internationally, which makes cartel or monopoly behavior more difficult. Indeed, given the recent entry of new wineries and micro breweries, it appears that any attempt by existing producers to raise prices would be frustrated by new firms entering the industry, increasing supply, and driving prices down. Still, we cannot rule out prices greater than marginal cost that result from imperfect competition at home or abroad.

We are not aware of any empirical studies on tax shifting of alcohol prices; however, we expect little movement. For example, U.S. consumption of alcoholic beverages is less than 10 percent of world consumption. Doubling the tax on alcohol (as is suggested in Chapter 5) would lead to *at most* a 2 percent shift in world demand. If the supply of alcohol or the factors of production were perfectly inelastic (an extreme assumption), the price of alcohol would fall by at most 2 percent, much less than the change in price to the U.S. consumer. Despite the lack of empirical evidence that the price of alcohol is close to marginal cost, we believe our qualitative conclusion that alcohol prices will increase by nearly the amount of the tax to be robust.

3

Data and Statistical Methods

Our study used a number of data sources, primarily the RAND Health Insurance Experiment (HIE) and the National Health Interview Survey (NHIS). The HIE was the principal source for people younger than 60 years, because of its detailed information on habits and the medical reasons for using health care. Because those age 62 or over at the time of enrollment were excluded from the HIE sample, we used data on the elderly from a 1983 supplement to NHIS. It includes information on poor health habits and overall measures of health care use and work loss. We also compared the NHIS data on the nonelderly with the HIE data. The Current Population Survey, the Centers for Disease Control, and other sources provided supplementary information.

This chapter describes the data sources, the outcome measures and explanatory variables derived from them, and our statistical methods. We deal explicitly with all three poor health habits.

Data from the RAND Health Insurance Experiment

Nature of the Experiment

The HIE was a randomized trial of alternative health insurance arrangements in fee-for-service and prepaid group practices.[1] It collected detailed information on health status and the use of medical services, demographic and socioeconomic characteristics, and the poor health habits of interest here—smoking, drinking, and lack of exercise.

Between November 1974 and February 1977, the HIE enrolled families in six sites: Dayton, Ohio; Seattle, Washington; Fitchburg, Massachusetts; Franklin County, Massachusetts; Charleston, South Carolina; and Georgetown County, South Carolina. The sites were selected to (1) represent the four census regions; (2) represent the range of city sizes (a proxy for the complexity of the medical delivery system); (3) cover a range of waiting times to appointment and physician per capita ratios (to test how having to wait for health care affects demand); and (4) include both urban and rural sites in the North and in the South. In each site families were randomized to an enrollment term of either three or five years. Families participating in the experiment were assigned to one of fourteen different fee-for-service insurance plans.[2]

The Sample

The sample was taken randomly from each site's population, but the following groups were not eligible: (1) those 62 years of age and older at the time of enrollment; (2) those with incomes in excess of $25,000 in 1973 dollars (or $62,000 in 1986 dollars—this excluded 3 percent of the families contacted); (3) those eligible for the Medicare disability or end-stage renal programs; (4) those in jails or institutionalized for indefinite periods; (5) those in the military or their dependents; and (6) veterans with service-connected disabilities. The sample size for each site is given below, excluding persons enrolled in the Health Maintenance Organization portion of the experiment.

Dayton, Ohio	1,137 persons
Seattle, Washington	1,222
Fitchburg, Massachusetts	723
Franklin County, Massachusetts	889
Charleston, South Carolina	778
Georgetown, South Carolina	1,060
Total	5,809

Data on Outcome Measures

To estimate how poor health habits influence external costs, we examined, among other effects, the use of medical care services (excluding dental care) and work-loss days.[3]

USE OF MEDICAL CARE SERVICES

The measures of medical use included the number of episodes of outpatient medical treatment and the number of continuous periods of hospitalization. Both measures were based on claims data filed during the experiment. An episode of treatment is defined as all of the visits and related charges associated with the treatment of a bout of illness. The aggregation was based on information from claims data on diagnoses, time since last charge for related diagnoses, and information from the provider on treatment history.

Outpatient episodes fell into one of three classes—acute, routine chronic treatment, or well-care—defined as follows:

- Acute episodes: all unforeseen and undeferrable outpatient episodes (in particular, chronic flareups).

- Routine chronic treatment: the foreseen annual care for each chronic condition.

- Well-care episodes: conditions and services that are deferrable without great loss, such as immunizations and gynecological examinations.

Keeler et al. (1982, 1988) and Keesey et al. (1985) describe the theory and construction of episodes in greater detail.

CLASSIFICATION OF DIAGNOSES RELATED TO HABITS

Although use of medical care may differ for people with and without each habit, the differences may or may not be "caused" by the habit. We addressed this problem by examining two kinds of health care usage. First, we looked at use of all services except well-care and maternity: it seemed implausible that those could have any causal relation to the habits.[4] We also examined use for only those diagnoses that evidence suggests are causally related to poor health habits. This approach should increase the chances that medical usage is caused by the habits. In both cases we adjusted for differences, across individuals, in age, sex, race, education, income, and other habits.

Smoking. Employing a substantial body of literature, we compiled two lists of diagnoses—those *probably* related to smoking (Table 3–1) and those *possibly or probably* related to smoking (Table 3–2). Probably related are cancers at several sites: buccal cavity and pharynx, esophagus, larynx, trachea, bronchus, and lung. Smoking is also probably a contributory factor in cancer of the bladder, kidney, and pancreas (USDHHS, 1982). The other probably related conditions are arteriosclerosis and the slightly broader category of ischemic heart disease (USDHHS, 1983b), as well as chronic bronchitis, pulmonary emphysema, and chronic obstructive lung disease (USDHHS, 1984b).

Table 3–2 shows the second list of diagnoses, which comprises

TABLE 3-1. Diagnostic categories probably related to smoking

Code[a]	Condition
140–149	Malignant neoplasms of buccal cavity and pharynx
150	Malignant neoplasms of esophagus
157	Malignant neoplasms of pancreas
161	Malignant neoplasms of larynx
162	Malignant neoplasms of trachea, bronchus, and lung
188	Malignant neoplasms of bladder
189.0, 189.1	Malignant neoplasms of kidney
410–414	Ischemic heart disease
440	Arteriosclerosis
491	Chronic bronchitis
492	Pulmonary emphysema
496	Chronic obstructive lung disease (COLD), NEC[b]

a. Diagnostic codes are based on Commission on Professional and Hospital Activities (1973) 8th revision H-ICDA.

b. Not elsewhere classified.

TABLE 3-2. Diagnostic categories possibly or probably related to smoking

Code[a]	Condition
140–149	Malignant neoplasms of buccal cavity and pharynx
150–159	Malignant neoplasms of digestive organs and peritoneum
160–163	Malignant neoplasms of respiratory system
188, 189.0, 189.1	Malignant neoplasms of bladder and kidney
410–414	Ischemic heart disease
415–416	Disorders of heart rhythm
430–438	Cerebrovascular disease
440	Arteriosclerosis
460–470	Acute upper respiratory infections
480–486	Pneumonia
490–493, 496	Bronchitis, emphysema, asthma, COLD
502	Chronic pharyngitis and nasopharyngitis
503	Chronic sinusitis
506	Chronic laryngitis
508	Other diseases of upper respiratory tract
519	Other diseases of respiratory system
531–534	Ulcer: stomach, duodenal, gastrojejunal, site unspecified

a. Diagnostic codes are based on Commission on Professional and Hospital Activities (1973) 8th revision H-ICDA.

TABLE 3-3. Diagnostic categories possibly related to drinking

Code[a]	Condition
140–149	Malignant neoplasms of buccal cavity and pharynx
150	Malignant neoplasms of esophagus
151	Malignant neoplasms of stomach
153	Malignant neoplasms of large intestine
154	Malignant neoplasms of rectum
155	Malignant neoplasms of liver
157	Malignant neoplasms of pancreas
161	Malignant neoplasms of larynx
251.1	Hypoglycemia
260–269	Other nutritional deficiencies and malabsorption
299.8	Presenile dementia
302	Mental disorders associated with alcohol
305.6	Senile or presenile brain disease
309.9	Unspecified psychoses, including mental deterioration
313	Alcoholism
347.1	Cerebral and cortical atrophy
357.9	Peripheral neuropathy, NOS[b]
401	Hypertension
425	Other diseases of myocardium, including other cardiomyopathies
427.9	Congestive heart failure
429.0	Cardiomegaly
531–534	Peptic ulcer disease
535	Gastritis
571	Cirrhosis of liver, including alcoholic hepatitis
577	Diseases of pancreas
790.9	Ketoacidosis

a. Diagnostic codes are based on Commission on Professional and Hospital Activities (1973) 8th revision H-ICDA.
b. Not otherwise specified.

conditions both probably and possibly related to smoking. The indications for possibly related diseases were as follows. Malignant neoplasms of the digestive organs, peritoneum, buccal cavity, and pharynx were included because cancer of the stomach has been associated with cigarette smoking (USDHHS, 1982). We also included cancers of all sites within the respiratory system because of their direct exposure to the carcinogenic components of smoke, and other acute and chronic conditions of the respiratory tract because of an observed increase in incidence and prevalence of these conditions among cigarette smokers (USDHEW, 1979). As for diseases of the circulatory system, experimental evidence implicates nicotine in disorders of heart rhythm, and data from prospective mortality studies support an association between cerebrovascular disease and cigarette smoking (USDHHS, 1983b). Observations also indicate an increase in incidence of and mortality from peptic ulcer disease among cigarette smokers (USDHEW, 1979).

Drinking. The association between drinking and disease has been investigated, but the conclusions are not as strong or as consistent as they are for smoking and disease. So we compiled only Table 3-3, conditions *possibly* related to drinking.[5] Several of the conditions are more strongly implicated than that, however. Alcoholism and cirrhosis of the liver are closely related to alcohol consumption. Evidence indicates that alcohol is probably or possibly implicated in cancers of numerous sites: buccal cavity and pharynx, esophagus, stomach, large intestine, rectum, liver, pancreas, and larynx (USDHHS, 1981).

Various conditions of the nervous system have been associated with chronic heavy drinking: presenile dementia, mental disorders associated with alcohol, senile or presenile brain disease, psychoses, cerebral and cortical atrophy, and peripheral neuropathy. Heavy users of alcohol exhibit heart muscle disorders without a specific cause (cardiomyopathies) and a higher prevalence of hypertension, as well as symptoms associated with congestive heart failure and cardiomegaly (USDHHS, 1981).

The irritating effects of alcohol on the digestive tract lead to the stomach disorders and malnutrition common among alcoholics (USDHHS, 1983a), including nutritional deficiency, peptic ulcer disease, and gastritis. Ketoacidosis may occur in nondiabetic alcoholic patients in conjunction with alcohol-induced hypoglycemia, or the two metabolic states may occur separately (Berkow, 1982). Chronic alcoholics account for more than 75 percent of cases of chronic pancreatitis in the United States (USDHHS, 1983a). We include this condition and other disorders of pancreatic function as "diseases of pancreas."

Lack of exercise. Identifying conditions related to exercise is less straightforward than for the other two habits, because people may need medical care as a result of either exercise or lack of exercise. As Table 3–4 shows, we included diagnostic categories related to both. On the one hand, exercise can result in damage to the musculoskeletal system (Koplan et al., 1985). We listed several diagnoses falling into this category: fractures of upper or lower limb, dislocations, and other musculoskeletal injuries. On the other hand, numerous chronic

TABLE 3-4.   Diagnostic categories possibly related to lack of exercise or to exercise

Code[a]	Condition
Related to exercise	
810–817	Fractures of upper limb
820–829	Fractures of lower limb
830–839	Dislocations
840–848	Other musculoskeletal injuries
Related to lack of exercise	
001–136	Infective and parasitic diseases
140–209	Malignant neoplasms
250	Diabetes mellitus
272	Hypercholesterolemia
273.0	Cystic fibrosis
277	Obesity
401	Hypertension
410–414	Ischemic heart disease
415–416	Disorders of heart rhythm
430–438	Cerebrovascular disease
443	Other peripheral vascular disease, including peripheral arterial disease
460–470	Acute respiratory infections
480–486	Pneumonia
490–492, 496	Bronchitis, emphysema, COLD
712	Rheumatoid arthritis
723.0	Osteoporosis
789.1	Lower back pain

a. Diagnostic codes are based on Commission on Professional and Hospital Activities (1973) 8th revision H-ICDA .

conditions can be aggravated by lack of exercise. Or increased exercise can provide effective management for some conditions, decreasing the need for outpatient and hospital care.

Kottke et al. (1984) discuss the benefits of physical activity in the treatment of coronary artery disease, peripheral vascular disease, chronic obstructive pulmonary disease, cystic fibrosis, rheumatoid arthritis, and osteoporosis. Although they suggest that these conditions may be improved by exercise, they caution that the results are preliminary and must be validated through well-designed clinical trials. Paffenbarger and Hyde (1984, 1986) and Paffenbarger et al. (1986) concluded that exercise lowers the risk of developing coronary heart disease and events associated with it. A review by Siscovick et al. (1985) suggests that increased physical activity is associated with lower blood pressure. The reduced prevalence of hypertension should, therefore, reduce the incidence of cerebrovascular disease.

In addition, research has indicated that exercise may reduce blood glucose levels, increase insulin receptors, and raise the effectiveness of insulin (Richter et al., 1981) and thus may have a positive effect on diabetic patients. Physical exercise is frequently recommended in weight-reduction regimens (Berkow, 1982), and obesity seems to be associated with sedentary habits. Clinical recommendations in the treatment of hyperlipidemia often include a regimen of physical activity (Haskell, 1984).

If habitual exercise protects against infection, as some suppose, diseases responding to an impaired immune state may be associated with lack of exercise (Simon, 1984). Given this possibility, we have included several conditions, including infective diseases and malignant neoplasms, in Table 3–4.

Work Loss

We based the work-loss measure on responses to a health diary that HIE participants filled out biweekly. Work loss included time lost from work because of illness (the individual's or someone else's) and visiting a physician. A half-day or more away from work was counted as a work-loss day. We summed work-loss days on an annual basis up to two years for each participant.[6] Because the data do not include reasons for work loss, we could not measure specifically those sick days that might relate to poor health habits. We simply estimated the difference in total work-loss days between persons with and without the habit, controlling for other habits and covariates.

Data on Explanatory Variables

The base-case analysis for each habit controlled for the other poor health habits, sex, age, health insurance coverage, health status, and sociodemographic and economic measures.

HEALTH HABITS MEASURES

Smoking. In the HIE sample smoking status was based on responses to a questionnaire filled out when the families enrolled. For everyone aged 14 years or older, the HIE used a ten-question battery on current and past smoking to obtain a smoking history (see Appendix C). Each person responded individually. Our study placed everyone 20 years or older in one of four categories: former cigarette smokers, current cigarette smokers, current pipe or cigar smokers, and never smokers. People were classified as pipe or cigar smokers only if they were currently smoking pipes or cigars *and* had never smoked cigarettes.[7]

To people younger than 20 and never smokers 20 or older, we assigned a passive smoking status. That status was based on the worst smoking habit of adults in the family when they enrolled. We ordered smoking habits, from best to worst, as follows: never smoker, current pipe or cigar smoker, former cigarette smoker, current cigarette smoker. In this scheme a former-smoker household is one with a former but no current cigarette smoker. The approach understates the number of never smokers exposed to smoking when they were married to former or current smokers but were subsequently widowed or divorced. We have no estimate of passive smoking at the workplace or at school.

Drinking. To establish drinking habits, we used data from the HIE's twenty-question battery on present and past consumption of beer, wine, and liquor (see Appendix C). This battery was administered at enrollment and filled out by every individual. We divided the population into abstainers (people who never or rarely drink or drank), former drinkers, and current drinkers. A person qualified as an abstainer if he or she had never had more than twelve drinks per year. Former drinkers had imbibed more than twelve drinks per year in the past, but none in the last year.[8]

For current drinkers, we collapsed the information on consumption of beer, wine, and spirits into a single variable—monthly consumption of ethanol in ounces. Because an ounce of alcoholic beverage contains less than an ounce of ethanol, to calculate ethanol consumption we treated a bottle of beer as 12 ounces of fluid, a glass of wine as 4 ounces, a bottle of wine as 26 ounces, and a fifth of liquor as 30 ounces. To convert ounces of fluid to ounces of ethanol, we multiplied the beer volume by 0.04, the wine volume by 0.15, and the liquor volume by 0.45. Given the small number of heavy drinkers, we could not separately estimate the effects of the three sources of alcohol.

Lack of exercise. Data on the exercise variables came from the HIE's eight-question battery on the frequency and strenuousness of exercise (see Appendix C), also filled out at enrollment. We put each person in one of four exercise categories—those with role or physical limitations due to health, those who exercised lightly or not at all (mostly sitting or walking), those who exercised moderately or strenuously several times a week, or those who exercised strenuously almost every day.

We placed people with role or physical limitations in a separate category. People with such limitations use more medical and mental health services than others, and because of their limitations they probably exercise less. Had we included them among the low exercisers, we would attribute the effects of their limitations to lack of exercise. But lack of exercise can lead to physical or role limitation; so our approach was conservative.

INSURANCE PLAN VARIABLES

We estimated equations for the use of health services as a function of the family's insurance coverage in the experiment (log of their average coinsurance rate + 1), health habits, and other explanatory variables. The HIE insurance plans had nominal coinsurance rates of 0, 25, 50, or 95 percent, and one plan with free inpatient care but 95 percent coinsurance for outpatient services.[9] We used an indicator variable for the fifth plan. The value of the average coinsurance rate is the plan mean for out-of-pocket expenses, divided by the plan mean for total medical expenses ($\times$ 100).[10]

For the cost comparisons reported here, we used that equation, substituting the value of the family's preexperimental coverage for their experimental coverage, to predict their use of health services—because we wanted the cost projections to reflect a cross-section of actual coverage rather than experimental coverage.[11] We used the values of the preexperimental plan because some of our plans, especially the free plan, were more generous (lower cost sharing) than commonly available insurance plans. As the HIE established empirically, the lower people's cost, the more likely they are to use health care services. Thus, cost projections based on experimental coverage alone could overstate the medical costs for individuals with both good and bad health habits. See Marquis (1986) for further details on the preexperimental coverage variable.

MEASURES OF HEALTH STATUS

For some of our analyses, it was important to see how sensitive the results were to including health status measures as covariates in equations for work-loss and medical services. We used four measures: (1) general health perceptions; (2) physical or role limitations; (3) chronic diseases and complaints; and (4) mental health status.

Each measure is based on the responses to the HIE medical history questionnaire.[12] All data on health status were collected at the beginning of the HIE study and are summarized below.

General health perceptions. The General Health Index is a continuous score (0–100, 100 being best) based on questionnaire items about perceptions of past, present, and future health. The items also address resistance to illness and self-concern about health. Twenty-two questions were asked of individuals 14 and over, and seven of younger children. The index refers to health in general and does not focus on a particular component.

The scale is a subjective assessment of personal health status. The reliability and validity of the index have been extensively studied and documented (Ware, 1976; Davies and Ware, 1981; Eisen et al., 1980). For example, the impact of hypertension, everything else being equal, is equivalent to 5 index points (Brook et al., 1983). The death rate in the study was 25 in 1,000 for those with index values lower than 63, 6 in 1,000 for those with index values from 63 to 76, and 1 in 1,000 for those with index values from 77 to 100.

Physical or role limitations. This measure is scored dichotomously ($= 1$ if limited, $= 0$ otherwise) to indicate one or more limitations in four categories: self-care (eating, bathing, dressing); mobility (confined, or able to use public or private transportation); physical activity (walking, bending, lifting, stooping, climbing stairs, running); and usual role activities (work, home, school). Data for this measure came from twelve questionnaire items for adults and five items for children. The reliability and validity of these measures have been studied and documented by Stewart et al. (1977, 1978, 1981a,b), and Eisen et al. (1980).

Chronic diseases and complaints. This measure is a simple count of diseases or health problems (from a possible twenty-six) for individuals aged 14 or older (Manning et al., 1981). The list of conditions includes kidney disease and urinary tract infections, eye problems, bronchitis, hay fever, gum problems, joint problems, diabetes, acne, anemia, heart problems, stomach problems, varicose veins, hemorrhoids, hearing problems, high blood pressure, hyperthyroidism, and so forth.

Mental health status. The Mental Health Inventory for adults is a continuous score (0–100) based on thirty-eight questionnaire items. They measure both psychological distress and psychological well-being, as reflected in anxiety, depression, behavioral and emotional control, general positive affect, and interpersonal ties. The reliability and validity of this measure have been studied and documented by Veit and Ware (1983), Ware et al. (1979, 1980b), and Williams et al. (1981). A similar construct has been developed for children aged 5 to 13, based on twelve questionnaire items (Eisen et al., 1980).

OTHER COVARIATES

Our analysis also included covariates for age, sex, race, family income, family size, education, and the use of seat belts. With the exception of family income, all these variables were measured before the study or at enrollment.[13]

We used measures of education and seat-belt use to reduce any bias that might result from differences in health attitudes between people who do and do not have poor health habits. These attitudes may affect work loss and use of medical services—independent of smoking, drinking, or lack of exercise. For example, cautious individuals may have fewer illnesses because they take better care of themselves. They may also be less likely to smoke. Consequently, we might find a negative association between smoking and use of medical care that reflects caution rather than the effects of smoking. Similarly, individuals with more future orientation are more likely to go to college and to get preventive care, and are less likely to smoke. Adding measures of seat-belt use and education should reduce the bias from possible differences in health attitudes among those with different habits.

Data from the National Health Interview Survey (NHIS)

Throughout our analyses we used data from the NHIS for the elderly (those aged 60 and older). We also compared the nonelderly NHIS responses on habits with the HIE data. The former are from a 1983 supplemental questionnaire on habits that was administered to 20 percent of the NHIS sample (N = 22,418 persons) aged 18 or older.

Outcome Measures

We used the responses to questions about the twelve-month physician visit and hospitalization rates as our medical use measures. The two-week work-loss response provides our measure of work loss.

Prices from the National Medical Care Utilization and Expenditure Survey (NMCUES) and wages from the CPS were employed to convert medical utilization and work loss into dollar values.

Explanatory Variables

We classified people as never smokers, former smokers, or current smokers, based on responses about past and present cigarette smoking habits. The NHIS did not ask about pipe or cigar smoking. For nonsmoking adults we created a second-hand or passive smoking measure in the same way as described above for the HIE. Neither the HIE nor the NHIS provides data on exposure to cigarette smoke at work or in school.

We based drinking status on responses about current and past consumption of alcohol. Monthly volume of ethanol was calculated from reported consumption of beer, wine, and liquor, using the same conversion factors described for the HIE.

The exercise categories were based on responses to a single question: Are you less active, about as active, or more active than others your age? Those with physical or role limitations form a separate category. Thus, the NHIS categories differ substantially from those for the HIE in that the NHIS measures the perceived amount of exercise relative to the average for that age, rather than the more objective HIE measure of how often a person exercises.

Comparing the NHIS and HIE

We compared the habit responses in the HIE data with those in the NHIS data for three reasons. First, we wanted to see whether the HIE results could be generalized to the nonelderly (those under age 60). The HIE sample is close to representative of the six sites studied, but the sites could differ from the United States as a whole. Second, we wanted to estimate possible changes in habits and their effects for data collected at two different points in time. Finally, and most important, when estimates are based on small to moderate sample sizes, the analyses should be replicated. If the studies agree, we can be more confident of the results.

To compare the two data sources, we examined the prevalence of poor health habits, the average amount of medical use and work loss, and the response of medical use and work loss to poor health habits. (The comparison was necessarily limited to people less than 60 years old.) Chapters 4, 5, and 6 discuss differences in habit prevalence between the two studies.

Among our various analyses of the relationship between health habits and use of medical care, we found a (nominally) statistically significant difference between the NHIS and HIE samples only for the relationship between outpatient visits and alcohol consumption. The nominal statistical significance is uncorrected for the multiple comparisons that were made. Estimated responses to the various habits were not significantly different between the two samples for either hospital admissions or work loss. For smoking and exercise, there were no significant differences between the two samples for any of the three measures of medical use and work loss.

Although differences in most responses were not statistically significant, we found appreciable differences in the magnitude of some estimated coefficients. Some were so large that we performed the cost analysis two ways. First, we used data from the NHIS only, that is, for all age groups. Second, we used data from the HIE for those under age 60 and the NHIS for those 60 and older. As we show below, our qualitative conclusions were not changed by which data set we used (for those under 60), but the magnitude of some of the costs of poor health habits was somewhat sensitive to the source used.

Appendix E provides further details on differences in the response of medical use and work loss to poor health habits.

Statistical Methods

The unit of analysis in our study is a person. For our analyses of HIE information, we collapsed multiple years of data for each individual into a single observation. We used the person as the unit of observation because the major determinants of the use of services are individual (age, sex, health status) rather than familial (insurance coverage, family income). We corrected for differences among families by including measures for family variables (family income and size) and by correcting for intrafamily correlation in the use of health services and work loss.

Methods

We used analysis of variance (ANOVA) techniques (after direct age and sex adjustment) as well as multiple regressions to estimate the effects of poor health habits on the use of medical services (outpatient visits, outpatient episodes of treatment, and inpatient admissions) and on work loss. We used direct age and sex adjustment to provide simple contrasts for these outcomes, purged of the known association between age, sex, and habits.

We augmented these results with estimates based on a negative binomial regression model. We chose the negative binomial technique because of three characteristics of the distribution of medical expenses and work loss. First, a large proportion of the participants used no medical services or had no work loss during the year. Second, the distribution of expenses among users and work loss among workers is strongly skewed. Third, the distribution of medical use is quite different for individuals with only outpatient use than it is for individuals with inpatient use. Accordingly, we examined inpatient and outpatient use separately.

Because of these characteristics, techniques like ANOVA (including direct age and sex adjustment) and the analysis of covariance (ANOCOVA) yield imprecise though consistent estimates of the effects of health habits on the use of medical services and work loss, even for a sample as large as the NHIS 1983 habits supplement. A model that exploits the characteristics of the distributions of medical expense and work loss yields more precise and robust estimates.

We used a model based on the negative binomial distribution to estimate how admissions, outpatient episodes of treatment, and work loss respond to poor health habits. The negative binomial is an appealing distribution because it can yield a large proportion of zeros and a skewed distribution of positive outcomes. It is also attractive because of its ability to adjust the estimates for different time frames for different individuals—that is, its convolution properties with respect to time observed. We have counts on episodes of treatment, admissions, and work loss that cover varying periods of time—from one day to five years. The technique can effectively annualize all of our estimates, while controlling for age, sex, and other confounding variables. See Appendix D for a formal description of the statistical methods.

The negative binomial regression model is more appealing than a Poisson regression because it allows for unmeasured characteristics generating overdispersion, that is, a variance greater than the mean. (Indeed a Poisson regression can be a special case of the negative binomial model.)

Correlation in the Responses

Although we have several thousand observations, we do not have the information we would get from the same number of *independent* observations, because of substantial positive correlations in the error terms among family members and over time among observations on the same person. These correlations exist in all of our outcome measures. Failure to account for them in the analysis yields inefficient estimates of the coefficients and statistically inconsistent estimates of the standard errors. As a result, the inference statistics (t, F, and χ^2) calculated in the usual way (without adjusting for these correlations) can be too large.

In the results presented in the rest of the text, we have used a nonparametric approach to correct the inference statistics for this positive intrafamily correlation. The correction is similar to that for the random effects least-squares model, or equivalently the intracluster correlation model (Searle, 1971). The model is described in Rogers (1983) and Brook et al. (1984), based on prior work by Huber (1967) on the variance of a robust regression.

4

The External Costs of Smoking

Our results provide still more evidence that smoking is a pernicious habit for smokers and for the rest of society as well. To recapitulate, the Health Risk Appraisal model applied to our data shows that it reduces the life expectancy of a 20-year-old by about 4.3 years, or 7 minutes per cigarette. Current smokers are more likely than former smokers or people who have never smoked to (1) be hospitalized for any reason and (2) visit their doctors for conditions related to smoking. Nonsmokers subsidize this higher demand for medical services. Because nonsmokers live longer, however, smokers effectively subsidize their pensions. In fact, if the costs of smoking are not discounted, smoking has negative external costs. With a 5 percent discount rate, smoking has net lifetime external costs of $1,000 per smoker. The external cost per pack of cigarettes (at a 5 percent discount rate) is 15 cents.

This chapter describes the analyses that led to these and other findings on the effects of smoking. It shows the prevalence of smoking in the two HIE and NHIS samples and smoking's association with both the use of medical services and work loss. It presents results adjusted only for age and sex, as well as results controlled for a fuller set of factors that may affect health outcomes: age, sex, education, family income and size, and other health habits. Finally, it presents our estimates of the external costs of smoking, that is, the costs imposed by smokers on others through health insurance, sick leave, retirement, and other collectively financed programs.

Prevalence of Smoking

As noted earlier, to establish the prevalence and incidence of smoking, we classified the samples into four groups: never smokers, former cigarette smokers, current cigarette smokers, and pipe or cigar smokers. We then subdivided the groups by age, sex, race, residence, and years of education.

Health Insurance Experiment Data

CIGARETTE SMOKING

Patterns. Table 4–1 shows this breakdown for the HIE sample.[1] At the beginning of the HIE, 42 percent of people 20 through 59 years of age smoked cigarettes and an additional 17 percent were former smokers. The prevalence of cigarette smoking was highest for persons with less than a high school education (52 percent) and men in their thirties (49 percent). It was lowest for individuals with postgraduate education (25 percent) and women in their fifties (33 percent). The relationship between smoking and education was particularly striking: the more education, the less likely people were to smoke. The highest prevalence of never smokers for any subgroup was among those with postgraduate education (55 percent). People in nonmetropolitan areas (Franklin County, Massachusetts, and Georgetown County, South Carolina) were also much less likely to smoke than city dwellers were. There was no appreciable racial difference in prevalence of smoking. More blacks reported never smoking and more nonblacks claimed to have quit.

Duration. Table 4–2 shows the duration of cigarette smoking for current and former smokers. Among former smokers, 11 percent reported less than two years and about 14 percent reported more than twenty years of smoking. Not surprisingly, duration was higher among current smokers: fewer than 5 percent had smoked less than two years and about 25 percent had smoked longer than twenty years. The two groups had similar percentages of heavy smokers. Because former smokers had not smoked as long or quite as much as current smokers, their pack-year exposure was lower.[2]

Stability of status. Cigarette smoking status in the HIE was very stable, as Table 4–3 shows. From enrollment to the end of the experiment, 94 percent of never smokers, 75 percent of former smokers, and 82 percent of current smokers maintained their status. Overall, 86 percent of persons 20 through 59 years of age did not change their smoking status during the three to five years of the experiment, and 6 percent changed from smoker at enrollment to former smoker at exit.

TABLE 4-1.   Smoking status of persons 20 through 59 years of age, Health Insurance Experiment[a]

		Cigarette Smoking			
Subgroup	Sample Size (N)	Never Smoker (%)	Former Smoker (%)	Current Smoker (%)	Current Pipe or Cigar Smoker[b] (%)
TOTAL	3,059	41.3	16.9	41.8	9.1
Males aged —					
20–29	488	38.5	14.6	46.9	13.3
30–39	422	28.0	22.8	49.3	18.4
40–49	264	25.0	27.3	47.7	16.5
50–59	214	28.5	31.8	39.7	16.5
Females aged —					
20–29	593	47.9	11.6	40.5	3.9
30–39	491	50.9	12.6	36.5	2.5
40–49	280	50.4	10.4	39.3	4.0
50–59	307	50.2	16.6	33.2	2.6
Race					
Black	439	49.2	8.9	41.9	11.0
Nonblack	2,620	39.9	18.3	41.8	8.7
Years of education					
0–11	823	34.8	13.0	52.3	10.5
12	1,177	40.4	17.5	42.1	8.6
13–15	555	44.0	18.0	38.0	7.4
16	323	48.9	21.4	29.7	8.3
More than 16	181	54.7	19.9	25.4	12.1
Residence					
Dayton, Ohio	615	40.2	15.8	44.1	11.9
Seattle, Wash.	717	41.1	17.7	41.1	8.1
Fitchburg, Mass.	374	34.8	21.1	44.1	8.9
Franklin, Mass.	472	37.9	24.4	37.7	7.0
Charleston, S.C.	384	43.5	10.4	46.1	10.5
Georgetown, S.C.	497	49.1	12.1	38.8	8.0

a. Status as of enrollment, 1974–1978.

b. Current pipe or cigar smoking and cigarette smoking are not mutually exclusive; all persons in the final column may also appear in one of the three cigarette smoking categories.

TABLE 4-2.   Cigarette smoking habits of former and current smokers among persons
20 through 59 years of age, Health Insurance Experiment[a]

Smoking Characteristic	Former Smoker (N = 516) (%)	Current Smoker (N = 1,275) (%)
Years of smoking		
Less than 2	10.9	4.7
2–5	26.7	15.6
6–10	21.7	22.9
11–20	26.9	32.2
21–35	11.6	20.6
More than 35	2.1	4.1
Average packs per day		
Less than 1	35.1	31.4
About 1	44.2	45.6
About 2	17.8	20.8
More than 2	2.9	2.2
Pack-years		
Less than 2	21.9	11.0
2–5	20.5	15.3
6–10	15.9	19.0
11–20	22.3	26.8
21–30	8.7	12.0
31–50	7.4	10.9
51 or more	3.3	5.2
Physician advice to stop smoking		
Yes	16.7	24.7
No	83.3	75.3

a. Numbers represent percentage of former or current smokers. Data as of enrollment, 1974–
1978.

There were slight differences (not shown in our tables) in stability
among different subgroups. Women (87 percent) and people older
than 25 (86 percent) were slightly more likely than men (84 percent)
and people under 25 (83 percent) to maintain their status. Similarly,
a slightly higher percentage of those enrolled in the experiment for
three years maintained the same smoking status than those enrolled
for five years (86 and 84 percent, respectively).

PIPE OR CIGAR SMOKING

The most striking fact about pipe and cigar smoking is that its relationship to education is the reverse of the relationship for cigarette

TABLE 4-3.   Cigarette smoking status at enrollment and at exit among persons 20
                through 59 years of age, Health Insurance Experiment[a]

	Status at Enrollment[b]		
Status at Exit	Never Smoker (N = 1,159)	Former Smoker (N = 477)	Current Smoker (N = 1,134)
Never smoker	93.5	10.5	2.2
Former smoker	3.5	75.1	15.8
Current smoker	3.0	14.5	82.0
Total	100.0	100.0	100.0

a. Numbers represent percentage of column total.
b. Stability (agreement) of cigarette smoking status between enrollment and exit significantly
better than chance (kappa = 0.77, z = 55.7).

smoking. The highest percentage of pipe or cigar smokers was among
people with postgraduate education. Overall, 9 percent of the HIS
population were currently smoking pipes or cigars (Table 4–1) and,
not surprisingly, more men (13 to 18 percent) than women (3 to 4
percent) indulged. We found no major differences in pipe or cigar
smoking among the six study sites.

National Health Interview Survey

As Table 4–4 indicates, smoking patterns in the NHIS differed from
patterns in the HIE ($p < 0.0001$ based on χ^2 test). Overall, fewer
people in the NHIS currently smoked cigarettes and more were never
and former smokers. These differences probably reflect the secular
decline in smoking, especially for males, between the mid-1970s, the
time of the HIE, and the early 1980s, the time of the NHIS.

The differences held for most of the subgroups in Tables 4–1 and
4–4. In both there is a higher percentage of former and current smokers among males than females in all age groups and a strong inverse
relationship between years of education and percentage of current
cigarette smokers. The racial difference was stronger for the NHIS:
an appreciably higher percentage of blacks were current smokers. We
had no information on pipe or cigar smoking for the NHIS sample.

The Effect of Smoking on Health Care and Work Loss

Having established the prevalence and incidence of smoking, we
then calculated its costs in terms of medical service use and work

TABLE 4-4.   Cigarette smoking status of persons 20 through 59 years of age, National Health Interview Survey, 1983[a]

Subgroup	Sample Size	Never Smoker	Former Smoker	Current Smoker
TOTAL	16,309	44.7	19.8	35.5
Males aged —				
20–29	2,310	49.0	13.2	37.8
30–39	1,895	36.2	24.6	39.2
40–49	1,423	27.3	31.6	41.0
50–59	1,407	24.6	40.2	35.3
Females aged —				
20–29	3,011	52.9	12.3	34.8
30–39	2,632	51.2	15.8	33.0
40–49	1,863	48.6	17.6	33.8
50–59	1,768	50.7	18.1	31.2
Race				
Black	1,634	48.0	12.8	39.2
Nonblack	14,614	44.4	20.5	35.1
Years of education				
0–11	3,232	34.6	17.8	47.6
12	6,599	41.8	19.0	39.2
13–15	3,236	49.7	19.3	30.9
16	1,854	55.4	22.8	21.8
More than 16	1,312	57.0	24.9	18.1

a. Numbers represent percentage of row total.

loss. We first conducted a descriptive analysis, which adjusted only for age and sex. It compared the use of current and former smokers with the use of *actual* never smokers—rather than the "nonsmoking smokers" discussed in Chapter 2. Implicitly, this comparison attributes all of the differences in results to smoking.

We next conducted regression analyses, in which we controlled for all three habits and other characteristics of individuals as well. This procedure estimated differences in health care and work loss between smokers and never smokers, controlling for other differences between the two groups. Thus, we obtained the incremental effect of smoking on our outcomes, rather than the effect of smoking and any correlated drinking, exercise, or other covariates. For example, cigarette smokers might be less likely to exercise strenuously and

TABLE 4-5.   Annual utilization of services among persons 20 through 59 years of age, by smoking status, Health Insurance
Experiment[a]

	Never Smokers		Former Smokers		Current Smokers	
Utilization	% with 1 or more en- counters	Average per person	% with 1 or more en- counters	Average per person	% with 1 or more en- counters	Average per person
All outpatient episodes[b]	78.3	3.20	84.0	3.58	78.3	3.11
All episodes possibly or probably related to smoking	16.1	0.22	17.8	0.25	19.1	0.27
All episodes probably related to smoking	1.0	0.01	2.3	0.04	2.3	0.03
All hospitalizations[c]	7.8	0.09	7.9	0.10	10.4	0.14
All hospitalizations possibly or probably related to smoking	0.9	0.01	1.6	0.02	1.9	0.02
All hospitalizations probably related to smoking	0.3	0.00	0.8	0.01	0.8	0.01

a. All figures adjusted for age and sex using the direct method with HIE enrollment sample as standard.
b. Excludes episodes related to maternity and well-care.
c. Excludes hospitalizations related to maternity and pregnancy.

more likely to be heavy drinkers. If so, then the observed correlation between smoking and use of services could be due in part to lack of cardiac conditioning or the adverse effects of alcohol abuse rather than to cigarette smoking alone.

The importance of using multiple regressions for estimating external costs is implied by the differences between the multiple regression and the descriptive results.

Descriptive Results for Health Care

OUTPATIENT EPISODES

Smokers could be expected to use more medical services than non-smokers because smoking causes morbidity. As Table 4–5 shows, that was not the case for outpatient care. Current smokers had no more overall outpatient contacts than never or former cigarette smokers. In fact, former smokers (84 percent) proved to be greater users of general outpatient services than either current or never smokers (78 percent for both). Former smokers averaged almost 3.6 episodes of outpatient treatment each year, while never smokers and current smokers had 3.2 and 3.1, respectively.

The picture changes somewhat for conditions *possibly or probably* related to smoking (Table 4–5, row 2; see Table 3–2 for a list of these conditions). Both current and former smokers were more likely than never smokers to have one or more episodes of outpatient treatment, although differences were modest. These differences held when we narrowed outpatient services to episodes *probably* related to smoking (Table 4–5, row 3; see Table 3–1 for a list of these conditions).

HOSPITALIZATION

The findings for hospitalization were different: current smokers had more chance than former or never smokers of being hospitalized for any reason (bottom half of Table 4–5). Those who currently smoked also had an increased chance of inpatient admission for the subsets of diagnoses possibly or probably related to smoking. Still, the magnitude of the difference between the two kinds of hospitalizations does not account for the large difference between current smokers and the other two smoking subgroups for all hospitalizations.

There are two possible explanations for the discrepancy. First, smoking may have a broader set of adverse consequences than those included in Tables 3–1 and 3–2. Second, smokers may engage in activities other than smoking that undermine their health. With the data available to us, we could not make that distinction. Later on, we shall describe our sensitivity analysis to check the robustness of our conclusions.

PASSIVE SMOKING

In the HIE, exposure to cigarette smoke at home did not increase the probability of using any outpatient care. In fact, as Table 4–6 indicates, never smokers who lived with current smokers were less likely to have any outpatient care than those who lived with never smokers and former smokers, in that order. This pattern holds for outpatient care limited to diagnoses possibly or probably related to smoking.[3] It does not hold for hospitalizations. Never smokers living with current smokers were most likely, whereas never smokers living with never smokers were least likely, to be admitted to a hospital (bottom half of Table 4–6). This pattern was consistent for all hospitalizations and for the two subsets related to smoking.

Multiple Regression Results

HIE RESULTS

Outpatient use for smokers. We first examined hypothesis tests and then the estimated magnitudes of the differences by smoking status. Using the HIE data on the nonelderly adults (aged 20–59), we found a mixed pattern of results for outpatient care: smoking was significantly

TABLE 4-6.   Annual utilization of services among never smokers, 20 through 59 years of age, by second-hand smoking status,
Health Insurance Experiment[a]

| | Never Smokers Living with — | | | | | |
| | Never Smokers | | Former Smokers | | Current Smokers | |
Utilization	% with 1 or more	Average per person	% with 1 or more	Average per person	% with 1 or more	Average per person
All outpatient episodes[b]	78.0	3.10	86.0	3.54	73.4	3.07
All episodes possibly or probably related to smoking	15.9	0.21	16.7	0.21	15.0	0.23
All episodes probably related to smoking	0.9	0.01	1.0	0.02	0.9	0.01
All hospitalizations[c]	6.9	0.08	8.7	0.10	8.9	0.12
All hospitalizations possibly or probably related to smoking	0.5	0.01	1.2	0.01	1.6	0.02
All hospitalizations probably related to smoking	0.2	0.00	0.3	0.00	0.5	0.01

a. All figures adjusted for age and sex using the direct method, with HIE enrollment sample as standard.
b. Excludes episodes related to maternity and well-care.
c. Excludes hospitalizations related to maternity and pregnancy.

TABLE 4-7.   Wald tests (χ^2) for smoking response of persons 20 through 59 years of age, Health Insurance Experiment[a]

| | | Outpatient Use | | Inpatient Use | |
Smoking Habit	df	Excluding Well-Care	Habit-Related Diagnoses[b]	Excluding Maternity	Habit-Related Diagnoses[b]
Cigarette	2	6.88**	2.22	14.00***	6.19**
Pipe or cigar	1	0.62	1.99	0.01	0.02

a. Significance levels: ** 5 percent, *** 1 percent; otherwise insignificant at the 10 percent or better level; df = degrees of freedom.
b. Habit-related diagnoses from Tables 3-1 through 3-4.

related to all outpatient episodes, but only for former smokers. Although current and former smokers had more episodes for habit-related diagnoses than nonsmokers had, the differences were not statistically significant.

As Table 4–7 shows, cigarette smoking status was significantly related to the number of outpatient episodes (excluding maternity and well-care; $p < 0.05$), but not to episodes for diagnoses known to be related to habits.

When we compare current smokers with people who have similar demographic and other characteristics but who never smoked (labeled "never smokers"), Table 4–8 indicates that the increase in episodes occurred for former but not for current smokers. Former smok-

TABLE 4-8.   Effects of smoking, Health Insurance Experiment (t versus never smoker)[a]

	Outpatient Use		Inpatient Use		
Smoking Habit	Excluding Well-Care	Habit-Related Diagnoses	Excluding Maternity	Habit-Related Diagnoses	Male Work Loss
Never	100(–)	100(–)	100(–)	100(–)	100(–)
Pipe or cigar	106.0(0.98)	113.1(1.39)	107.8(0.51)	110.3(0.43)	125.2(1.64)*
Former cigarette	112.4(2.50)**	108.5(1.10)	113.3(0.97)	120.6(0.88)	87.4(–0.99)
Current cigarette	99.2(–0.22)	97.3(–0.46)	138.2(3.56)***	144.4(2.30)**	100.1(0.01)

a. Ages 20–59 years at enrollment. Number in parentheses = t-test. Significance levels: *10 percent, **5 percent, ***1 percent; otherwise insignificant at the 10 percent or better level. The t's are from negative binomial estimates and are on the log scale. Effects are rates of use (work loss) relative to never smokers with similar characteristics (= 100). Habit-related diagnoses from Tables 3-1 through 3-4.

ers had 12 percent more episodes of outpatient treatment, other things being equal, than never smokers ($p < 0.05$).[4] But current smokers were not significantly different from never smokers. Indeed, they had 1 percent fewer episodes of outpatient treatment than never smokers.

For episodes of outpatient treatment for the habit-related diagnoses (Table 4–8), the observed effect was of roughly the same magnitude but no longer statistically significant. Former smokers had 9 percent more episodes than never smokers. Comparing the significance levels in the first two columns shows that none of the habit-related estimates were statistically significant. Again, current smokers did not differ significantly from never smokers.

Inpatient use for smokers. As Table 4–8 shows, current smokers had more inpatient care than never smokers for all diagnoses (excluding maternity and well-care) and for habit-related diagnoses alone. For all hospital care, current cigarette smokers had 38 percent more hospitalizations than never smokers ($t = 3.56$), while for the narrower definition smokers had 44 percent more ($t = 2.30$). For both categories of diagnoses, former smokers also had more hospitalizations (13 to 21 percent) than never smokers, but the differences were not statistically significant.

Pipe or cigar smoking. Individuals who smoked a pipe or cigar, but had never been cigarette smokers, had higher inpatient and outpatient use than never smokers (see Table 4–8, row 2). The estimated effects were not statistically different from never smokers at conventional significance levels, and the results were insensitive to the set of diagnoses examined.

Passive smoking. The effects of passive smoking are a contentious public issue. As noted above, to examine those effects for the HIE sample, we assigned children (under 20 years of age) and never-

TABLE 4-9.   Wald tests (X^2) for passive smoking effects[a]

| Group | Habit (Current or Former) | df | Outpatient | | Inpatient | | Work Loss |
			All	Habit-Related[b]	All	Habit-Related[b]	
Health Insurance Experiment							
Children (0–19)	Cigarette smoking	2	2.31	0.14	1.57	1.94	NA
	Pipe or cigar	1	0.31	1.30	0.53	2.11	NA
Nonsmoking adults (20–59)	Cigarette smoking	2	4.33	0.65	2.10	9.73***	1.83[c]
	Pipe or cigar	1	0.04	0.76	0.37	0.04	0.89
National Health Interview Survey							
Nonsmoking adults (20–59)	Cigarette smoking	2	1.28	NA	2.41	NA	0.89

a. All outpatient care excludes well-care for HIE. All inpatient care excludes maternity for HIE. Significance level: *** 1 percent; otherwise insignificant at the 10 percent or better level; df = degrees of freedom.

b. Habit-related diagnoses from Tables 3-1 through 3-4.

c. Males only.

smoking adults the smoking status of the adult in their household who had the "worst" smoking habit.[5] As rows 1 and 2 in Table 4–9 indicate, passive cigarette smoking had no statistically significant effect on children's use of either inpatient or outpatient services, for all care or for habit-related diagnoses. Pipe or cigar smoking did have an effect on children's inpatient use, but in an unexpected direction. For habit-related diagnoses, children who lived with pipe or cigar smokers had 50 percent less inpatient care than children who lived with never-smoking adults (not shown in the tables; $t = -2.11$, $p < 0.05$; significance level uncorrected for multiple comparisons).

As rows 3 and 4 in Table 4–9 indicate, for nonsmoking adults passive smoking had no significant effect on any outpatient care. For inpatient care, however, passive smoking had a significant effect on smoking-related diagnoses (for nonsmoking adults). Although the use rates for all inpatient diagnoses were not statistically significant, the magnitude of the difference was large (26 percent; not shown) relative to rates for adults in never-smoking households. Given our sample size and the fact that passive smoking effects are probably less than active smoking effects, we may not have had the statistical precision to detect clinically meaningful effects of passive smoking.

Because we lack information on exposure to passive smoke outside the home, we are unable to estimate the possible effects of passive smoking at work or other locations.

Work loss. As the last column of Table 4–8 shows, former and current cigarette smokers did not have significantly more work loss than never smokers in the HIE sample.[6] Current pipe or cigar smokers lost 25 percent more work days ($p = 0.10$) than never smokers. Passive smoking had a surprising effect on never-smoking men, which mirrors the effect of passive smoking on children: never-smoking men who lived with a current or former cigarette smoker lost 42 to 51 percent fewer work days than those who lived in never-smoking households ($p < 0.05$). The magnitude and statistical significance of the result were not affected by the inclusion of health status measures.

NHIS RESULTS

We also examined separately the effects of smoking using the 1983 NHIS for all adults and for the elderly (aged 60 or older). The NHIS findings for outpatient use were almost identical to those from the HIE. Both the HIE and the NHIS data showed higher inpatient use for current smokers than for never smokers, although the difference was greater for the NHIS. The NHIS found considerably more inpatient use for former smokers, but the difference between the two data sources was not significant at conventional levels. Only for work loss did the two data sources diverge markedly, with the NHIS data showing a much greater response to smoking.

Table 4–10 shows that cigarette smoking was significantly related to hospitalizations for both the elderly and all age groups (20+) but was significantly related to outpatient use only for all ages combined.[7] Table 4–11 indicates that current smokers had negligibly higher outpatient visit rates than never smokers (less than 1 percent higher), but former smokers had 10 percent more visits ($p < 0.01$). Both current and former smokers had higher inpatient admission rates, 19 and 31 percent greater, respectively, than never smokers ($p < 0.001$).

TABLE 4-10.   Wald tests (χ^2) for effects of smoking on all adults and elderly,
National Health Interview Survey, 1983; smoking response[a]

| Health Outcome | df | Age Range | |
		20+	60+
Outpatient visits	2	9.00**	3.48
Hospitalizations	2	25.17***	5.84*
Work loss	2	10.13***	8.38**

a. Significance levels: * 10 percent, ** 5 percent, *** 1 percent; otherwise insignificant at the 10 percent or better level; df = degrees of freedom.

TABLE 4-11.   Effects of smoking, National Health Interview Survey, 1983[a]

Smoking Habit	Outpatient Use	Inpatient Use	Work Loss (Workers Only)
Never	100	100	100
Former cigarette	110**	131***	131*
Current cigarette	101	119***	152***

a. Significance levels: * 10 percent, ** 5 percent, *** 1 percent; otherwise not significant at the 10 percent or better level. Level for each habit stated as percentage of rate of use (or work loss) for never smokers with similar characteristics.

TABLE 4-12.   Smoking response per person, age- and sex-adjusted annual rates,
National Health Interview Survey, 1983[a]

Smoking Habit	Doctor Visits	Admissions	Work-Loss Days
Never	3.73	0.14	1.03
Former cigarette	4.23	0.18	1.31
Current cigarette	3.84	0.17	1.50

a. Adjusted using weights by age and sex from the 1983 NHIS sample, ages 20 and older.

As the last column of Table 4–11 shows, cigarette smokers also had more work loss days. Among working adults, former smokers had 31 percent more work loss days ($p < 0.10$) and current smokers had 52 percent more ($p < 0.01$), other things equal, than never smokers. Table 4–12 provides estimates using only direct age and sex adjustment. With the exception of work-loss days, the qualitative pattern was similar to the results from the multiple regression results for HIE data (see Table 4–8).

TABLE 4-13.   Lifetime external costs of smokers

	Discount Rate			
	0% Total	0% Women	5% Total	10% Total
Number of packs	16,300	16,800	6,400	3,700
Life expectancy at age 20 (years)	55.5	58.7	18.6	10.2
Costs[a]				
Medical care[b]	59	67	10	3.9
Sick leave	6	2	2	1.2
Group life insurance	5	2	1	0.4
Nursing home care	10	13	1	<0.05
Retirement pension	133	122	15	3.1
Fires	0.2	0.3	0.1	0.1
Taxes on earnings[a]	201	112	26	7.4
Total net costs[a,c]	13	94	3.0	1.3

a. Measured in thousands of dollars.
b. Excludes maternity and well-care.
c. (Sum of costs) minus taxes on earnings. Because of rounding, categories may not sum to total.

We could detect no significant passive smoking effect for adult never smokers living in households with former or current cigarette smokers (see last row of Table 4–9). Without data on passive smoking at the workplace, however, we are missing a source of exposure to cigarette smoke.

Cost Analysis Results for Smoking

Average Lifetime External Costs for Smokers

The average lifetime external costs in each category for smokers are given in Table 4–13 for our base case, which used data from the HIE on those aged 20–59 and data from the NHIS on older people. For the nonelderly, the costs include all external medical expenses except maternity and well-care, and all covered work loss from the HIE. For the aged, they include all medical services and retirement costs. The first two columns show undiscounted lifetime costs, first for all smokers (assuming half are men and half are women) and then just for women smokers. These nondiscounted costs are the easiest to understand but are misleading for policy. Because of time preference and the possibilities for productive investment of society's resources, future costs must be discounted (see Chapter 2).

We estimated that, on average, smokers will smoke 16,300 packs in their lifetime.[8] Because their life expectancy at age 20 is 55.5 additional years (that is, the average 20-year-old smoker will live to be 75.5), this amounts to a little less than a pack a day (including zero for the nonsmoking years of people who quit).

In addition to the external costs associated with collectively financed programs, such as medical and pension programs, the external costs of smoking include the cost of fires caused by smoking. Luce and Schweitzer (1978) estimate the fire cost associated with cigarette smoking to be $340 million per year (1986 dollars). Because of fire insurance, almost all of these costs are external. Thus, fires add about $340 million annually to the external costs of smoking, or about $5 per smoker per year.

As the table shows, medical costs and retirement pensions are the biggest cost categories. When we subtract taxes on earnings, the total net undiscounted costs are $13,330 per person.[9]

Comparing undiscounted costs for all smokers with undiscounted costs for female smokers, we see that the latter have higher net costs because they live longer. Specifically, they have higher medical and nursing home costs, but lower in the other categories—and much lower taxes on earnings than the average smoker (including both men and women).

Comparing the costs discounted at 5 percent with the undiscounted costs, we see a tremendous drop in medical, nursing home, and pension costs. The other costs do not fall as much, because a portion occurs early in adulthood.

Difference in Costs between Smokers and Nonsmoking Smokers

Table 4–14 gives the average lifetime external costs in each category for our hypothetical group of nonsmoking smokers. It shows the effect on these costs if ever smokers retained all their other characteristics and habits, but had never started smoking. We subtracted the values in Table 4–14 from the values for smokers in Table 4–13 to get the external costs of smoking shown in Table 4–15. The differences in costs for the two groups are the external costs caused by smoking.

Life expectancy increases more than four years overall, but medical

TABLE 4-14.   Lifetime external costs of nonsmoking smokers

	Discount Rate			
	0% Total	0% Women	5% Total	10% Total
Life expectancy at age 20 (years)	59.8	62.1	18.9	10.2
Costs[a]				
Medical care[b]	53	58	9	3.2
Sick leave	6	2	2	1.1
Group life insurance	4	1	1	0.3
Nursing home care	14	17	1	0.05
Retirement pension	163	144	16	3.1
Fires	0	0	0	0.0
Taxes on earnings[a]	211	115	26	7.4
Total net costs[a,c]	28	108	2.1	0.4

a. Measured in thousands of dollars.

b. Excludes maternity and well-care.

c. (Sum of costs) minus taxes on earnings. Because of rounding, categories may not sum to total.

costs and group life insurance decrease. Because nonsmoking smokers live longer, their nursing home and pension payments are increased. But because they live longer and have less disability, their taxes on earnings increase. Consequently, the net effect of smokers not smoking is an increase in undiscounted external costs to society. As we have said, however, the discounted external lifetime costs are more relevant to policy.

Both the 5 and 10 percent discounts show that total net costs to society of nonsmoking smokers are lower than those of smokers. The decreased medical costs and group life payouts and increased taxes by nonsmokers are somewhat offset by higher nursing home and retirement payments. These "gains" to society come far in the future, however, so discounting greatly reduces them.

External Costs per Pack and the Efficient Tax per Pack

We divide the differences due to smoking (Table 4–15) by the lifetime number of packs to get the external costs per pack shown in Table 4–16. In undiscounted costs, for example, each pack of cigarettes

TABLE 4-15.   Difference in lifetime external costs between smokers and nonsmoking
              smokers

	Discount Rate			
	0% Total	0% Women	5% Total	10% Total
Difference in life expectancy at age 20 (years)	−4.25	−3.38	−0.34	−0.04
Differences in costs[a]				
Medical care[b]	6	9	1.6	0.7
Sick leave	*	1	0.1	0.1
Group life insurance	2	1	0.3	0.1
Nursing home care	−4	−4	−0.2	*
Retirement pension	−30	−22	−1.5	0.1
Fires	0.2	0.3	0.1	0.1
Taxes on earnings[a]	−11	−3	−0.6	−0.1
Differences in total net costs[a,c]	−15	−14	1.0	0.9

NOTE: * indicates value less than 0.05.
a. Measured in thousands of dollars.
b. Excludes maternity and well-care.
c. (Sum of costs) minus taxes on earnings. Because of rounding, categories may not sum to total.

causes a 38 cent increase in medical costs, a saving of $1.82 in pensions due to a reduction of 2.28 hours in life expectancy, and a net saving of 91 cents in total undiscounted costs. The change in life expectancy is about 7 minutes per cigarette.

As Table 4–16 shows, for each pack of cigarettes discounted at 5 percent, society pays on average 26 cents more for medical costs, 1 cent more for covered work loss, 2 cents more for fires, and 5 cents more for group life insurance payments. Society pays 3 and 24 cents less in nursing home care and retirement pensions, respectively, and receives 9 cents less in taxes on earnings. This leads to a total cost of 15 cents per pack overall, with women exhibiting a cost considerably higher than men (not shown in table). The loss of discounted life expectancy per pack is 0.46 hour (28 minutes), which means that the lost 2.28 nondiscounted hours occur, on average, in the smoker's late fifties. At a 10 percent discount rate, the cost is 24 cents per pack, which is due primarily to medical costs related to smoking. (The other

TABLE 4-16.   External costs per pack of cigarettes (1986 dollars)[a]

Cost	Discount Rate (percent)		
	0	5	10
Costs per pack (dollars)			
Medical care[b]	0.38	0.26	0.18
Sick leave	0.00	0.01	0.01
Group life insurance	0.11	0.05	0.02
Nursing home care	−0.26	−0.03	0.00
Retirement pension[c]	−1.82	−0.24	−0.02
Fires[d]	0.02	0.02	0.02
Taxes on earnings to finance above programs (dollars)	−0.65	−0.09	−0.02
Total net costs per pack (dollars)[e]	−0.91	0.15	0.24
Life expectancy at age 20 per pack (minutes)	−137	−28	−6

NOTE: Packs of cigarettes are corrected for underreporting.

a. Costs per pack are calculated by dividing by the discounted number of packs smoked.

b. All but maternity, well-care, and dental.

c. Includes disability insurance.

d. Calculated by dividing annual costs by annual packs smoked.

e. (Sum of costs) minus taxes on earnings; e.g., costs at 5 percent equal $0.15 = 0.26 + 0.01 + 0.05 − 0.03 − 0.24 + 0.02 − (−0.09)$. Because of rounding errors, cost categories may not sum to total net costs, as in this example.

costs are negligible at this discount rate.) Because any cigarette tax would be collected over the lifetime of the smoker, the number of packs smoked must also be discounted (assuming the tax stays the same in real terms). That is, we wish to find the tax rate that equates the discounted tax revenues with the discounted costs.

Sensitivity of Costs to Assumptions

Figure 4–1 shows total external costs discounted at various rates from 0 to 10 percent. Between 5 and 10 percent the external costs per pack are not sensitive to the choice of discount rate, but below 5 percent the rate has a substantial effect.

Table 4–17 shows the effect of varying some of the other assump-

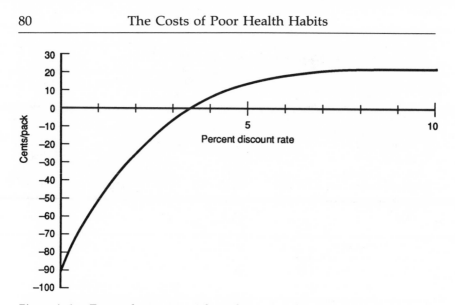

Figure 4–1.   External cost per pack at alternative discount rates

tions of the cost model. (For comparison, column 1 repeats the results from column 2 of Table 4–16.) First, to test the sensitivity to data source, we used values based entirely on NHIS data (for the young as well as the old). With these NHIS-only data, medical costs per pack do not change but covered work loss rises to 5 cents per pack and the total costs rise from 15 to 20 cents per pack.

Second, to test sensitivity to our assumptions about the health effects of smoking, we contrasted smokers with actual never smokers, rather than the hypothetical nonsmoking smokers. As we have explained, this procedure should give an upper bound on health effects because (with the exception of taxes on earnings) it assigns all the differences between smokers and nonsmokers to smoking. Column 3 of Table 4–17 gives the net never smoker versus smoker result of 28 cents per pack. With the NHIS data there is no change in discounted life expectancy (not shown) at 5 percent. Nonsmoking smokers are less healthy than never smokers at young ages, but become more healthy at older ages.[10] Never smokers have slightly lower pension and nursing home costs, lower medical costs, and less covered work loss than nonsmoking smokers. The wage rates for never smokers are higher than for nonsmoking smokers, even after controlling for education. It seems implausible that these differences are causally related to smoking. We have therefore continued to use the wages

TABLE 4-17. Sensitivity of external costs per pack to assumptions at 5 percent discount rate (1986 dollars)

Cost	Base Case[a]	All NHIS Data	Comparison to Never Smoker	Lower Bound[b]	Total Costs[c]
Costs per pack					
Medical care	0.26	0.26	0.30	0.15	0.36
Sick leave	0.01	0.05	0.04	0.01	0.03
Group life insurance	0.05	0.05	0.06	0.05	0.05
Nursing home care	−0.03	−0.03	−0.02	−0.03	−0.06
Retirement pension[d]	−0.24	−0.24	−0.20	−0.38	−0.24
Fires	0.02	0.02	0.02	0.02	0.02
Taxes on earnings per pack	−0.09	−0.09	−0.09[e]	−0.05	−0.93[f]
Total net costs per pack[g]	0.15	0.20	0.28[e]	−0.15	?[h]

a. From Table 4-16, column 2. Effect of changing current smokers and former smokers to never smokers; other characteristics held constant.

b. Narrow definition of medical effects; no effects of smoking on early retirement.

c. Include internal costs.

d. Includes disability insurance.

e. Value shown is nonsmoking smoker's differential; never smokers actually pay 51 cents more earnings tax per pack than smokers because of higher earning rates. It is implausible that their higher earnings rates are causally related to smoking, and we have assumed they are not so related. Had we used the figure of 51 cents, total net costs would be 63 cents.

f. Earnings, not taxes on earnings.

g. (Sum of costs) minus taxes on earnings. Because of rounding, cost categories may not sum to total net costs.

[h]Loss of life, and pain and suffering by smoker and family are not included; see text.

of smokers in our calculations. If we had used the actual wage rates of never smokers, the figure of 9 cents would increase to 51 cents.

Smokers may have different patterns of medical use for reasons unrelated to smoking. As a sensitivity test, we examined the use of services thought to be related to poor health habits (Table 4–17, column 4). This lower bound results in a net saving of 15 cents per pack.

Finally, for those interested in total costs rather than external costs, column 5 of Table 4–17 gives total, not just external, costs for several components. These figures may permit comparison with other estimates in the literature. Total medical costs are 36 cents per pack, sick leave 3 cents per pack, nursing home payments 6 cents per pack, and the difference in total earnings is 93 cents per pack, which stems from the nonsmoking smoker's greater life expectancy. The differences between the total costs shown in the last column and the external costs shown in the earlier columns occur because different areas are collectively financed to different degrees; for example, group life insurance is fully financed collectively and does not change at all. Our estimate of the proportion of work-loss costs financed collectively is unreliable. Nevertheless, column 5 shows that even if coverage were complete, it would not have much of an effect on results for the components shown in the table.

Two other costs borne by the smoker are larger than any of the costs shown in Table 4–17. The biggest component of total costs is the cost to the smoker of premature death and disability. Because this cost is borne by the smoker, we have not included it in the tables. What is the cost to a person and his or her family of losing 28 discounted minutes for each pack of cigarettes smoked? In monetary terms, this is 93 cents of wages (see Table 4–17).[11] But surveys have shown that most people are willing to pay many times their expected increase in earnings for additional safety. Thus, this component of costs may be as much as $5.00 a pack (Howard, 1978). Another large component of costs to the smoker is, of course, the retail price of the cigarettes themselves, about $1.00 a pack. Because of the imprecision in the magnitude of this cost, we left the lower right entry in Table 4–17 a question mark.

Sensitivity of Costs to Medical Prices and Wage Growth

In our calculations we assumed that medical prices and wages are constant over time in real terms. This assumption ignores the possibility of increases in real medical prices as well as real wage growth. To correct for such increases, we would clearly need to know how much medical care prices and wages will grow relative to other goods and services. But given the history of medical prices and wages over the last three decades, it would be difficult to predict their future course.

We *can* determine how sensitive our estimates are to changes in real medical prices. If real medical prices were to rise by 5 percent per year, then the medical costs per pack at a 5 percent discount rate would just equal the nondiscounted medical costs with no medical inflation—in other words, medical inflation would cancel out the discounting factor. Thus, at a 5 percent discount rate with 5 percent inflation, the external medical cost per pack would be 38 cents (rather than 26 cents with no inflation in real medical prices) and the total external cost would be 27 cents (rather than 15 cents). It is likely that the 5 percent real rate of medical inflation would also apply to nursing home costs and would decrease nursing home costs by 23 cents (= −26 + 3), thereby *reducing* the total external economic cost per pack to 4 cents. Moreover, if in the future we develop an effective cure for lung cancer (or heart disease), this treatment would have a strong effect on costs. If the treatment were inexpensive, costs would fall; but if it were more expensive than the current ineffective treatments, costs would rise.

Thus, it appears that the tax necessary to correct for the external costs of smoking is somewhat sensitive to assumptions about the future course of medical prices. The likely direction of error is that we have overstated the external costs; that is, if we were to assume that medical prices would increase, the tax necessary for smokers to pay their way exactly would fall.

Other External Costs

Our estimates of the costs of smoking do not include *all* the external effects of cigarette smoking. They ignore the adverse effects of passive smoking on those outside the smoker's family, especially non-smokers, as well as mortality effects within the smoker's family and certain costs of fires.

The Surgeon General (USDHHS, 1986) reports that passive smoking is responsible for about 2,400 deaths per year due to lung cancer. Passive smoking has also been linked to reduced lung function in children of smokers, a higher incidence of respiratory problems for children and others, as well as the displeasure of consuming unwanted cigarette smoke.

Many of these costs are within the family and therefore, under our assumptions, internal. If, to compute an upper bound, we treated all 2,400 deaths as external costs and valued them at $1.66 million in 1986 dollars (based on Shepard and Zeckhauser, 1984), we would add about 14 cents per pack to external costs.

By omitting maternity costs from our calculations, we have also omitted the extra costs of neonatal care incurred because some women smoke during pregnancy. These women are twice as likely as nonsmokers to have low-birthweight babies, and those babies average 200 grams lower in birthweight than the babies of nonsmokers.

Low birthweight is one of the strongest predictors for use of neonatal intensive care units (NICUs). An Office of Technology Assessment report (1987) on neonatal intensive care indicates that between 150,000 and 200,000 infants are treated annually in NICUs, and 50 to 80 percent are low-birthweight babies. The average cost per baby of NICU use is $12,000 to $39,000. If we use the midpoint of each range, the estimated total cost for neonatal care of low-birthweight babies is $2.9 billion.

According to the NHIS, 35 percent of all women between 20 and 29 years were current smokers in 1983. If as many as one-third of pregnant women persist in smoking, then smoking may be responsible for as many as one-quarter of all NICU costs for low-birthweight babies. In 1986 Americans purchased 652 billion cigarettes (*Statistical Abstract of the United States, 1988*, p. 719). Our estimates of the direct dollar costs of smoking, then, are probably too low by up to 2 cents per pack.

In addition, the Surgeon General estimates that 2,500 fetal deaths occur because of smoking during pregnancy. If we were to value these infant deaths at the same $1.66 million that we use for adult deaths, and assume that the smoking mothers ignore the risks to their babies, then the external cost not considered by the smoker is 14 cents per pack.

Our estimates for the external cost of fires take into account the likelihood that an innocent bystander will be killed in a smoking-related fire. In 1984 there were 1,600 smoking-related deaths from fires in the United States (John Hull, National Fire Protection Association, and John Ottoson, U.S. Fire Administration, personal communications). Based on a willingness-to-pay for a human life of $1.66 million in 1986 dollars,[12] and the total volume of smoking from the NHIS 1983 survey (corrected for underreporting), we estimate the value of the lost lives in smoking-related fires to be 9 cents per pack of cigarettes. Because virtually all of these deaths are smokers or members of their families, these costs can be considered internal, not external.

Summary

The major determinants of the external costs of cigarette smoking are medical costs, pensions, and taxes on earnings. Although the results from our two data sets are similar, the estimated magnitude of the external costs of smoking are quite sensitive to methods, especially to the discount rate used. Because smoking increases these costs among the young and middle-aged but decreases the need for support of the aged, the discount rate is a critical determinant of the net costs of smoking. Without discounting, smoking appears to save nonsmokers money because it reduces the period of aged dependency. At reasonable (real) discount rates, smoking appears to cost nonsmokers 15 or more cents per pack. Including all of the other costs discussed, the estimated external costs of smoking range from 31 to 52 cents per pack.

5

The External Costs of Heavy Drinking

People who consume more than five drinks a day reduce their life expectancy at age 20 by about 20 minutes per excess ounce of ethanol.[1] (We define excess ounces as anything over two drinks per day.) These individuals also ring up heavy external costs for the set of collectively financed costs we examined for smokers. For that set, the lifetime external costs per heavy drinker are $3,200 (at a 5 percent discount rate)—a great deal more than smokers' costs. In addition, drinkers impose steep external costs through crime and auto accidents. When those costs are added, the net external lifetime cost per heavy drinker is a daunting $42,000, or $1.19 per excess ounce consumed. As explained earlier, it is not possible to tax only "excess" ounces. When we prorate the costs over all alcohol consumed, every ounce of ethanol imposes 48 cents in external costs.

This chapter describes the statistical and cost analyses from which we derived those estimates. As we did for smokers, we examine the prevalence of drinking and discuss its association with collectively financed costs. We also estimate the other major costs: the value of the lives of innocent bystanders lost in auto accidents related to drinking, property damage, and crime. We present findings from both descriptive and multiple regression analyses. We conclude with estimates of the external costs heavy drinkers impose on others, including the results of our sensitivity analysis.

Prevalence of Drinking

Our purpose in this project was to estimate the external costs of heavy drinking. Thus, we did not simply categorize people as abstainers, former drinkers, and current drinkers. We further divided current drinkers into four categories by the amount of ethanol *they*

TABLE 5-1.   Drinking status of persons 20 through 59 years of age, Health Insurance Experiment[a]

				Current Drinker[b]			
Subgroup	Sample Size	Abstainer	Former Drinker	0.01–0.21 ounce/day	0.22–0.99 ounce/day	1.0–2.99 ounces/day	3.0 or more ounces/day
TOTAL	3,011	35.9	2.8	25.6	25.2	8.5	2.0
Males aged —							
20–29	478	15.9	1.9	24.5	37.7	17.0	3.1
30–39	412	18.0	3.4	24.5	35.4	14.3	4.4
40–49	260	24.6	4.6	20.8	29.6	14.2	6.2
50–59	215	27.4	7.0	22.3	27.9	13.0	2.3
Females aged —							
20–29	585	46.0	1.5	29.9	18.8	3.3	0.5
30–39	481	49.3	2.1	27.2	17.9	3.5	0.0
40–49	274	55.5	1.5	22.6	17.2	2.2	1.1
50–59	306	48.7	3.9	27.5	17.0	2.9	0.0
Race							
Black	438	52.5	4.1	14.4	16.7	8.5	3.9
Nonblack	2,573	33.0	2.6	27.6	26.6	8.5	1.7
Years of education							
0–11	811	47.2	5.7	18.6	18.4	7.3	2.8
12	1,159	37.3	2.3	26.6	23.2	8.6	2.0
13–15	543	30.2	1.5	28.6	29.8	8.5	1.5
16	320	21.6	0.9	31.9	34.1	10.0	1.6
More than 16	178	18.0	0.6	31.5	38.8	10.7	0.6
Residence							
Dayton	602	45.2	1.8	19.4	22.9	10.0	0.7
Seattle	701	23.4	1.9	33.0	31.4	8.8	1.6
Fitchburg	359	32.0	2.2	26.7	29.0	7.2	2.8
Franklin	465	24.5	0.9	31.6	30.3	10.8	1.9
Charleston	387	42.1	3.4	23.8	18.4	9.0	3.4
Georgetown	497	50.7	7.2	17.9	16.9	4.6	2.6

a. Numbers represent percentage of row total.

b. Represents average volume of ethanol consumed daily, based on reported intake of beer (0.04 ounce ethanol per ounce beer), wine (0.15 ounce ethanol per ounce wine), and liquor (0.45 ounce ethanol per ounce liquor).

reported consuming, on average, per day. The heaviest drinkers were those who reported imbibing 3.0 or more ounces per day (over six drinks of hard liquor or six cans of beer).[2]

Health Insurance Experiment

Prevalence. When the HIE began, 61 percent of people 20 to 59 years of age classified themselves as current drinkers. As Table 5–1 shows, about 36 percent of the sample were "abstainers" (people who said they had never drunk alcohol on a regular basis), and almost 3 percent were former drinkers (people who reported consuming alcohol on a regular basis in the past, but not during the previous year). Just over half the sample *reported* drinking less than 1 ounce of ethanol per day, and only about 10 percent said they drank more than that.

Patterns. More men than women identified themselves as current

TABLE 5-2.   Drinking status at enrollment and at exit among persons 20 through 59 years of age, Health Insurance Experiment[a]

	Status at Enrollment		
Status at Exit	Abstainer (N = 981)	Former Drinker (N = 67)	Current Drinker (N = 1,640)
Abstainer	73.7	34.3	13.0
Former drinker	3.1	37.3	2.4
Current drinker	23.2	28.4	84.6

a. Stability (agreement) of drinking status between enrollment and exit significantly better than chance (kappa = 0.59, z = 33.2). Numbers represent percentage of column total.

drinkers, and they reported drinking more per day. More nonblacks were current drinkers than blacks and, in most categories, reported drinking more. But more blacks fell into the "heaviest drinker" category, saying they drank 3.0 or more ounces of ethanol a day.

Recall that in the case of smoking, we found that the more education people had, the less likely they were to smoke. For drinking we found the reverse. With the exception of the heaviest drinking category, the more education, the higher the percentage of people who drank. Among the heaviest drinkers, the situation reversed: the less education, the higher the percentage who drank. As for sites, Dayton, Charleston, and Georgetown had much higher percentages of abstainers than the other three sites. Franklin and Charleston also had a higher percentage than all the other sites of people who fell into the two heaviest drinking categories (combined).

Stability of status. Drinking status was fairly stable during the experiment, but not as stable as smoking. About 79 percent of the sample maintained their status over the course of the experiment.[3] Table 5–2 shows that 74 percent of abstainers, 37 percent of former drinkers, and 85 percent of current drinkers maintained their status from enrollment to the end of the HIE. Men were more stable in their drinking habits than women (82 and 78 percent, respectively).

National Health Interview Survey

A comparison of Tables 5–1 and 5–3 reveals that the NHIS sample had fewer self-reported abstainers than the HIE sample (30 and 36 percent, respectively), but more of the NHIS sample reported being former or light drinkers ($p < 0.0001$ based on χ^2 test). Sex and race

TABLE 5-3.   Drinking status of persons 20 through 59 years of age, National Health Interview Survey, 1983[a]

Subgroup	Sample Size	Abstainer	Former Drinker	Current Drinker[b]			
				0.01–0.21 ounce/day	0.22–0.99 ounce/day	1.0–2.99 ounces/day	3.0 or more ounces/day
TOTAL	15,877	29.8	5.5	32.1	22.8	8.2	1.7
Males aged —							
20–29	2,262	16.3	3.0	28.7	34.7	14.2	3.3
30–39	1,844	13.3	6.8	31.8	32.7	12.8	2.6
40–49	1,374	17.2	10.1	29.8	25.8	13.6	3.6
50–59	1,352	18.0	12.2	29.2	22.9	14.6	3.2
Females aged —							
20–29	2,938	35.2	2.7	36.9	20.3	4.1	0.8
30–39	2,567	38.2	4.2	36.7	17.5	3.2	0.3
40–49	1,817	42.8	4.4	31.7	15.2	5.4	0.6
50–59	1,723	49.2	5.9	26.2	14.4	3.8	0.5
Race							
Black	1,572	46.3	5.8	25.0	15.7	5.6	1.7
Nonblack	14,247	28.0	5.4	32.9	23.6	8.5	1.7
Years of education							
0–11	3,132	41.8	9.2	23.6	16.1	7.5	1.9
12	6,427	31.1	5.3	33.2	21.4	7.6	1.6
13–15	3,149	23.4	4.2	35.3	26.1	9.3	1.7
16	1,811	21.7	3.3	34.6	29.2	9.4	1.8
More than 16	1,288	20.7	3.4	36.1	29.3	9.0	1.5

a. Numbers represent percentage of row total.

b. Represents average volume of ethanol consumed daily, based on reported intake of beer (0.04 ounce ethanol/ounce beer), wine (0.15 ounce ethanol/ounce wine), and liquor (0.45 ounce ethanol/ounce liquor).

differences in drinking roughly mirrored the differences in the HIE, except for the heaviest drinker category. In the NHIS, blacks did not have a higher percentage in that category. Education outcomes were also similar, except that education did not have as strong an inverse relation for the heaviest drinkers.

The Effects on Health Care and Work Loss

As we did for smoking, we calculated the effects of heavy drinking on collectively financed programs, both descriptively and with multiple regression. In considering outpatient and inpatient use, we looked at effects under two definitions: all care (excluding well-care and maternity) and care for diagnoses related to all three poor health habits. The descriptive analysis adjusted only for age and sex, and compared use of medical services by abstainers and the four categories of current drinkers. The regression analyses controlled for all three habits

TABLE 5-4. Annual utilization of services among persons 20 through 59 years of age, by drinking status, Health Insurance Experiment[a]

| | Abstainers | | Current Drinkers | | | | | | | |
| | | | 0.01–0.21 ounce/day | | 0.22–0.99 ounce/day | | 1.0–2.99 ounces/day | | 3.0 ounces/day or more | |
Utilization	% with 1 or more	Average per person	% with 1 or more	Average per person	% with 1 or more	Average per person	% with 1 or more	Average per person	% with 1 or more	Average per person
All outpatient episodes[b]	76.7	3.21	82.7	3.24	80.4	3.23	78.2	3.31	44.5	1.74
Episodes possibly related to drinking	8.6	0.10	6.5	0.08	7.8	0.09	11.6	0.13	11.7	0.14
All hospitalizations[c]	10.2	0.13	7.5	0.10	8.1	0.10	10.6	0.13	6.1	0.09
Hospitalizations possibly related to drinking	1.3	0.01	0.9	0.02	1.1	0.01	2.0	0.02	0.9	0.01

a. All figures adjusted for age and sex using the direct method, with HIE enrollment sample as standard.
b. Excludes episodes related to maternity and well-care.
c. Excludes hospitalizations related to maternity and pregnancy.

and other characteristics of individuals as well. Thus, the regression results are more likely to represent the effects of heavy drinking alone.

Descriptive Results for Health Care

Tables 5–4 and 5–5 present the descriptive results for the HIE and the NHIS sample, respectively. As Table 5–4 indicates, people in the HIE sample who reported consuming large quantities of alcohol (3.0 ounces or more per day of ethanol) were much *less* likely to have outpatient episodes than the rest of the sample. Only 45 percent of them had one or more episodes, while 77 percent of the abstainers

TABLE 5-5. Drinking response: age- and sex-adjusted annual rates, National Health Interview Survey, 1983[a]

Drinking Status	Doctor Visits	Admissions
Abstainers	3.75	0.17
0.01–0.21 ounce/day	3.98	0.15
0.22–0.99 ounce/day	3.42	0.13
1.00–2.99 ounces/day	3.70	0.11
3+ ounces/day	5.71	0.20

a. Weighted to NHIS-1983 population mix if age ≥ 20.

and 83 percent of lighter drinkers had one or more episodes. Vogt and Schweitzer (1985) report a similar finding. This was not true of the NHIS sample, where the heaviest drinkers had the highest number of doctor visits (5.7), followed by the light drinkers (3.9).[4] For diagnoses related to drinking, however, the HIE heavy drinkers were the most likely to have outpatient episodes (Table 5–4, row 2, column 9; see Table 3–3 for a list of these diagnoses).

Hospitalizations were highest for moderately heavy drinkers and abstainers in the HIE. In the NHIS, the very heaviest drinkers had the highest rates, followed by the abstainers.[5]

Multiple Regression Results

In the multiple regressions we estimated the effect of drinking on outpatient episodes, inpatient use, and work-loss days, controlling for a large set of variables in the HIE and NHIS 1983 data. The contrast group was "light drinkers" (those with a monthly consumption of 1.0 ounce of ethanol).[6]

HIE RESULTS

Outpatient episodes. As Table 5–6 indicates, the number of outpatient episodes was not significantly related to our drinking variables taken as a group—former drinker, abstainer or infrequent drinker, logarithm of monthly volume of ethanol, and logarithm squared of monthly volume. This result largely reflects the fact that increased monthly volume has no effect. Table 5–7 shows how insignificant the monthly volume terms were. The indicator variables for being a former drinker or abstainer were individually significant at better than the 10 percent level. Abstainers tended to have 13 to 17 percent

TABLE 5-6. Wald tests (X^2) for drinking response of persons 20 through 59 years of age, Health Insurance Experiment[a]

Habit	df	Outpatient Use		Inpatient Use	
		Excluding Well-Care	Habit-Related Diagnoses	Excluding Maternity	Habit-Related Diagnoses
Drinking	4	7.48	4.51	13.18**	14.21***

a. Significance levels: ** 5 percent, *** 1 percent; otherwise insignificant at the 10 percent or better level; df = degrees of freedom. Habit-related diagnoses from Tables 3-1 through 3-4.

TABLE 5-7.   Health Insurance Experiment drinking coefficients (*t* statistics)[a]

Type of Care	Former Drinker	Abstainer	ln (Monthly Volume Ethanol)	ln^2 (Monthly Volume Ethanol)	Chi Squared(4)
Outpatient care					
All except well-care or maternity	0.197 (1.72)*	0.123 (2.32)**	0.0389 (0.86)	−0.00674 (−0.66)	7.48
Habit-related diagnoses	0.286 (1.70)*	0.153 (1.82)*	0.0741 (1.08)	−0.010 (−0.75)	4.51
Inpatient care					
All except well-care or maternity	0.744 (2.34)**	0.323 (1.89)**	−0.00811 (−0.06)	0.0150 (0.59)	13.18**
Habit-related diagnoses	1.054 (2.20)*	0.371 (1.24)	−0.135 (−0.58)	0.0619 (1.45)	14.21***

a. Significance levels: * 10 percent, ** 5 percent, *** 1 percent; otherwise insignificant at the 10 percent or better level. Units for dependent variables are log visits or admissions. Essentially, this model is a multiple regression of log visits or log hospitalizations versus the variables listed across the top of the table and other covariates.

more outpatient episodes than those who drank very little (the equivalent of a couple of drinks per month), based on the exponentiated value for abstainer coefficient in Table 5–7 ($e^{-0.123} − 1 = 0.13$, or 13 percent). In contrast, former drinkers had 22 percent more of the broadly defined episodes of outpatient care and 33 more percent of the narrower habit-related episodes than light drinkers.[7] The significance of the former drinkers is surprising, given the small number of such individuals in the HIE sample.

Inpatient care. Table 5–6 shows that drinking had a significant effect on the number of admissions under both the broader (everything except maternity) and the narrower (habit-related diagnoses) definitions of use ($p < 0.05$). As with outpatient care, we could not detect an effect of increased drinking within the group of current drinkers. Table 5–7 indicates that, compared with light drinkers, former drinkers had higher rates under either definition of use and abstainers had higher rates under the broad definition. Compared with light drinkers, former drinkers had 110 percent more hospitalizations under the broad definition and 187 percent more under the narrow definition.[8]

An issue to be considered is how much of the drinking effect is due to adverse effects of drinking and how much to related problems (depression, for example). A person can be depressed because of alcohol, or drink because of depression or anxiety. We tested the sensitivity of our findings to this phenomenon by including health status variables as explanatory variables. To the extent that drinking is mediated through health status, the significance of the drinking variables is reduced. This reasoning applies with special force to the mental health index, which is based to a large degree on items related to depression.

Including mental and other health status covariates did not alter any of our earlier conclusions. After health status was added, the estimated differences among the groups were less precise, but still significant. The size of the variable coefficients for former drinkers and abstainers fell by one-quarter to one-half. The coefficients of the monthly volume variables remained insignificant.

Work-loss days. For HIE men, we found that drinking had a significant effect on work loss—primarily for former drinkers. They had 38 percent more work loss than either abstainers or infrequent current drinkers ($p < 0.01$; not shown). Among current drinkers, work loss was not significantly related to the volume of monthly consumption.

National Health Interview Survey Results

As Table 5–8 indicates, the NHIS data show that drinking has a significant effect on outpatient visits and hospitalizations for all age groups combined, but not for work loss (both males and females). Among the elderly we observe significant drinking effects only for

TABLE 5-8.   National Health Interview Survey, 1983, drinking response (χ^2)[a]

Outcome	df	All Ages	60+
Visits	4	18.98***	5.75
Hospitalizations	4	42.02***	14.15***
Work loss (workers only)	4	2.18	6.57

a. Significance level: *** 1 percent; otherwise insignificant at the 10 percent or better level; df = degrees of freedom.

TABLE 5-9.   Drinking coefficients for National Health Interview Survey, 1983[a]

Outcome	Former Drinker	Abstainer	ln (Monthly Volume Ethanol)	$\ln^2$ (Monthly Volume Ethanol)	Chi Squared(4)
Outpatient	−0.162***	−0.003	−0.159***	0.0334***	18.98***
Inpatient	0.121*	0.353***	−0.062	0.0071	42.02***
Work loss (workers only)	0.216	0.356	0.121	−0.0212	2.18

a. Significance levels: * 10 percent, *** 1 percent; otherwise insignificant at the 10 percent or better level. Units for dependent variable are log visits, admissions, or work-loss days.

hospitalization. Table 5–9 shows that NHIS former drinkers have 15 percent ($e^{-0.162} = 0.85$) fewer visits ($p < 0.01$) and 13 percent ($e^{-0.121} = 1.13$) more admissions ($p < 0.10$) than infrequent drinkers. Abstainers do not have a significantly different visit rate than infrequent drinkers, but (as Table 5–9 indicates) they have 42 percent ($e^{0.353} = 1.42$) more hospitalizations ($p < 0.01$) than that group. (In the HIE results shown in Table 5–7, abstainers had 13 percent more episodes and 38 percent more admissions.)

For those who are currently drinking, we observed no relationship between monthly ethanol consumption and hospitalization rate. For office visits, however, there is a significant U-shaped relationship. As with work loss, the number of outpatient episodes falls with increased consumption up to about 0.8 drink per day and rises after that point. (The estimates for NHIS are derived from the coefficients in Table 5–9.)

Cost Analysis Results

Our cost analysis for drinking differs from the analyses for smoking and lack of exercise because drinking imposes an additional category of external costs. These costs arise from property damage, loss of innocent lives, and expenditures on the criminal justice system because of drunk driving.

Average Lifetime External Costs for Heavy Drinkers

Table 5–10 gives the lifetime external costs in each category for current heavy drinkers and former drinkers. We defined heavy drinkers

TABLE 5-10.   Lifetime external costs for heavy drinkers[a]

Cost	Discount Rate			
	0% Total	0% Women	5% Total	10% Total
Total ounces	70,400	53,200	27,800	15,700
Excess ounces	41,100	25,500	15,800	8,600
Years of life expectancy at age 20	54.1	57.5	18.1	10.1
Collectively financed costs[b]				
Medical care[c]	56	68	10	3
Sick leave	11	2	4	2
Group life insurance	8	2	2	1
Nursing home care	8	13	0.4	<0.05
Retirement pension	134	122	15	3
Immediate costs for motor vehicle accidents and criminal justice[d]				
Lives of nondrinkers	24	15	9.2	5.0
All other costs	14	9	5.5	3.0
Taxes on earnings[b]	246	118	32	9
Total net costs[b,e]	9	113	15	9

a. Ounces corrected for underreporting.

b. Measured in thousands of dollars.

c. Excludes maternity and well-care.

d. Assumes all alcohol-related immediate costs are due to excess drinking. If instead costs are proportional to amount drunk, these costs need to be multiplied by 0.68, the fraction of total alcohol that is consumed by heavy drinkers. Costs are computed by multiplying estimated immediate costs per ounce by (discounted) lifetime ounces.

e. (Sum of costs) minus taxes on earnings. Includes the value of innocent lives, crime, fires, and property damage. Because of rounding, categories may not sum to total.

as those who reported an average two or more drinks per day (five or more actual drinks, with correction for underreporting).[9] As a base case, we used data from the HIE on those aged 20–59 and data from the NHIS on older people. For the HIE sample, we included all medical expenses (except maternity and well-care) and all covered work loss. For the aged, we included all medical use. From the NHIS 1983 sample, we assumed that men would account for 80 percent of the heavy and former drinkers. We averaged the results for men and women accordingly, to make up the drinkers' total.

The first two columns show nondiscounted lifetime costs. We estimated that heavy drinkers will drink 70,400 ounces in their lifetime (and report drinking 25,600 ounces). This can be converted into drinks by multiplying by 2.2 drinks per ounce. Because the life expectancy at age 20 of these drinkers is 54 years, this number amounts to slightly more than three reported (seven actual) drinks a day on average (including zero for the nondrinking years of those who quit).[10] More than half of the drinks (the 41,100 ounces in row 2) are in excess of five actual (two reported) drinks per day.

The costs of drinking include more than the medical, sick leave, and other collectively financed costs that we examined for smoking. They include also the substantial costs of the criminal justice system, fire, and costs to others hurt or killed in traffic accidents caused by drinkers.

Because our two data sets, the HIE and the NHIS, do not contain information on these costs, we have relied on the work of others. Estimating these costs poses particular challenges. We could not model the way in which a person's drinking and other habits and characteristics affect the probability that he will damage property or kill an innocent bystander in an auto accident. For fatal accidents, we found no data that had the same structure as the HIE or NHIS on habits, socioeconomic variables, and whether or not an individual was implicated in a fatal accident. Such a data set would have allowed us to model the effect of drinking on these drunk-driving costs in the same way that we modeled its effect on collectively financed programs.

Instead, we had to rely on a less direct approach. We assumed that these external costs could be measured by the number of nondrinkers killed in accidents reportedly involving someone who was "driving under the influence." In much the same fashion we used others' estimates of the costs of fires and property damage associated with drinking.

Our estimates of mortality, based on the HRA, include the differential probability that a drinker will have a fatal accident but do not include the likelihood that an innocent bystander or nondrinking passenger will be killed in a drinking-related accident. The U.S. Department of Transportation (1986) estimates that there were 22,360 deaths in alcohol-related traffic accidents. Of those killed, two-thirds had been drinking. Thus, the external costs of drinking should include at least the lives of the 7,400 nondrinkers who were killed.

The problem is how to apportion the cost of innocent lives, crime, fire, and property damage to heavy drinking. We have two straightforward alternatives: (1) assign all of the costs of innocent lives to heavy drinkers; and (2) prorate the costs according to alcohol consumption. The first overstates the costs of heavy drinking, while the latter understates it. For this part of the analysis we chose the first alternative.

Our measure of heavy drinking is average consumption per day. An individual may have a low daily average, but occasionally drink heavily and drive. Such an individual is not a heavy drinker by our formal definition, but his behavior—drinking and driving—could impose heavy social costs. On the other hand, someone who drinks heavily on average is more likely to drink and drive (although not all heavy drinkers do so).

To estimate the costs of innocent lives, we assigned all of the 7,400 deaths to the excess drinking of heavy drinkers (approximately 10 percent of the adult population) and used a willingness-to-pay for a human life of $1.66 million in 1986 dollars (based on Shepard and Zeckhauser, 1984). The result, per heavy drinker, is an estimated $23,800, nondiscounted, for the lives of innocent bystanders killed in drinking-related accidents.[11] This figure is an upper bound on the costs of heavy drinking—heavy drinkers have been assigned the costs of all drunk driving, including accidents caused by individuals who do not regularly drink heavily. Had we chosen to prorate the costs by total rather than by excess consumption, the costs of excess drinking would be 60 percent less.

We based our costs of fire, crime, and property damage on the estimates of Harwood et al. (1984): motor vehicle accidents (property)—$3.6 billion; criminal justice—$3.1 billion; fires (property)—$507 million; and social programs (largely administration)—$54 million (all in 1986 dollars). If we attribute all these $7.2 billion in costs to excess consumption of alcohol, the external cost is about $14,000 per heavy drinker.

Rough though they are, these calculations indicate that the costs of fire, crime, and auto accidents (for both property and innocent lives) are much larger than one might expect—$38,000 per heavy drinker, nondiscounted.

Gender differences. Comparing nondiscounted total costs with costs for women, we see that women drinkers have substantially higher net costs because they live longer than men. Specifically, they have higher medical and nursing home costs, but less sick leave, group life insurance costs, pensions, and much lower taxes on earnings.

Discounting and total external costs. To this point, we have discussed only nondiscounted costs, but discounted costs are more relevant for policy. Comparing the collectively financed costs discounted at 5 percent with the nondiscounted costs, we see a tremendous drop in nursing home and pension costs. The other costs do not fall as much because some of them occur early in adulthood.

Whichever discount rate we use, the results are swamped by the costs of innocent lives lost, fire, crime, and property damage. These are immediate costs and therefore are not discounted. As the discount rate rises, the other components (especially the distant nursing home costs) become smaller and relatively less important, because the immediate costs do not change. Thus, at a 5 percent discount rate taxes on earnings paid by heavy drinkers are barely sufficient to pay for insured medical care, pension, nursing home, and other collectively financed costs. They are not sufficient to offset the costs of innocent lives lost, fire, crime, and property damage. When we add all the costs and subtract taxes on earnings, the total net lifetime cost per heavy drinker is $38,000.

The Difference between Heavy Drinkers and Controlled Heavy Drinkers

Table 5–11 shows the effect on all these costs if the former and heavy drinkers had never drunk to excess but retained all their other characteristics and habits (that is, if their drinking status changed to exactly five actual, or two reported, drinks a day). We constructed a table (not shown) similar to Table 5–10 for these "controlled or limited drinkers" and subtracted the resulting values from the values in Table 5–10. Controlling drinking increases life expectancy by 1.55 years overall (row 3), and greatly reduces medical costs. Because controlled drinkers live longer, their nursing home payments increase. For pension payments, however, two effects conflict. Many heavy drinkers retire and start to receive pensions early. This offsets their shorter

TABLE 5-11. Difference between heavy drinkers and controlled heavy drinkers

Cost	Discount Rate			
	0% Total	0% Women	5% Total	10% Total
Total ounces	41,100	25,500	15,800	8,600
Excess ounces	41,100	25,500	15,800	8,600
Years of life expectancy at age 20	−1.55	−0.55	−0.24	−0.06
Collectively financed costs[a]				
Medical care[b]	11	16	1.6	0.5
Sick leave	2	0.1	0.8	0.3
Group life insurance	0.7	0.1	0.3	0.2
Nursing home care	−0.6	−0.3	<0.05	<−0.05
Retirement pension	−1.5	2.1	0.5	0.2
Immediate costs for motor vehicle accidents and criminal justice[c]				
Lives of nondrinkers	24	15	9.2	5.0
All other costs	14	9	5.5	3.0
Taxes on earnings[a]	−14	−5	32	9
Total net external costs[a,d]	64	47	19	9

a. Costs are external. Measured in thousands of 1986 dollars.

b. Excludes maternity and well-care.

c. Assumes all alcohol-related immediate costs are due to excess drinking. If instead costs are proportional to amount drunk, these costs need to be multiplied by 0.40, the fraction of total alcohol that is excess drinking by heavy drinkers. Costs are computed by multiplying estimated immediate costs per ounce by (discounted) lifetime ounces.

d. (Sum of costs) minus taxes on earnings. Includes lives lost, crime, fires, and property damage. Because of rounding, categories may not sum to total.

life, so controlling drinking increases nondiscounted pension payments only slightly. Early disability also decreases the lifetime wages of drinkers.

The net effect of controlled drinking is a large decrease in nondiscounted external costs. These results differ from nondiscounted smoking results because drinking has a substantial effect on innocent bystanders. Also, early in life, drinking has a larger effect on medical costs, sick leave, early retirement, and so on, and does not have such a significant effect on life expectancy. Heavy drinkers live longer than smokers, but have more expenses along the way.

The discounted external lifetime costs, which are more relevant to policy, show a similar pattern. Total net costs to society of controlled drinkers are much lower than those of heavy drinkers. In all categories except nursing home payments, heavy drinkers impose external costs on society. The largest of these costs are due to crime, property damage, and the loss of innocent lives.

It may seem paradoxical that the nondiscounted external costs of heavy drinkers are only $9,000 in Table 5–10, but the external costs of heavy drinking are $64,000 in Table 5–11. In the former, we are simply reporting that drinkers cost $9,000 more than they pay in. In contrast, Table 5–11 indicates that if heavy drinkers had never been heavy drinkers they would have cost society even less (no extra medical care, no extra sick leave, no extra fires and property damage, and no extra lives lost). They would also have paid even more into the system in taxes. The difference between what they did as drinkers and what they would have done if they had never been heavy drinkers is $64,000 nondiscounted. The removal of the fires, property damage, and innocent lives effects an immediate saving of $38,000. Heavy drinking also results in a loss of $14,000 in taxes on discounted earnings that would otherwise have been paid into the system. The reason is that men earn more than women, and heavy drinkers are disproportionately male: according to the NHIS 1983, over all ages men are about four times more likely than women to be heavy drinkers. These two components alone account for $52,000 of the $64,000 nondiscounted external costs of heavy drinking. Discounted at 5 percent, the lifetime costs of heavy drinking are $42,000.

External Costs per Excess Ounce

To estimate the external costs of drinking per excess ounce, we divided the costs due to drinking by the lifetime number of excess ounces. Table 5–12 gives the results.

TABLE 5-12.   External costs of heavy drinkers per excess ounce (1986 dollars)[a]

Cost per Excess Ounce	Discount Rate		
	0%	5%	10%
Medical and pension costs			
Medical care[b]	0.26	0.10	0.05
Sick leave	0.06	0.05	0.04
Group life insurance	0.02	0.02	0.02
Nursing home care	−0.01	<0.005	<0.005
Retirement pension[c]	−0.04	0.03	0.02
Taxes on earnings	−0.35	−0.06	−0.02
Net medical and pension costs	0.63	0.26	0.15
Motor vehicle accidents and criminal justice costs			
Lives of nondrinkers	0.58	0.58	0.58
All other costs[d]	0.35	0.35	0.35
Total net costs[e]	1.56	1.19	1.08
Minutes of life expectancy at age 20	−20	−8	−4

a. Costs per excess ounce are calculated by dividing by the discounted number of excess ounces.

b. Excludes maternity, well-care, and dental. Also does not include costs of medical care to others caused by drunk driving.

c. Includes disability insurance.

d. The 35-cent figure is high because certain of the costs are internal, such as the property damage in motor vehicle accidents paid by the alcoholic driver in deductibles or other copayments and higher premiums. Any overstatement, however, is probably offset by our omission of the external costs associated with the effects of alcoholism on spouses and children (e.g., their use of insured mental health services) and those associated with the increased risk of alcoholism for these dependents, some costs of which will be external.

e. (Sum of costs) minus taxes on earnings. Because of rounding, categories may not sum to total.

Each actual (as opposed to reported) excess ounce of alcohol causes a loss of 20 minutes of life expectancy (10 minutes per drink). It also leads to a 26 cent increase in nondiscounted external medical costs; a 6 cent rise in covered work loss; small effects on group life, pension, and nursing home costs; 35 cents less in taxes on earnings; 58 cents for lost lives of innocent bystanders; and 35 cents for fire, crime, and other property damage—for a total external cost of $1.56 per excess ounce.

As discussed earlier, from a policy standpoint discounted costs are more relevant than nondiscounted costs in considering problems that have long-term effects. Table 5–12 shows total external costs discounted at 0, 5, and 10 percent. Throughout this range the costs per excess ounce fall gradually as the discount rate rises. (Some drinking costs are for hospitalization and early retirement, which occur later than much of the drinking.) At a 5 percent discount rate each excess ounce of ethanol imposes an external cost of $1.19, while at 10 percent the external cost is $1.08.

From a policy perspective, particularly for tax purposes, it makes more sense to divide costs of drinking by *all ounces for all drinkers*, instead of excess ounces for heavy drinkers. Prorated over all consumption, our best estimate of the cost of drinking is about 48 cents per ounce of ethanol.

Sensitivity Analysis

We conducted sensitivity analyses varying some of the assumptions of the cost model. For comparison, column 1 of Table 5–13 repeats column 2 of Table 5–12. Because our sensitivity analyses focused on the collectively financed programs (such as medical care and pensions), Table 5–13 does not include the substantial external costs associated with crime and drunk driving. Those costs would add 93 cents to the net in each column, except column 3: light drinkers might well be responsible for drunk-driving accidents, but abstainers could not be.

To test the sensitivity to data source, we used NHIS data for all age groups instead of only the old. Column 2 shows that the principal change with the NHIS data is that covered work loss is not affected by drinking and hence the net external costs (excluding the drunk-driving costs) are 23 to 26 cents per actual excess ounce. The consistency of the other findings is reassuring.

To test the sensitivity to how we estimated the health effects of drinking, we contrasted heavy drinkers with abstainers and light drinkers rather than with the hypothetical controlled drinkers. We should thereby get an upper bound on health effects and on the tax, because it assigns to drinking all the differences between heavy drinkers and others. Column 3 gives the results. The difference in life expectancy between heavy drinkers and the group of moderate, light, and never drinkers is more than twice the difference between heavy and controlled drinkers (19 versus 8 minutes per excess ounce).

There are two reasons for this variance. First, we assume that con-

TABLE 5-13.   Sensitivity to assumptions: medical and pension costs per excess ounce, 5 percent discount rate (1986 dollars)

Cost per Excess Ounce	Base Case[a]	All NHIS Data	Abstainers and Light Drinkers	Lower Bound[b]	Total Costs[c]
Medical and pension costs					
Medical care[d]	0.10	0.11	0.07	0.11	0.16
Sick leave	0.05	<0.01	0.10	0.05	0.13
Group life insurance	0.02	0.01	0.04	0.02	0.02
Nursing home care	<0.01	<0.01	−0.01	<0.01	<0.01
Retirement pension[e]	0.03	0.05	−0.15	−0.05	0.03
Taxes on earnings	−0.06	−0.06	−0.14[f]	−0.03	−0.64[g]
Net medical and pension costs[h]	0.26	0.23	0.20	0.15	?[i]
Life expectancy at age 20 (minutes)	−8	−7	−19	−8	−8

a. From Table 5-12, column 2. Effect of changing heavy drinker to controlled drinker; other characteristics held constant.

b. Narrow definition of medical effects; no effect on early retirement.

c. Includes internal costs.

d. Excludes maternity, well-care, and dental.

e. Includes disability insurance.

f. Earnings of abstainers and light drinkers used to compute taxes are considerably higher than earnings of drinkers, even after controlling for education. To the extent that these earnings differences are not caused by drinking, drinkers' earnings should be used; in that case the −0.14 figure would be −0.03.

g. Earnings, not taxes on earnings.

h. (Sum of costs) minus taxes on earnings. Because of rounding, categories may not sum to total.

i. Loss of life, and pain and suffering are not included.

trolled drinkers consume fourteen reported drinks a week and so have more automobile accidents than the abstainers and light drinkers. Second, drinkers have other poor habits. Differences in sick leave and group life are doubled, but medical costs are smaller (heavy drinkers are less apt to get medical care). The additional years of life mean that abstainers and light drinkers get more retirement income than heavy drinkers, even after the early retirement of heavy drinkers is taken into account.

After we have controlled for education, the earnings for abstainers and light drinkers still are considerably higher than for controlled drinkers. Part of the reason is the lower wage rates of former drinkers, and part is the early retirement of drinkers. To the extent that earnings differences are not effects of drinking, we should use drinkers' earnings; the 14 cent figure in Table 5–13, column 3, should be 3 cents.

To compute a lower bound for the external costs of drinking, we restricted medical services to those known to be related to drinking. The resulting estimate of medical costs is 11 cents per excess ounce, about the same as the overall estimate. Even though drinking-related medical costs are less than 10 percent of the discounted total medical costs, they contain all the differences between the controlled drinker and the heavy drinker. This finding implies that the higher total medical costs are causally related to drinking, and does not support the view that heavy drinkers are hypochondriacs or that there is some other noncausal connection.[12]

Early retirement can have a substantial effect on both pensions and taxes paid on earnings.[13] Because we have few longitudinal data, we attributed early retirement to prior heavy drinking. It is possible, however, that retirement for other reasons permits people to drink, rather than that drinking causes people to retire early. To test the impact of our assumption that the difference is caused by drinking, we recalculated retirement values and taxes on earnings assuming that drinking had no effect on early retirement. This result is also shown in the lower bound column. The retirement payments change enormously: the earlier deaths of heavy drinkers cause them to receive 8 cents per ounce less than if they were controlled drinkers. Also, if drinking has no effect on early retirement, the earnings taxes paid are 3 cents less than for controlled drinkers. All together, the lower bound on net medical, pension, and other collectively financed costs of drinking is 15 cents per excess ounce. Adding crime and the losses from drunk driving (not shown) yields a lower bound estimate of the total net cost per excess ounce of $1.08.

Several components of total costs are shown in the last column to permit comparison with other estimates in the literature. Per excess ounce, total medical costs are 16 cents; sick-leave costs are 13 cents; group life, nursing home, and retirement payments do not change; and the difference in total earnings is a loss of 64 cents. These changes from external costs relate to the differing rate of collective financing in the various areas.

Two other costs borne by the heavy drinker are larger than any shown in Table 5–13. The biggest component of total costs, his or her own premature death and disability, is borne by the heavy drinker and so is not included in the tables. What are the costs to a person and his family of losing 20 minutes of life and bearing a larger amount of disability? We have calculated that on average this is 64 cents of wages per excess ounce. But surveys have shown that most people are willing to pay many times their expected increase in earnings for safety. This component of costs may well be up to $2.00 an ounce (Howard, 1978). Another sizable component of costs to the drinker is the price of the drinks themselves, about $1.00 per ounce of ethanol.

Finally, the external cost of drinking is sensitive to the loss of innocent lives, because that loss accounts for nearly half of external costs. Phelps (1988) suggests that the usual estimates of drunk driving are underestimates, because some states are less likely to test those involved in motor vehicle fatalities for evidence of alcohol abuse. If we were to base our estimate of lives lost on states with more thorough testing, there would be 9,400 lost innocent lives, which would add 16 cents per excess ounce to the external costs of heavy drinking. Also, if we were to use a less conservative estimate of the value of a lost life, say $3 million instead of $1.66 million, the cost per excess ounce would increase by 46 cents.

Our estimates are also conservative in that they omit the external costs associated with the effects of alcoholism on spouses and children (for example, the use of insured mental health services) and those associated with the measured risk of alcoholism for these dependents.

Summary

The major determinants of the external costs of drinking are the value of the lives of innocent bystanders in drinking-related auto accidents (58 cents per excess ounce) and the cost of crime and property damage (35 cents per excess ounce). Of secondary importance are the costs of collectively financed programs such as medical insurance and retirement; these come to 26 cents per excess ounce. The total external costs of heavy drinking are $1.19 per excess ounce. If we divide the costs of drinking by *all ounces for all drinkers,* instead of excess ounces for heavy drinkers, our best estimate of the cost of heavy drinking is about 48 cents per ounce of ethanol.

Results from our two data sets are quite similar, but our assumption that the connection between early retirement and heavy drinking is causal has a sizable effect on external costs. Compared to smoking, heavy drinking imposes higher external costs but has less effect on own-life expectancy. The external costs of drinking are higher in part because of the number of innocent lives lost to drunk driving; with smoking, the loss of life is largely the smoker's.

6

The External Costs of Sedentary Life-Styles

The sedentary 20-year-old reduces his or her life expectancy by 10 months and imposes surprisingly high external costs. Sedentary people consume more benefits than active people from collectively financed programs such as sick leave and health, disability, and group life insurance. Because they die earlier, they pay lower lifetime taxes on earnings. But they collect less in public and private pensions. As a result of these differences, the sedentary person imposes $1,650 in discounted lifetime external costs—almost double the costs of smoking.

This chapter describes the analyses from which that estimate derives. As we did for smoking and drinking, we begin by examining the prevalence of exercise and its association with use of medical services and work loss. We also present the results of a descriptive analysis, which controlled only for age and sex, and of a regression analysis, which controlled for other factors that may affect health outcomes.

Prevalence of Exercise

The HIE and NHIS data present a problem for comparative estimates, because the questions asked do not produce comparable categories. The HIE asked about the frequency and intensity of exercise (see Appendix C, questions 29 to 34). In contrast, the NHIS questionnaire asked respondents how much they exercised *relative* to other people of their age and sex. These differences led to large apparent differences in activity level between the two samples.

Prevalence and Stability in the HIE Sample

Based on answers to the HIE questionnaire, we categorized individuals as light, moderate, or heavy exercisers. We subdivided the groups by age and sex, race, years of education, and site of residence. Table 6–1 shows the results.

Overall, only 24 percent of the HIE sample claimed to be light exercisers, while more than 75 percent claimed to exercise moderately (63.4 percent) or heavily (12.6 percent). These totals mask differences among the subgroups:

(1) Men were more likely than women to be heavy exercisers and women were more likely to be light exercisers. Approximately the same percentage of both sexes reported exercising moderately.

(2) For both sexes the older the age group, the higher the percentage of light exercisers. In general, the percentage of moderate and heavy exercisers declined with age for both sexes, except for women who reported heavy exercise. For that group, the percentage of heavy exercisers was higher among 40- to 59-year-olds than among the 20 to 39 age group.

(3) As for race, a higher percentage of blacks reported light and heavy exercise, while a higher percentage of nonblacks reported moderate exercise.

(4) The correlation with education was also mixed. The more education, the more likely people were to be moderate exercisers, and the less likely they were to be light or heavy exercisers.

Our site results require some clarification. Table 6–1 suggests that Dayton had a radically lower percentage of moderate exercisers and a radically higher percentage of heavy exercisers than we found at the other sites. In fact, these findings probably result from dissimilarity in the wording of the question about exercise in Dayton and at the other sites. Where the question was worded the same, we found that the two rural sites (Franklin and Georgetown) had a higher percentage of heavy exercisers than the urban sites.

Our findings suggest that people are less stable in their exercise habits than they are in smoking and drinking. Overall, only 64 percent of the sample maintained the same exercise status from enrollment to exit. Table 6–2 shows that this overall rate broke down to 78 percent for moderate, 48 percent for light, and 25 percent for heavy exercisers.[1] Stability percentages did not differ by age or sex.

Prevalence in the NHIS

Because the NHIS and HIE asked different questions, it is problematical to compare exercise prevalence for the two samples. The HIE asked how often and how strenuously respondents exercised. The NHIS asked if they were more, less, or about as active as others

TABLE 6-1. Level of physical exercise of persons 20 through 59 years of age, Health Insurance Experiment[a]

Subgroup	Sample Size	Level of Exercise		
		Light	Moderate	Heavy
TOTAL	3,074	24.0	63.4	12.6
Males aged —				
20–29	495	11.5	70.9	17.6
30–39	424	18.2	63.0	18.9
40–49	264	21.6	60.2	18.2
50–59	217	30.0	55.8	14.3
Females aged —				
20–29	593	22.3	71.7	6.1
30–39	495	28.5	62.6	8.9
40–49	279	33.3	55.2	11.5
50–59	307	37.8	52.4	9.8
Race				
Black	441	28.1	55.6	16.3
Nonblack	2,633	23.3	64.7	12.0
Years of education				
0–11	832	29.6	54.6	15.9
12	1,180	22.4	65.1	12.5
13–15	555	20.7	68.8	10.5
16	325	20.9	69.2	9.9
More than 16	182	24.7	65.4	9.9
Residence				
Dayton (see text)	615	28.9	44.2	26.8
Seattle	723	22.4	71.1	6.5
Fitchburg	376	22.9	69.4	7.7
Franklin	474	15.4	73.6	11.0
Charleston	386	29.0	61.4	9.6
Georgetown	500	25.4	63.0	11.6

a. Status at enrollment, 1974–1978. Numbers represent percentage of row total.

their age. People may unconsciously compare themselves with others when they are asked how often and how strenuously they exercise; nevertheless, the HIE was asking for an absolute answer, whereas the NHIS asked for a comparative one.

As Table 6–3 shows, about half of the NHIS respondents reported that they were about as active as other people their age, while 13

TABLE 6-2.   Physical exercise status at enrollment and at exit among persons 20
              through 59 years of age, Health Insurance Experiment[a]

	Status at Enrollment		
Status at Exit	Light Exerciser (N = 662)	Moderate Exerciser (N = 1,779)	Heavy Exerciser (N = 357)
Light exerciser	47.6	15.6	8.4
Moderate exerciser	50.0	78.0	66.4
Heavy exerciser	2.4	6.4	25.2

a. Stability (agreement) of exercise status between enrollment and exit significantly better than
chance (kappa = 0.27, z = 18.6). Numbers represent percentage of column total.

TABLE 6-3.   Level of physical exercise of persons 20 through 59 years of age, National
              Health Interview Survey, 1983[a]

		Level of Exercise		
Subgroup	Sample Size	Less Active than Average	Average	More Active than Average
Total	16,267	13.2	49.6	37.2
Males aged —				
20–29	2,310	9.3	46.7	44.0
30–39	1,895	9.1	47.0	43.9
40–49	1,414	12.2	44.7	43.1
50–59	1,398	14.0	44.3	41.8
Females aged —				
20–29	3,008	16.5	57.2	26.3
30–39	2,626	15.0	52.4	32.6
40–49	1,855	12.2	51.1	36.8
50–59	1,761	16.1	45.3	38.6
Race				
Black	1,630	17.2	47.0	35.8
Nonblack	14,576	12.8	49.9	37.4
Years of education				
0–11	3,218	18.1	50.6	31.3
12	6,584	12.3	52.0	35.7
13–15	3,231	12.7	47.0	40.4
16	1,848	10.9	47.2	41.8
More than 16	1,310	10.6	44.4	45.0

a. Numbers represent percentage of row total.

percent felt they were less active and 37 percent felt they were more active.

Despite the differences, the two samples showed some similar patterns. At all ages, a higher percentage of men than women saw themselves as more active than their peers. For men, comparative self-rating of exercise generally dropped with age, but as women aged an increasing percentage classified themselves as more active than their peers.

With regard to race, the patterns differed for the two samples. In both data sets blacks had a higher percentage of less active (light) exercisers and a lower percentage of average (moderate) exercisers. Nonblacks in the NHIS, however, had a higher percentage of more active (heavy) exercisers than were found in the HIE. Patterns according to education also differed in the NHIS: the higher the education level, the more likely people were to say that they exercised more than others their age.

Effects of Sedentary Life-Style

Causality presents a major problem in analyzing how exercise relates to use of health care and work loss. If exercise causes injuries, the analysis should show a higher incidence of health care for exercise-related conditions. The causal relationship should be fairly straightforward. Nonetheless, the relationship between lack of exercise and health care use is not that simple to establish. People in general may use health care more because they have conditions that exercise might prevent or ameliorate. Alternatively, people may exercise less or not at all because they have such conditions. Either way, analysis would show a correlation between use of medical services and lack of exercise.

The association between exercise and mortality raises the same chicken-and-egg issue. The HRA model treats exercise as an important risk factor for heart disease. Many epidemiologic studies have shown dramatic differences in future heart disease between those who are sedentary and those who exercise (Paffenbarger et al., 1986; Powell et al., 1987; Burdette and Mohr, 1979). These analyses have controlled for age and other health habits. Still, it is hard to rule out the possibility that heavy exercisers are inherently more healthy than sedentary people in unmeasured ways, so that inactive persons who take up exercise will not enjoy the gains in life expectancy that models based on those studies would predict. Because of this uncertainty, the forthcoming HRA model revision says only that exercise is probably good for one's health, and does not attempt to quantify its life-extending benefits.

We attempted to control for this problem in two ways. In the descriptive analysis, we included a category of people with physical or role limitations. In the regression analysis, we excluded such people. To check the sensitivity of our results to the possibility that health status may affect exercise, to our list of covariates we added general and mental health indexes and a count of the number of chronic diseases affecting each individual. In other ways the exercise analyses were similar to those described for smoking and drinking.

Descriptive Results

The descriptive analyses did not support the hypothesis that those who exercise heavily use more health care because of injuries. For the HIE, Table 6–4 shows that, in general, those who have a physical or role limitation (the "physically limited") are more likely to receive outpatient or inpatient care than the other three exercise subgroups. This relationship holds for all diagnoses and the diagnoses related to exercise or lack of exercise. (See Table 3–4 for list of diagnoses.) For both kinds of diagnoses, outpatient and inpatient use are higher for light exercisers than moderate exercisers. There is a small difference in the opposite direction for all outpatient care, excluding well-care. The chance of having one or more hospitalizations is also consistently higher for those reporting light exercise than those with moderate exercise, and higher for those reporting moderate exercise than those with heavy exercise. Again, it is also higher for hospitalizations possibly related to both exercise and lack of exercise.

For overall care we found generally the same pattern in the NHIS data, except for the advantages of more strenuous exercise. As Table 6–5 shows, people who reported more than average exercise had the same hospitalization rates as average exercisers and somewhat higher rates of work loss; there were negligible differences in their rates of doctor visits.

The presence of an acute or chronic health problem is quite likely to deter an individual from exercising, a case in which causality clearly runs from health and associated medical use to exercise rather than vice versa. The increase in outpatient and inpatient care for injuries among those who reported physical limitation or light exer-

TABLE 6-4. Annual utilization of services among persons 20 through 59 years of age, by exercise status, Health Insurance Experiment[a]

	Physically Limited		Light		Moderate		Heavy	
						Level of Exercise		
Utilization	% with 1 or more	Average per person	% with 1 or more	Average per person	% with 1 or more	Average per person	% with 1 or more	Average per person
All episodes[b]	85.7	4.36	77.9	3.20	78.9	2.95	76.9	2.81
Episodes possibly related to lack of exercise	34.3	0.54	25.3	0.37	24.6	0.35	24.8	0.38
Episodes possibly related to exercise	14.2	0.21	9.9	0.15	7.8	0.10	7.5	0.09
Episodes possibly related to lack of exercise or to exercise	42.7	0.75	30.9	0.52	29.9	0.45	29.5	0.47
All hospitalizations[c]	14.1	0.20	9.6	0.12	7.4	0.09	6.9	0.08
Hospitalizations possibly related to lack of exercise	3.4	0.04	1.6	0.02	1.5	0.02	1.3	0.01
Hospitalizations possibly related to exercise	0.6	0.01	0.7	0.01	0.2	0.00	0.2	0.00
Hospitalizations possibly related to lack of exercise or to exercise	3.9	0.05	2.3	0.03	1.7	0.02	1.4	0.02

a. All figures adjusted for age and sex using the direct method, with HIE enrollment sample as standard.
b. Excludes episodes related to maternity and well-care.
c. Excludes hospitalizations related to maternity and pregnancy.

TABLE 6.5. Annual rates of outcomes per person by exercise status, National Health Interview Survey, 1983[a]

Group	Doctor Visits	Admissions	Work-Loss Days
Physical or role limitation	8.34	0.34	2.44
Less than average exercise	4.06	0.20	1.31
Average exercise	2.82	0.12	1.05
More than average exercise	2.86	0.12	1.19

a. Age- and sex-adjusted to NHIS-1983 population mix if age ≥ 20.

cise may be evidence of reverse causality. As we have said, the role of reverse causality can be reduced by controlling for observed differences between those getting various degrees of exercise, which we did in the multiple regression analyses.

Multiple Regression Results

The multiple regression analyses used both the HIE and NHIS 1983 data. For HIE outpatient exposdes and inpatient use, we also employed a broader definition (all use excluding well-care and maternity, respectively) and a narrower definition related to poor health habits; see Tables 3–1 to 3–4. Although the regression analyses excluded people with physical limitations, our limitation measure is dichotomous and thus only a crude measure of ability to exercise. To check the sensitivity of our results to the possibility that health status may affect exercise, for the HIE data we added to our list of covariates the general and mental health indexes and the count of the number of chronic diseases.

HIE RESULTS

Analytical results for the HIE data were mixed. In the first analysis, which excluded only people with physical limitations, exercise made some significant differences in outpatient and inpatient use. In the second analysis, when we added the health status indexes, these differences were no longer significant. Evidently the magnitude of the effects of exercise depends on how one treats the causal relationship between health status and exercise.[2]

As Table 6–6 indicates, a joint test on all exercise variables (light versus moderate versus heavy exercisers) failed to show that exercise was significantly related to the number of outpatient episodes. There was weak evidence that exercise reduced use. Table 6–7 shows that moderate exercisers had a significant 12 percent fewer episodes than light exercisers, but strenuous exercisers had an insignificant 8 percent fewer overall episodes and 7 percent fewer habit-related episodes. We also found that heavy and moderate exercise were not significantly different from each other. The pattern of the effects was consistent across use in general and for habit-related diagnoses.

For inpatient use, Table 6–6 indicates that exercise did not relate significantly to overall care, but was significant for use involving the habit-related diagnoses ($p < 0.10$). Table 6–7 shows that amount of exercise had uneven effects. On the one hand, heavy exercisers had

TABLE 6-6. Wald tests (χ^2) for exercise response of persons 20 through 59 years of age, Health Insurance Experiment[a]

	df	Outpatient Use		Inpatient Use	
		Excluding Well-Care	Habit-Related Diagnoses[b]	Excluding Maternity	Habit-Related Diagnoses[b]
Exercise variables	2	0.89	1.66	3.94	5.06*

a. Significance level: * 10 percent; otherwise significant at the 10 percent or better level; df = degrees of freedom.

b. Includes all diagnoses related to poor health habits listed in Tables 3-1 through 3-4.

about 30 percent lower use rates than light exercisers, but the difference was significant only for overall care. On the other hand, moderate exercisers had inconsistent results across the two definitions. They had 10 percent less general inpatient use, but 15 percent higher use for exercise-related diagnoses; neither result was statistically significant.

When we tested the sensitivity of our results to the possibility that health status affects exercise, the significance disappeared. The new analyses yielded statistically insignificant exercise coefficients for both inpatient and outpatient care (results not shown in tables). The results were insensitive to the definition of health services used—the broader definition (excluding only well-care and maternity) or the narrower (habit-related) diagnoses. For inpatient care, the heavy exercisers had an insignificant 20 to 23 percent lower hospitalization

TABLE 6-7. Exercise response at enrollment of persons 20 through 59 years of age, Health Insurance Experiment[a]

Habit	Outpatient Use		Inpatient Use		Male Work Loss
	Excluding Well-Care	Habit-Related Diagnoses[a]	Excluding Maternity	Habit-Related Diagnoses[b]	
Exercise					
Light	100	100	100	100	100
Moderate	87.5***	84.4**	89.8	114.9	82.5
Heavy	92.1	92.8	72.2*	71.3	67.9**

a. Significance levels: * 10 percent, ** 5 percent, *** 1 percent; otherwise not significant at the 10 percent or better level. Significance levels not corrected for multiple comparisons.

b. Includes all diagnoses related to poor health habits listed in Tables 3-1 through 3-4.

rate than those with little or no exercise. For outpatient care, there was an insignificant 6 to 8 percent decline.

For adult males we did observe a significant and beneficial effect of exercise on work loss. As Table 6–7 shows, moderate exercisers had 18 percent fewer work-loss days than those with little exercise, while those with heavy exercise had 32 percent lower work loss ($p <$ 0.05). We could not do a sensitivity analysis for work loss, because we were unable to tell which work-loss days were attributable to which complaint.

NHIS RESULTS

We also examined the effects of lack of exercise using the 1983 NHIS for all adults and separately for the elderly (aged 60 or older). As Table 6–8 indicates, level of exercise was significantly related to outpatient and inpatient use for both the elderly and the nonelderly. It was significantly related to work loss only for the nonelderly.

The NHIS results show more pronounced exercise effects than the HIE results do. As a comparison of Tables 6–7 and 6–9 indicates, moderate exercisers in the NHIS had 28 percent lower rates than light exercisers, but only 12 percent lower in the HIE. Because of the difference in definitions, comparison of the two sources is somewhat problematical. Unfortunately, we had no alternative. We wanted to see if our results would have been measurably different had we used the NHIS approach—with its different population and definition.

In the NHIS, people who reported exercising less than average for their age group had 39 percent ($[100/72] - 1$) more office visits ($p <$ 0.001) and 52 percent ($[100/66] - 1$) more hospitalizations ($p < 0.001$) than those who exercised more than average, other things being equal. For both use rates, the differences were negligible between people who reported average and more than average exercise.

Cost Analysis Results

Because there has never been a direct trial of the lifetime costs of sedentary habits, we had to use several observational studies to estimate the components of external costs. The main uncertainty comes from the validity of our assumptions, rather than from statistical noise. Therefore, we undertook extensive sensitivity analyses to show how our computed costs vary with the assumptions.

TABLE 6-8.   Wald tests (χ^2) for adult exercise response, National Health Interview Survey, 1983[a]

Habit	df	20+	60+
Visits	2	48.91***	45.41***
Hospitalizations	2	41.10***	70.53***
Work loss (workers only)	2	5.07*	0.69

a. Significance levels: * 10 percent, *** 1 percent; otherwise insignificant at the 10 percent or better level; df = degrees of freedom.

Average Lifetime External Costs for Lifelong Sedentary People

We first estimated the costs for people who do not exercise even when young, and even though they are not physically limited. They constitute about 12 percent of the men and 20 percent of the women in our population. Table 6–10 gives the lifetime external costs in each category for those who classify themselves as not very active physically.

In this base case we used data from the HIE on those aged 20–59 years and data from the NHIS on older people. For those 20–59, we included all medical expenses (except maternity and well-care) and all covered work loss. For the aged, we included all medical use. Based on the male-female proportion just cited, we assumed the not very active population to be 36 percent male.

Columns 1 and 2 of Table 6–10 show nondiscounted lifetime costs, which are easiest to understand but misleading for policymaking. Medical costs and retirement pensions are the largest external costs. When we subtract taxes on earnings, the total net nondiscounted costs are $27,000 per person (for both sexes).

The nondiscounted costs for women only are considerably higher,

TABLE 6-9.   Exercise response, National Health Interview Survey, 1983[a]

Level of Exercise	Outpatient Use	Inpatient Use	Work Loss
Little	100	100	100
Moderate	72***	66***	70
Strenuous	73***	65***	78

a. Significance level: *** 1 percent; otherwise insignificant at the 10 percent or better level. Entry indicates effect of exercise on use of services or work loss, stated as a percentage of those with little exercise who have similar nonexercise characteristics.

TABLE 6-10.   Lifetime external costs of a relatively inactive person (1986 dollars)

	Discount Rate			
Cost	0% Total	0% Women	5% Total	10% Total
Years of life expectancy at age 20	56.9	59.4	18.7	10.2
Costs[a]				
Medical care[b]	60	66	10	4
Sick leave	5	2	2	1
Group life insurance	4	2	0.8	0.3
Nursing home care	11	14	0.6	<0.05
Retirement pension	129	121	14	3
Taxes on earnings[a]	183	112	24	7
Total net costs[a,c]	27	92	3	1

a. Measured in thousands of dollars.

b. Excludes maternity and well-care.

c. (Sum of costs) minus taxes on earnings. Because of rounding, categories may not sum to total.

for several reasons. In our data more women than men were sedentary. Inactive women have higher net costs because they live longer and pay less taxes on earnings than men do. Specifically, they have less sick leave, smaller group life costs, and lower pensions, but have higher medical and nursing home costs and, again, much lower taxes on earnings.

Discounting at 5 percent yields much lower nursing home and pension costs. The other costs fall less because a portion of them occur early in adulthood. The discounted lifetime external costs fall to $3,000 at a 5 percent discount rate, and to $1,000 at a 10 percent rate.

Difference in Costs If Sedentary People Were Active

To estimate the external costs that may be attributed to lack of exercise alone, we compared the costs for the sedentary with costs for "active inactive" people—a group analogous to our nonsmoking smokers and controlled heavy drinkers. These individuals retain all the other characteristics and habits of the sedentary, except that they exercise regularly.

TABLE 6-11. Difference between external costs of relatively inactive persons and those same individuals had they been active[a]

Cost	Discount Rate			
	0% Total	0% Women	5% Total	10% Total
Days of life expectancy at age 20	−300	−161	−21	−2
Differences in costs				
Medical care[b]	15	17	1.6	0.5
Sick leave	1	0.6	0.4	0.2
Group life insurance	0.3	*	0.1	*
Nursing home care	−1	−0.7	−0.1	− *
Retirement pension	−7	−3	−0.5	− *
Taxes on earnings	−1	− *	−0.1	− *
Differences in total net costs[a,c]	9.3	13.9	1.65	0.7

a. Measured in thousands of 1986 dollars; * indicates figure is less than $50.

b. Excludes maternity and well-care.

c. (Sum of costs) minus taxes on earnings. Because of rounding, categories may not sum to total.

For reasons to be given below, we uniformly altered the HRA's age-specific relative mortality risks of not exercising so that male exercisers lived 1.5 years longer than male nonexercisers.[3] We did not adjust values for women because very little is known quantitatively about the effects of exercise on women. The principal studies have all dealt with middle-aged men. As a result, our estimates of the external costs are probably conservative.

Table 6–11 shows the effect on costs if the sedentary changed only their exercise habits. The net effect is a decrease in nondiscounted external costs. According to our recalibrated HRA model, increasing exercise increases total life expectancy by 300 days overall, while reducing medical costs. Because active individuals live longer, nursing home payments increase. We did not have firm data on the effects of exercise on early retirement, so we assumed that less active people would retire at the same rate as more active people. The low total benefit on life expectancy is the result of two factors: (1) our assumption that exercise adds only 1.5 years of life for men, and less for women; and (2) the low proportion of men (36 percent) in the sedentary group.

The discounted external lifetime costs tell a similar story. Relative to the nondiscounted figures, external costs would fall in all categories except pensions and nursing home payments. At a discount rate of 5 percent, lifetime external costs of relatively sedentary people are $1,650, a figure greater than the cost of smokers ($1,000), but less than those of drinkers ($42,000).[4]

Sensitivity Analysis

For several reasons, we have less faith in our exercise results than in our drinking and smoking results:

(1) Less is known about the effects of exercise, and problems of reverse causality are potentially substantial.

(2) The HRA model attributes improbably high life expectancy benefits to exercise.[5] Further, with regard to smoking and drinking the HRA model has been checked on several data sets. Despite its methodological flaws, it seems to work quite well on average (Wiley, 1981; Brown and Nabert, 1977; Smith et al., 1987). No similar checking has been done for exercise.

(3) Our data are more complete for drinking and smoking. These considerations merit further discussion because they inform the assumptions in our sensitivity analysis.

The HRA model estimates are implausible for two reasons: first, the model fails to account for the fact that better health may lead a person to exercise rather than vice versa; second, the adjustments for declining effects with age are inadequate. Studies have shown that exercisers have lower mortality (especially from heart disease) than nonexercisers. But better health may permit exercise, rather than exercise's causing better health. Furthermore, sick people may be unable to exercise.[6] The resulting bias probably causes the HRA's large estimated effects of exercise.

The exact source of the HRA model's figures is not documented, but the multiples match *unadjusted* observed mortality differentials in some reports on (mostly) young and middle-aged men (Paffenbarger et al., 1986; Chave, 1978). In several studies that estimated multivariate relationships, the ratios for exercise were much smaller than those for smoking.[7]

In addition, the HRA model inadequately adjusts the exercise risk multipliers for age. This creates three main problems.

First, the current HRA model multiplies the risk of dying from a disease by a factor that depends on the habit level *but not on age*. This method is not a bad approximation when the risk of dying is small, that is, when the multiple is close to 1. It does not work well, however, for exercise of older men. If we alter exercise from the least possible to the most possible, the model halves the risk of dying from heart disease. For 75-year-old men in our sample, the average risk of dying from heart disease is 26 percent, with a mortality of 64 percent from all causes over ten years.

In the HRA model generally, the risk multipliers are applied to the probability of dying itself, rather than to more statistically tractable alternatives such as the logit of dying. This practice leads to problems such as probabilities of dying of more than 100 percent for old people with multiple risk factors. Even if we truncate the probability of any individual's dying in the next ten years at 100 percent, the model predicts that our group of sedentary 75-year-olds has an unreasonably high 88 percent average probability of dying in ten years. This figure contrasts with 63 percent if the same individuals were very active. Modeling mortality with these multiplicative constants can be misleading. In short, the same constant that changes a 6 percent chance of death to 8 percent (94 and 92 percent survival) should not be used to change a 60 percent chance of death to 80 percent (40 and 20 percent survival).[8]

Second, the model's multipliers for smoking are more realistic than those for exercise because there are more data specifically on smoking and mortality for older men. Thus, the multiplier for smoking on death from heart disease for older men is 1.3, as opposed to the 2.0 value for exercise, which applies to all ages. There is little or no evidence on the effect of exercise in elderly people: it should fall with age, because survivors among those who are sedentary are a more select group than survivors among those who exercise.[9] Natural selection reduces the effect of heart disease factors such as smoking and blood pressure at older ages, and it probably does so for exercise as well.

Third, people become more sedentary as they age. In Alameda County data the percentage of very active men drops steadily from 48 to 14 percent with increasing age (Schoenborn and Cohen, 1986), while those labeled sedentary rise from 35 to 73 percent. With a higher percentage of sedentary individuals, even if the mortality ratio of sedentary to active is preserved at about 3, both multipliers should fall (relative to moderately active) so that the average risk would stay at 1. This correction would reduce the estimated effect of exercise on total mortality because the multipliers affect only heart disease.[10] The most recent versions of the HRA model do not use exercise status to compute the probability of dying.

To compound the problems, our data on exercise are not as complete as our data on drinking and smoking and do not always mesh well with the HRA categories. We have no information on past exercise. We had to assume that current exercise patterns represent life-long patterns, instead of (as in the case of smoking) having actual data on the history of the habit. Because exercise is not as stable as drinking or smoking, our assumption could lead to misestimates of the effects of exercise.[11] Furthermore, we did not have information on how exercise affected the probability of early retirement. If there is a causal effect, the quantitative impact is likely to be large. Finally, different measures of exercise are used in our samples, in the HRA model, and in the literature on exercise. HIE questions are based on self-reported intensity and frequency of exercise, as is the HRA. By contrast, most of the epidemiological studies compute kilocalories per week, which decrease sharply with age. NHIS questions ask about exercise relative to the average for one's age.

We therefore decided to estimate the external costs of exercise in three ways. The middle estimate is our estimate, described above, of the differences in external costs for sedentary and active inactive people. For convenience, column 1 of Table 6–12 repeats the results from column 3 of Table 6–11 (the external costs at a 5 percent discount rate). Column 2 gives the lower bound on costs, for which we assumed that exercise had no effect whatever on mortality. We used the standard United States life table for both groups. Only medical costs and sick leave differ in this case, and these are both higher for sedentary people than they would be if those individuals were active. The last column gives the upper bound, which is based on the unaltered HRA results. It shows an enormous beneficial effect of exercise on mortality. The mortality changes strongly affect pensions and use of nursing homes. Even when discounted at 5 percent, these late-life costs make exercise more expensive to others. In sum, the external costs of inactivity decrease as the assumed beneficial effect of exercise on mortality increases.

We also investigated the sensitivity of our results to other assumptions and data sets, while holding the effect on life expectancy at its middle value of 1.5 years for men (Table 6–13). As a base of comparison, the first column repeats column 1 of Table 6–12.

First, to test the sensitivity to data source, we used parameters based entirely on NHIS data (for the young as well as the old). Col-

TABLE 6-12.   Sensitivity of external costs to assumptions on effects on mortality (5 percent discount rate)

Cost	Alternative Mortality Assumptions		
	Effect of Exercise 1.5 More Years for Men	No Effect on Mortality	HRA Model
Days of life expectancy at age 20	−21	0	−135
Costs[a]			
Medical care[b]	1.6	1.8	1.1
Sick leave	0.4	0.4	0.4
Group life insurance	0.1	0.0	0.4
Nursing home care	−0.1	0.0	−0.3
Retirement pension	−0.5	0.0	−3.0
Taxes on earnings[a]	−0.1	0.0	−0.4
Total net costs[a,c]	1.7	2.2	−1.0

a. Measured in thousands of 1986 dollars.

b. Excludes maternity and well-care.

c. (Sum of costs) minus taxes on earnings. Because of rounding, categories may not sum to total.

umn 2 gives the results. The major change was that estimated effects on medical costs were much larger, which caused the external costs of a sedentary life-style to double. Sick leave and nursing home estimates are consistent with the HIE results.

Second, to test the sensitivity to our estimate of the health effects of exercise, we contrasted sedentary individuals with current exercisers, rather than with the sedentary people made hypothetically active. Column 3 of Table 6–13 gives the results. In general, exercisers have higher external costs than sedentary people.[12] This difference reflects two facts. First, there is a slightly larger difference in life expectancy between the sedentary and exerciser groups (27 discounted days) than between the sedentary and the active inactive groups (21 discounted days). Second, sedentary people spend less than exercisers on medical services because they have other characteristics associated with lower medical use (for instance, less education). Although exercise would reduce external costs of inactive persons, as a group they do not impose external costs on current exercisers. Inactive people die sooner, according to the HRA model, with three-fourths of the

TABLE 6-13.   Sensitivity of costs to assumptions at 5 percent discount rate[a]

| | Alternative Assumptions | | | | | |
Cost	Inactive Individuals if Active	All NHIS Data	Active Individuals	Narrow Definition of Medical Costs[b]	Switch at 50	Total Costs
Costs[b]						
Medical costs[c]	1.6	3.9	−0.3	0.8	1.0	2.3
Sick leave	0.4	0.3	0.3	0.4	0.1	1.1
Group life insurance	0.1	0.1	0.1	0.1	*	0.1
Nursing home care	−0.1	−0.1	*	−0.1	*	−0.1
Retirement pension	−0.5	−0.5	−0.6	−0.5	−0.4	−0.5
Taxes on earnings	−0.1	−0.1	0.1	−0.1	*	−0.7[c]
Total net costs[d]	1.7	3.8	−0.7	0.7	0.7	?[e]

a. Measured in thousands of 1986 dollars; * indicates figure is less than 0.05. All costs are external, except last column.

b. Only costs in diagnoses that are "probably related" to exercise; costs for "active inactive" individuals.

c Earnings, not taxes on earnings.

d. (Sum of costs) minus taxes on earnings. Because of rounding, categories may not sum to total.

e. Loss of life, and pain and suffering to inactive and family are not included.

difference due to exercise itself and one-fourth to other characteristics.

Third, exercisers may have different patterns of medical use for reasons unrelated to exercise. As a sensitivity test, we examined the use of services known to be related to exercise. Column 4 gives the results (the comparison group here is the active inactive group). This estimate of the effect of exercise on medical costs is $800, about half of the overall difference from the base case in column 1. Work loss for conditions related to exercise is slightly smaller.

Fourth, because many people become less active later in life, we tried to estimate the costs that they impose on others. We assumed that they were like moderate or heavy exercisers up to age 50 and then became sedentary. Column 5 shows the differences in external costs between these people who become inactive at 50 and the inactive group that hypothetically exercises. Because the differences caused by a sedentary life-style start late in life, effects on sick leave and medical costs are diluted. Because dying before age 50 is rare, and the mortality model considers only current exercise status, the

TABLE 6-14.   External costs per mile-not-walked by a relatively inactive person[a]

Cost	Discount Rate			
	0% Total	0% Women	5% Total	10% Total
Minutes of life expectancy lost	21	11	4	1
Cost per mile (dollars)				
Medical care[b]	0.71	0.80	0.24	0.12
Sick leave	0.05	0.03	0.06	0.06
Group life insurance	0.02	*	0.01	*
Nursing home care	−0.05	−0.03	−0.01	− *
Retirement pension	−0.34	−0.15	−0.07	−0.01
Taxes on earnings	−0.05	− *	−0.01	− *
Differences in total net costs[c]	0.45	0.64	0.24	0.17

a. Costs are external measured in 1986 dollars, divided by discounted number of miles covered on foot; * indicates figure is less than 0.005.

b. Excludes maternity and well-care.

c. (Sum of costs) minus taxes on earnings. Because of rounding, categories may not sum to total.

effects on mortality and on old-age costs resemble those for people who were always sedentary. At a 5 percent discount rate, there is a loss of 16 minutes of life expectancy and external costs are $700 smaller than if this group exercised. The reason for the decrease in costs is that young workers pay into the system more than they receive. This money comes back later in life as medical and retirement benefits. People who become sedentary late in life contribute as much money in their young working years as lifelong exercisers, but they take out less because they die sooner.

Finally, the last column in Table 6–13 gives several components of total costs rather than external costs. By definition, total costs are higher in all areas where people pay only part of the costs themselves. We estimate that the total of these social costs would be $3,600, a figure that does not count what premature death or disability costs the sedentary person and his or her family. Although this cost is probably larger than any of the costs shown, it is hard to quantify.[13] Thus, we have left the total cost figure in column 5 as a question.

Table 6–14 presents the external costs per a unit of exercise—mile not walked—for sedentary people. Using Paffenbarger and Hyde's

(1984) estimate that time spent walking at 2.85 miles per hour is just returned (undiscounted) in later life, we can compute the amount of lifetime exercise equivalent to the 300 days of additional life expectancy that sedentary people might realize by changing to moderate exercise. At that speed 300 days of walking covers 20,520 miles. At age 20 the average sedentary person can expect to live 56.9 more years, or 20,780 days, as Table 6–10 shows. Dividing miles by days yields approximately one mile per day, which might reasonably be called "moderate" exercise. In Table 6–14 we have divided the costs shown in Table 6–11 by the appropriately discounted number of miles, to show the gains to the rest of society for each mile a sedentary person travels. (The gains from exercise per mile are about the same whether the exerciser walks, jogs, or runs.)

Summary

If sedentary individuals were more active, they would live longer and reduce the costs they impose on others. Lower covered medical and work-loss costs are associated with an active life-style, coupled with the higher taxes active individuals pay over their longer lifetimes. These more than offset the additional (collectively financed) pension payments active people get because they live longer. By our best estimate, a sedentary person imposes $1,650 in lifetime external costs. This figure falls well within the range of estimates that emerged from our sensitivity analyses. Under varying assumptions, the costs range from negative external costs of $1,100 to positive costs of $4,300.

Conclusions, Limitations, and Implications

In this book we have focused on the magnitude of the costs that people with poor health habits impose on others. Such external costs include the subsidies from health insurance of increased medical use and sick leave for additional time lost from work; the collective financing of excess disability and early retirement; and pension and life insurance effects. For smoking, they also include the damage from fires that smokers cause, and for drinking, the value of innocent lives lost and property damage from drunk driving and other crime-related costs.

Summary of External Costs

Cigarette Smoking

Our best estimate is that the external cost per pack of cigarettes is 15 cents. Smoking leads to higher medical costs (principally hospital costs), more covered work-loss days, less years of work and life, and more disability retirements than not smoking. The external financial impact of smoking is greatly reduced, however, by the effects of early death. Because smokers die younger on average, they receive less in pensions, Medicare benefits, and other long-term care.[1] Thus, smokers subsidize nonsmokers' Medicare and retirement benefits, while nonsmokers subsidize smokers' medical care, disability, and sick leave early in life.

Our estimate of 15 cents is sensitive to two assumptions: the appropriate rate of discount, and which health differences between smokers and nonsmokers are *caused* by smoking as opposed to merely associated with it.

The discount rate is crucial because smokers' costs come early in life whereas the "gains" to nonsmokers of lower pensions and Medicare come late in life. As a result, smoking actually reduces nondiscounted external costs by about a dollar a pack (that is, the costs are negative). Above a 5 percent rate, costs are not very sensitive; increasing the discount rate from 5 to 10 percent only increases our estimate of the external cost per pack from 15 cents to 24 cents.

On the causal relationships, if we attribute to smoking all differences between "ever" (current and former) and "never" cigarette smokers except the higher earnings of the latter, the estimated external cost is 28 cents per pack, at a discount rate of 5 percent. This estimate is almost certainly too high because it assigns all differences, not just smoking-caused differences, to smoking. At the other extreme, if we narrow the list of medical services to those associated with diagnoses known to be caused by smoking, and assume that smoking has no effect on early retirement despite its effect on health, the estimate of the external costs is only 4 cents per pack. This figure is probably an underestimate because of its overly restrictive scope. Our "best" estimate of 15 cents per pack lies in the middle of this range.

The costs are not as sensitive to other assumptions. For example, the estimated external costs varied by only 5 cents per pack depending on which of two data sources we used for the nonaged. But there are two exceptions to this generality. The first is the course of future technology. We have in effect extrapolated current technology. If, for example, a cure for lung cancer were discovered, our estimates would markedly change. Depending on how much the cure cost, they could either increase or decrease. Although our estimates are uncertain and sensitive to some modeling assumptions, under no reasonable assumptions could smoking cause external costs of several dollars per pack.[2] The second exception is our addition of the medical costs and lost lives of low-birthweight babies of smoking mothers. If we were to include only the medical costs, the external costs of smoking would rise by 2 cents a pack. If we were to include also the value of lost lives, the cost per pack would increase by 16 cents.

Heavy Drinking

Our best estimate is that the external cost per actual (not reported) excess ounce of ethanol consumed by heavy drinkers is $1.19 (or about 54 cents per excess mixed drink, four-ounce glass of wine, or twelve-ounce can of beer). This estimate includes 26 cents per excess ounce for medical care, sick leave, and pensions; other social costs for crime, fire, and property damage in auto accidents of 35 cents per excess ounce; and an estimate of 58 cents per excess ounce for the value of the lost lives of innocent bystanders of drinking-related accidents. Because one cannot tax only excessive drinking, this $1.19 per excess ounce becomes 48 cents per ounce of alcohol (22 cents per drink).

Of the external costs that we ourselves estimated, the major element is higher medical costs, with most of these costs arising from extra inpatient care, especially for former drinkers, as well as those who report consuming two or more drinks a day. More covered work-loss days, fewer years of work and life, and more disability retirements add up to an amount slightly smaller than the medical care component. Our estimates are in marked contrast to those of Berry and Boland (1977) and Harwood et al. (1984), who reported substantially higher costs in lost productivity than in medical care. But their estimates included lost earnings due to premature mortality (which are internal, not external costs), while ours included only the external costs associated with sick leave.

Our results of $1.19 per excess ounce or 48 cents per overall ounce again are sensitive to two assumptions: the value assigned to lives lost and the amount of underreporting of alcohol consumption.

Our estimates depend critically on the dollar value assigned to lost lives. If we had used a human capital approach to valuing lives, rather than willingness-to-pay, the cost per ounce would fall, because not all victims are working (children and the retired, for instance). If we use Rice and Hodgson's (1983) estimate of the value of life (as measured by lost productivity) for 30- to 35-year-olds, our estimated value of lives of innocent bystanders will fall by 13 cents per actual ounce.[3]

With regard to potential underreporting of alcohol consumption, Pernanen (1974) states that self-reported consumption of alcoholic beverages accounts for only 40 to 60 percent of alcoholic beverage sales. A comparison of apparent alcohol sales (USDHHS, 1983a) with NHIS 1983 estimates of consumption suggests underreporting by about two-thirds.[4] We have assumed that respondents report 40 percent of their actual consumption. A more truthful (higher) response would raise the cost in proportion to the ratio of the true rate to 40; for example, had we assumed respondents reported 60 percent of their actual consumption, our estimates of the costs per ounce would be 50 percent (60/40 = 1.5) higher.

Moreover, our estimated costs are too low because we omitted several categories of cost. Our calculations did not include certain external costs of alcoholism and alcohol abuse. The exclusion of maternity care means that we omitted the costly treatment of fetal alcohol syndrome. Our numbers also excluded the costs (psychological and financial) to the spouses and children of alcoholics. Some of the cost of their treatment or work loss is paid for by collectively financed health insurance and sick leave.

Our recommended alcohol tax is, if anything, too low because it is based on the average external cost per drink, rather than the conceptually correct incremental cost of someone's drinking more (see Appendix H). That is, our number is the average of the small or negligible costs of light drinkers and the high costs of heavier drinkers and drunk drivers. Our average includes single or occasional drinks, which have less potential for damage than heavy drinking at a single sitting, especially if such drinking is followed by driving. If a person drinks half a can of beer a night and does not drive, he is less dangerous than the person who consumes seven cans at one sitting every two weeks and then drives. Both generate the same average daily volume, but the second raises more concern and is the person we would like to target. Of course, this system also means that we overtax light or rare drinking.

Light drinkers may argue that it is both unfair and inefficient to tax their drinking because they impose few or no external costs. There are at least three arguments to counter this. First, although our proposed tax change would tax light drinkers more per drink, it almost certainly would leave them bearing a smaller share of the tax burden. As explained earlier, light and moderate drinkers constitute a majority of the population but a minority of the consumption. Especially because they are disproportionately highly educated, they almost surely pay more than half of all taxes (income, sales, payroll), but they pay only a third of alcohol taxes. Thus, higher alcohol taxes would shift taxes onto heavy drinkers and away from light and moderate drinkers, former drinkers, and abstainers.

Second, as our numbers indicate, the average heavy drinker is costing everyone, not just heavy drinkers. Because higher taxes deter alcohol abuse (Cook, 1981; Cook and Tauchen, 1982; Grossman et al., 1987), the resulting decrease in external costs will offset increases in the tax burden of light drinkers.

Third, penalizing light drinkers for damage they did not cause, so that we can penalize heavy drinkers, is in fact better than not raising the tax on alcohol at all. From an economic point of view, we are trading any losses from overtaxing nonabusive drinkers against the gains from making abusive drinkers pay more appropriate prices. As long as the gains from providing more appropriate incentives to moderate drinking are greater than the losses to light drinkers, society will benefit from a tax increase. We discuss this issue at greater length in Appendix H.

Lack of Exercise

We estimate that lack of exercise imposes external costs of 24 cents for very mile that sedentary people do not walk, jog, or run. The biggest uncertainty in our calculations concerns the degree of causality between exercise and health status. Although we excluded the physically limited and have controlled for several other differences between exercisers and nonexercisers, we cannot be certain that the association we have found between inactivity and health-related costs is causal.[5] The relationship between exercise and mortality raises the same issue. We conducted extensive sensitivity analyses to address these uncertainties, as well as assessing the sensitivity of our results to other assumptions and data sets.

Hypotheses about how exercise affects mortality have important implications for our results. The external costs of inactivity decrease the more we assume that exercise extends life. If exercise has no effect on mortality, the costs for sedentary people rise because they use more sick leave and medical care. In that case their lifetime external costs rise to $2,200. If, as the unadjusted HRA model assumes, exercise greatly increases life expectancy, sedentary people actually subsidize people who exercise. The latter live to collect the social security and nursing home benefits that the former helped pay for. In that implausible scenario the sedentary have negative external costs of $1,000.

Looking at health costs, we find an analogous effect when we contrast sedentary people with actual exercisers. In the base case we contrasted them with a hypothetical group of people who were like the sedentary in every way except amount of exercise. When we contrast them with actual exercisers, we find that the sedentary have negative costs of $700. There are two reasons for this: inactive people have other characteristics associated with lower use of medical care (less education, on average); and they die earlier.

Sedentary people might also have lower external costs if (1) the only medical costs they imposed were for specific diagnoses possibly related to poor health habits; and (2) they became inactive only after they reached age 50. Our sensitivity analysis revealed that under either assumption the lifetime external costs drop to $700. The effect for switching at age 50 comes about because medical and sick leave costs are lower for the period before 50 years of age.

Limitations of the Analyses

The first, and most important, limitation of this study is that it is observational. As such, it contains a measure of uncertainty about which differences between groups (smokers and nonsmokers, abstainers and drinkers, heavy and light exercisers) in the use of health services, work loss, and life expectancy are causally related to the habit in question and which are merely associated with it.

To reduce the quantitative magnitude of this problem, we have taken certain steps: (1) we have excluded services known to be unrelated causally to, but correlated with, the habits (maternity care and well-care); (2) as a sensitivity analysis, we have examined the use of health services for only those diagnoses thought to be related to poor health habits; and (3) we have used multiple regression methods to control for other habits and characteristics that influence use of health services and work loss. Although these methods limit the scope of the causality issue, some inherent uncertainty remains. At best, then, we can define a range for external costs.

Second, sample sizes for the two data sets we used are sufficient for detecting main effects—differences, say, in overall medical care use by overall smoking status—but are too small to permit reliable estimates of interactions. For example, we cannot determine whether people who both drink heavily and smoke cigarettes are especially affected. For purposes of assessing tax policy, however, a main effect is the most relevant because taxes are generally imposed per pack and per drink; it would not be feasible to tax heavy smokers more for their alcohol than light smokers are taxed. The sample size is also too small to assess reliably the external costs of various types of alcoholic beverages.

Third, as explained in Chapter 2, we have not explicitly accounted for externalities of pure public goods (such as national defense) and excludable services (for example, trash collection).[6] It could be argued that premature death and disability from bad health habits leave those with better habits paying a higher share of any given defense budget, and thus represent an external cost. We have assumed that such costs are offset by reductions in public evils such as congestion and pollution. That assumption, however convenient, is clearly speculative. In the case of excludable services, we assumed that consumption by people with varying habits equals the costs they pay.

Fourth, any assessment of the external costs of smoking needs to include the effects of passive smoking outside the home. Neither of our data sources included such information. Because we could not detect the effect of passive smoking on medical costs in the household, such costs from workplace smoking probably are also small. Yet the Surgeon General (USDHHS, 1986) estimates that 2,400 people a year die from lung cancers due to passive smoking alone, and additional lives are lost in cigarette-related fires. Using a value of $1.66 million per life lost (in 1986 dollars) and treating all these deaths as external would add 23 cents to the external costs of a pack of cigarettes. Because many of these deaths are actually within the family, the adjustment is likely to be overstated. Incorporating neonatal costs due to smoking adds 2 cents per pack. Including 2,500 infant deaths (also valued at $1.66 million per life and not considered by the mother who persists in smoking) adds another 14 cents per pack.

Fifth, we have relied on the estimates of others for the value of life, especially for nondrinkers killed in drinking-related traffic accidents. Although there are theoretically correct mechanisms for valuing lives ex ante (Schelling, 1968; Mishan, 1971), there is little consensus on appropriate empirical magnitudes. Nonetheless, our conclusion that alcohol taxes should be raised would not be altered under any reasonable estimate of the value of life.

Sixth, our estimates of the external costs of a sedentary life-style may be too low. The costs that sedentary people impose on others are indirect; sedentary people do not drive their armchairs into innocent bystanders. Most of these external costs are captured in the model, but the possible effects of inactivity on early retirement are not. In a study of those obtaining permanent disability Social Security benefits in 1975, the primary diagnosis of 38 percent of retiring workers aged 55–64 was cardiovascular disease (Burdette and Mohr, 1979). Assuming the year 1975 to be typical, we can estimate that 3 percent of those 55–64 years of age retire early because of cardiovascular disease, to which lack of exercise can contribute. Early retirement has large external costs associated with it, because it both decreases taxes paid and increases pension and disability insurance payments.

One of the largest uncertainties in our calculations concerns the degree of causality in the link between exercise and health status. Although we excluded the physically limited and controlled for several other differences between exercisers and nonexercisers, we cannot be certain that the association we found between inactivity and health-related costs is completely causal. In principle, this issue could be settled by a randomized experiment on the effects of exercise promotion, but such an experiment is not available. The issue of causality remains to plague any observational attempt to estimate external costs of inactivity.

The association between some exercise and mortality raises the same chicken-and-egg issue. Many epidemiological studies, controlling for age and other health habits, have shown dramatic differences in future heart disease between those who are sedentary and those who exercise (Burdette and Mohr, 1979; Paffenbarger and Hyde, 1986; Powell et al., 1987). Still, it is hard to rule out the possibility that heavy exercisers are inherently more healthy than sedentary people in unmeasured ways, so that inactive people who take up exercise will not enjoy the gains in life expectancy that models based on those studies predict. Of course, if exercising has no effect on mortality and morbidity, then there are no benefits to making sedentary people more active. Because of this uncertainty, the revised HRA model says only that exercise is probably good for you; it does not attempt to quantify any life-extending benefits.

Seventh, our estimates have not incorporated directly the altruistic concern of the rest of society for the welfare of smokers, heavy drinkers, or the inactive. Such concern may lead to public health interventions to prevent people from acquiring poor health habits. When individuals start a poor health habit, they may not be fully informed about its consequences. Society at large may be willing to pay more than we have calculated to protect these individuals from themselves.

Finally, there is the loss of human life of those addicted to smoking and alcohol who would prefer to quit (taking their present desire to quit rather than their earlier tastes as relevant to economic efficiency). To the extent that current smokers would stop if they could, or that heavy drinkers would moderate their drinking if they could, there is an argument for including the value of their lost lives in calculation of the optimal tax. For cigarettes the discounted cost is 0.4 hour per pack for the smoker, while for an ounce of pure alcohol it is 0.2 hour for someone who reports an average of two or more drinks per day. At $5 per hour, these costs amount to $1 to $2 per pack or per drink.

Implications for Policy

These limitations notwithstanding, some policy implications can be safely drawn from our analysis. First and foremost, there is compelling evidence that the current tax level for alcohol is too low generally, and far too low for beer and wine specifically. At a minimum, this suggests raising the tax rates on beer and wine to the same level as the rates for liquor. Preferably the overall taxes on alcohol should be at least doubled.

Second, it may be desirable to increase the tax on alcohol sold in bars and restaurants more than the tax on alcohol purchased for home consumption. A major element of the external costs of drinking is the loss of innocent lives caused by drunk driving. Taxes would have a more direct impact on drinking that is likely to be followed by driving if higher taxes were imposed on alcohol consumed in bars and restaurants than on alcohol in general.

Third, at the time of the Korean War, alcohol tax rates were at about the level we are suggesting. The rates were set in nominal terms, however, and over the years inflation has appreciably diminished their real value. To prevent future erosion, alcohol tax levels should be indexed by inflation.

We hope that our results will help to inform the public debate on these subjects. Because we have not tallied the costs of addiction, the regret of those with poor health habits (or of their families), or the costs of passive smoking, our numbers indicate where the minimum should be for taxes on alcohol and cigarettes as part of a wider public strategy for combating poor health habits.

Literature Review of the Costs of Smoking and Drinking

Costs of Smoking

The enormous literature on the costs of smoking gives quite varied estimates of costs. Some of the differences result from errors and differing data and assumptions, but most arise from the fact that the research asks different questions.

Many studies of the cost of smoking are descriptive: a good example is a study by Rice and Hodgson (1983). It addresses two questions: "In 1980, how many work days were lost and how much was spent on medical care for conditions caused by smoking? More important, how much future productivity was lost due to smoking-related deaths that occurred in 1980?" The authors first estimate the proportion of certain diseases that can be attributed to smoking, based on differences in mortality rates between smokers and nonsmokers. They then multiply the costs of illness, disability, and premature death for age- and sex-specific categories by the proportion of these diseases attributable to smoking to get a total cost of $61.7 billion (in 1985 dollars).

Rice et al. (1986) have updated their estimate of the economic costs of the health effects of smoking. For the three major diagnostic categories most clearly associated with smoking—neoplasms, diseases of the circulatory system, and diseases of the respiratory system—differences between smokers and never smokers in rates of medical care utilization, work loss, and disability were used to derive the proportion of these costs attributable to smoking. In Rice and Hodgson (1983) the proportion of each cost category attributed to smoking was based on differences between smokers and never smokers in *mortality rates*. The change in method improves the theoretical basis for the calculations, but, empirically, the estimated cost remains about the same. The more recent study estimates the total economic costs of smoking to be $56.4 billion (in 1985 dollars).

Studies using similar methods include Luce and Schweitzer (1978), which gives an estimate of $56.6 billion, and the 1985 Office of Technology Assessment report on the costs of smoking, which gives an estimate of $65 billion (both amounts converted to 1985 dollars). Dividing the $65 billion figure by the number of packs sold in 1985, the OTA estimates costs per pack to be $2.17. Thus, the three studies produce numbers that are relatively close to each other.

These descriptive studies show that the costs of smoking are enormous and that smoking issues should be taken seriously. The strengths of their methods are simplicity and use of readily available data. The analyses have several flaws, however. First, the lack of good data on smoking-related morbidity leads practitioners to apply the fraction of mortality that is smoking related to morbidity and medical costs as well. The only support for this assumption is in the Rice et al. (1986) study. Second, these studies do not distinguish between costs to the smoker and costs imposed on others, nor do they consider the benefits to the smoker of smoking. Third, they ignore the timing of the costs. Fourth, they typically use the expected loss in future earnings as a measure of the indirect costs of premature mortality. This method of valuation ("human capital") is simple but bears an uncertain relationship to the true economic costs of premature mortality, which in principle are what the families and friends of those dying early would pay for longer life; see Schelling, 1968, and Mishan, 1971. (For example, the human capital model assigns a zero value to the life of retired individuals.) Finally, mortality costs are mainly borne by the smoker and should be kept separate for purposes of most policy analyses.

These deficiencies mean that we cannot use the estimated "total" costs to quantify the economic consequences of reductions in current smoking, nor to compute the tax that would lead to no net subsidy of smokers by nonsmokers. We now elaborate on some of these deficiencies.

MEDICAL COSTS

Compared to the indirect mortality costs, the pure medical cost differences between smokers and nonsmokers are small. Assuming that medical cost differences are proportional to mortality differences, Stoddart et al. (1986) show that smoking-related medical costs are a small fraction of the tobacco taxes paid by Ontario smokers. Indeed, those who have looked at the differences in medical costs of smokers and nonsmokers directly find the assumption of Stoddart and colleagues is not conservative enough; medical cost differences tend to be smaller than mortality differences. Vogt and Schweitzer (1985) found more use of hospital care, but not of outpatient care, for smokers in an HMO; children of smokers used fewer outpatient services, primarily because they used fewer preventive services. Oakes et al. (1974) found higher hospitalization rates and fewer preventive services for smokers in data from another HMO.

OTHER COSTS

Reports from the Office of the Surgeon General (various dates) and from the National Resource Council (1986) have noted health consequences in addition to direct damage to the smoker. These include passive smoking, effects on birth outcomes, a link to other drugs, and fires. There are few good data to quantify these costs; researchers have generally either tried to guess them or ignored them in cost calculations.

Luce and Schweitzer (1978) discuss the costs of cigarette production, but properly exclude them from the costs of smoking effects. For most purposes it seems improper to mention the costs of producing cigarettes without balancing those costs with the benefits; none of the cost studies address the satisfaction of smoking. Other articles have included the costs of cigarettes as part of the costs of smoking and have been concerned with the loss of jobs in the tobacco industry, a question more of political than of economic interest.

Kristein (1983) combined Luce and Schweitzer's estimates with other data and guesses on the costs of ventilation and absenteeism, to estimate that the average smoking employee costs his or her employer between $336 and $601 per year. These estimates are conjectural for several reasons: Kristein lacks solid data; the differences other than smoking between smokers and non-smokers are not taken into account; and the reasons why smokers might be cheaper employees (for example, lower pension costs in a defined benefit plan) are not included.

LIFETIME MODELS

Forbes and Thompson (1983) and Leu and Schaub (1983) used lifetime simulation models of smoking to estimate the marginal health care costs due to smoking. Forbes and Thompson include effects on birth outcomes but do not adjust observed cost differences between smokers and nonsmokers for factors independent of smoking. Leu and Schaub do so, and in addition note that shorter life expectancy may lead to reduced costs for smokers,[1] and that the costs smokers impose on others should be distinguished from the costs they bear themselves. Leu and Schaub do not discount costs in their 1983 paper, but do so in a more recent paper (1985). Thus, their earlier work neglects the benefits of postponing the medical costs associated with dying.

The notion that smoking reduces pension payments is discussed by Wright (1986) and by Shoven, Sundberg, and Bunker (1988), who estimate the substantial effects on Medicare's hospital insurance fund needs if current smoking workers were to quit smoking. Atkinson and Townsend (1977) find that in Great Britain reduced smoking would lead to lower medical costs, increased pensions, and slightly reduced net government outlays. Leu and Schaub (1985) show that even with discounting, pension effects more than offset the costs of smoking in a cohort of 35-year-old Swiss male smokers.

Oster (1984) combines a lifetime model of costs with an incidence-based cost model to compute, for example, that a 45-year-old heavy-smoking male could save himself $46,000 (1980 dollars) over his lifetime by quitting. The incidence-based method attempts to predict lifetime costs on a disease-by-disease basis, rather than looking at costs and mortality for all diseases together and statistically trying to isolate the difference due to smoking. Because the incidence model has a sounder biological basis, it should in principle be better than the statistical methods, but it suffers from three practical problems. First, detailed data on habit-related incidence for all but the commonest conditions are hard to find. Second, a tremendous amount of work is involved in following the stochastic course of the disease. Finally, there are few data on joint incidence, but adding costs from different diseases overestimates their combined costs because of double counting (competing risks) and correlation of resistance to disease. Because the same person can get both lung cancer and heart disease, for example, it is improper simply to add estimated lifetime costs that follow the incidence of each. Moreover, variation in resistance implies that those smokers who resist getting one disease are less likely to get others, another reason why the sum of various disease-costs overestimates the total costs of smoking.

Costs of Alcohol Abuse

The literature in this area is considerably less extensive than the literature on the costs of smoking. Apart from published case studies on the costs of alcohol abuse incurred by individual firms, industries, and so on, only two comprehensive analyses have appeared thus far. The first, published by Berry and Boland in 1977, estimated the economic costs of alcohol abuse in 1971 to be just over $85 billion (in 1986 dollars); the second study, written by Cruze et al. at the Research Triangle Institute (RTI) in 1981 and updated in 1984 (Harwood et al.), estimated the 1983 costs at nearly $129 billion (1986 dollars).

Both of these estimates are considerably higher than the economic costs of smoking reported in the literature. Moreover, the authors claim that their estimates of the costs of alcohol abuse are conservative.

While the objectives of the two studies were similar in that both estimated the major costs attributable to alcohol abuse (health care, lost production, motor vehicle accidents, crime, fires, and social welfare programs), the methods used to generate estimates of particular components of the overall costs often differed.

HEALTH CARE COSTS

Perhaps the greatest difference in approach between the two studies lies in the method used to estimate health care costs due to alcohol abuse. Berry and Boland used a population-specific approach, which essentially entailed comparing per capita health care utilization of alcohol abusers with that of nonabusers and attributing any observed difference to alcohol abuse. The difference in per capita use was multiplied by an estimate of the prevalence of alcohol abuse to arrive at approximately $22.5 billion (in 1986 dollars) as the estimated total annual health care cost of alcohol abuse.

In contrast, an illness-specific or event-specific approach was used by Harwood and colleagues. They identified illnesses that are either partially or entirely attributable to alcohol abuse, estimating the costs associated with providing care to patients with each of the conditions and then summing across the conditions. The resulting estimated total health care cost was $16.4 billion (1986 dollars).

The population-specific approach tends to overstate the health care costs of alcohol abuse because it fails to correct for factors that are associated with but not caused by alcohol abuse. (To the extent that this approach fails to capture the health care costs associated with occasional drinks, these costs will be understated.) On the other hand, the illness-specific approach will understate the health care costs of alcohol abuse to the degree that it fails to include diseases caused or exacerbated by alcohol abuse.

LOST PRODUCTION

The results from both studies indicate that lost production, due to increased morbidity and premature mortality, accounts for the largest proportion of the total cost of alcohol abuse. Although details of the methods used to calculate these costs differ between the studies, both used a human capital approach for valuing the costs of premature mortality. Apart from the general limitations associated with this approach (mentioned in the review of the smoking literature), the Berry and Boland study suffers from an additional drawback in that it failed to include costs of reduced household (nonmarket) productivity and, more important, neglected to estimate productivity lost by women in the work force. In addition, Berry and Boland used data on total income rather than earnings to value productivity losses. This usage understates the differential between abusers and nonabusers because transfer payments to abusers appear as income.

The estimated value of lost production due to alcohol abuse differs markedly between the two studies. Specifically, Berry and Boland estimated it as over $40 billion (1986 dollars) in 1971, while the Harwood group's estimate for 1983 was over $98 billion (1986 dollars). Needless to say, a substantial part of the difference ($16 billion) in the two estimates can be explained by the Harwood inclusion of nonmarket production losses as well as lost productivity on the part of women in the work force. In addition, their estimate includes the costs of lost production due to motor vehicle accidents, crime, and fires, whereas the Berry and Boland study reports separately the lost production attributable to these events.[2]

MOTOR VEHICLE ACCIDENTS, CRIME, FIRES, AND SOCIAL
WELFARE PROGRAMS

For the most part, the two studies used the same methods and data sources for estimating the direct economic costs (which exclude "transfers" in the cases of crime and social programs) of motor vehicle accidents, crime, fires, and social programs due to alcohol abuse.[3] As already noted, the two studies reported the indirect costs differently, and the Harwood study included some indirect costs that were omitted by Berry and Boland (such as lost production due to incarceration). In order to minimize confusion, only the Harwood results are used in this text.

There is considerable uncertainty regarding the extent to which there is a causal link, as opposed to an association, between alcohol abuse and the occurrence of all these events. The estimates of the costs of crime due to alcohol abuse may be particularly problematic in this regard. Despite the fact that the authors of both studies made careful attempts—relying on both the literature and expert opinion—to arrive at an appropriate "causal factor," in the end they convey a strong sense of skepticism regarding the proportion of the costs of criminal activity that can be properly attributed to alcohol abuse.

The Harwood report estimated the direct and indirect costs of these activities due to alcohol abuse in 1983 (reported here in 1986 dollars) as follows: motor vehicle accidents, $3.6 billion; crime, $6.4 billion (external, $3.1 billion); fires, $507 million; and social programs, $54 million.

Survival Parameters from the HRA Model

Calculating Appraised Risk

Under the HRA method, questionnaire responses are translated into risk multipliers for related causes of death. (EXAMPLE: A two-pack-a-day 45-year-old smoker has twice the risk for lung cancer of the average male of that age, and ten times the risk of a nonsmoker.) If there is more than one risk multiplier (RM) for a cause of death, then a composite risk multiplier (CRM) is calculated as follows.

First, multiply all RM's < 1. Second, subtract 1.0 from all RM's > 1 and add. Third, add the results of steps 1 and 2. If all RM's are greater than 1.0, add 1.0 to the result.

EXAMPLE 1: RM1 $= 0.4$, RM2 $= 0.6$, RM3 $= 2.5$, RM4 $= 1.3$

CRM $= (0.4 \times 0.6) + (2.5 - 1.0) + (1.3 - 1.0) = 2.04$

EXAMPLE 2: RM1 $= 2.5$, RM2 $= 1.3$

CRM $= (2.5 - 1.0) + (1.3 - 1.0) + 1.0 = 2.8$

EXAMPLE 3: RM1 $= 0.4$, RM2 $= 0.6$

CRM $= (0.4 \times 0.6) = 0.24$

The composite risk multiplier for a particular cause applies to age-, sex-, and race-specific mortality rates for that cause. The procedure is repeated for the twelve leading causes of death. Cause-specific mortality rates for these twelve causes are then summed with the average rate for all other causes of death to yield an overall risk of death.

There is no result from the program if information on sex, age, height, weight, smoking status, or cigarettes per day is missing. If other data are missing, a value is imputed as shown in Table B–1.

Converting Ten-Year to Five-Year Survival Ratios

One technical problem arises because the HRA data give ten-year survival and we use five-year steps in our life table. To convert the HRA ten-year

APPENDIX TABLE B-1. Function of specific variables in HRA program

Variable	Use in Program	Response to Missing Data	HIE	NHIS
Sex	Group mortality rates	No appraisal	*	*
Race or origin	Group mortality rates	Assigns white, non-Hispanic	*	*
Age	Group mortality rates	No appraisal	*	*
Height	Recommended body weight	No appraisal	*	*
Weight	Recommended body weight	No appraisal	*	*
Tobacco	CHD, cancer, pneumonia	No appraisal	*	*
Alcohol	MVA, cirrhosis	Assigns average risk	*	*
Drugs or medications	MVA	Assigns average risk	*	
Miles driven per year	MVA	Assigns 1,000 miles	*	
Seat belt use	MVA	Assigns 0% usage	*	
Physical activity level	CHD	Assigns average risk	*	*
Family history of heart attack	CHD	Assigns average risk		
Family history of diabetes	Diabetes	Assigns average risk		
Personal history of diabetes	Heart disease	Assigns average risk	*	*
Rectal growth	Intestinal cancer	Assigns code 2 (no)		
Rectal bleeding	Intestinal cancer	Assigns code 2 (no)		
Annual rectal exam	Intestinal cancer	Assigns average risk	*	
Chronic bronchitis or emphysema	Pneumonia	Assigns code 2 (no)	*	
Blood pressure	Cardiovascular disease	Assigns average risk	*	
Cholesterol	CHD	Assigns average risk	*	
Description of physical health	Suicide	Assigns average risk	*	*
Life satisfaction	Suicide	Assigns average risk	*	
Strength of social ties	Suicide	Assigns average risk	*	
Hours of sleep	Suicide	Assigns average risk	*	*
Serious loss or misfortune	Suicide	Assigns average risk	*	
Witness to violence	Homicide	Assigns average risk		
Homicide risk habits	Homicide	Assigns average risk		
Hysterectomy	Cervical cancer	Assigns code 2 (no)	*	
Frequency of Pap smear	Cervical cancer	Assigns average risk	*	
Pap smear normal	Cervical cancer	Assigns average risk		
Family history of breast cancer	Breast cancer	Assigns code 2 (no)		
Breast self-exam	Breast cancer	Assigns code 3 (rarely, never)	*	
Current marital status	Suicide	Assigns average risk	*	

survival ratios of those with different habits to five-year survival ratios, we assume the effect of habits is to change the force of mortality from h to $h + k$. The population depends on the average force of mortality $h(t)$ according to $P'(t) = - hP$. Let $H(t)$ be the integral from 0 to t of $h(t)$. Then $\ln [P(t)/P(0)] = - H(t)$. Suppose the HRA ten-year survival value for those in a certain habit group is P^*. Let $\ln [P^*/P(0)] = - K - H(t)$. Since $\ln [P^*/P(0)]$ also is $[- kt - H(t)]$ by the force of mortality assumption, we have $K = 10k$. Adjusted five-year survival is $\exp [- H(5) - (K/2)]$. Thus, the square root of ten-year survival can be averaged to give the survival ratios at five years.

This process ensures that the survival·of our group of smokers is adjusted to the national smoker survival rates. We compute the survival ratio K_{10} at ten years for nonsmokers over ever smokers. The square root of K_{10} represents relative survival, K_5, at five years. Because we know the percentage of people who never smoked, P_N, in each age group, we can solve

$$K_5 S_5 P_N + S_5(1 - P_N) = \text{total 1980 survival}$$

for the national five-year smoker survival rates S_S. Once the values for the ever smokers are obtained, we can multiply by the survival ratios to get the values for the nonsmoking smokers and for the never smokers. The survival of the never smokers is simply $K_5 \times S_S$. The nonsmoking smokers have survival S_S/L, where L is the ratio of the square root of predicted ten-year survival for five-year age-sex groups with the habit to that of the same groups after changing to never smoking.

APPENDIX C

HIE Habit Batteries

SLEEP AND EXERCISE

28. IN AN AVERAGE <u>24 HOUR</u> PERIOD, ABOUT HOW MANY HOURS DO YOU SPEND SLEEPING?

(Circle one)

6 hours or less	1
7 hours	2
8 hours	3
9 hours or more	4

29. HAS ANY DOCTOR RECENTLY SUGGESTED THAT YOU GET MORE EXERCISE OR PRACTICE CERTAIN EXERCISES?

Yes .... 1 —*Answer 29-A-B*

No .... 2 —*Go to 30, next page*

29-A. WHAT IS THE REASON FOR THIS EXERCISE? (Circle one number on each line.)

	Yes	No
To improve your general health	1	2
To improve your athletic ability	1	2
To prevent heart disease	1	2
To lose weight	1	2
Treatment for sprain, sore muscle or broken bone	1	2
Treatment of arthritis	1	2
Some other reason	1	2

What? _____

29-B. HOW OFTEN DO YOU <u>DO</u> THE EXERCISE THE DOCTOR SUGGESTED?

(Circle one)

Always, never miss	1
Most of the time	2
About half the time	3
Less than half the time	4
Never, don't do it at all	5

30. SOME PEOPLE, IN THEIR JOBS OR IN THEIR WORK AROUND THE
     HOUSE, HAVE TO SPEND A GREAT DEAL OF TIME DOING <u>HEAVY</u>
     OR <u>STRENUOUS</u> WORK — LIKE LIFTING OR CARRYING HEAVY
     LOADS, PUSHING OR SCRUBBING THINGS, OR HANDLING HEAVY
     MACHINERY. OTHER PEOPLE DON'T DO ANY STRENUOUS WORK AT
     ALL.
     IN YOUR JOB, OR IN YOUR WORK AROUND THE HOUSE, ABOUT
     <u>HOW MANY HOURS</u> DO YOU SPEND DOING HEAVY OR STRENUOUS
     WORK <u>IN AN AVERAGE WEEK</u>?   (Circle one)

     None, don't do any heavy work 1
     1 hour or less 2
     2 to 3 hours a week 3
     4 to 5 hours a week 4
     6 to 10 hours a week 5
     More than 10 hours a week 6

31. THEN THERE ARE JOBS OR HOUSEHOLD TASKS THAT REQUIRE A
     <u>MEDIUM</u> AMOUNT OF PHYSICAL ACTIVITY — LIKE BEING ON YOUR
     FEET QUITE A BIT, STOOPING, BENDING, LIFTING OR CARRYING
     LIGHTER LOADS, HANDLING LIGHTER TOOLS OR MACHINERY, OR
     IRONING CLOTHES.
     IN YOUR JOB, OR IN YOUR WORK AROUND THE HOUSE, ABOUT
     <u>HOW MANY HOURS</u> DO YOU SPEND DOING THINGS THAT TAKE A
     <u>MEDIUM</u> AMOUNT OF PHYSICAL ACTIVITY <u>IN AN AVERAGE WEEK</u>?
                                              (Circle one)

     None, don't do any medium work 1
     2 hours or less 2
     3 to 5 hours a week 3
     6 to 10 hours a week 4
     11 to 15 hours a week 5
     More than 15 hours a week 6

32. IN THEIR <u>RECREATION</u> OR <u>LEISURE</u> ACTIVITIES, SOME PEOPLE
     SPEND A LOT OF TIME IN <u>STRENUOUS</u> ACTIVITY — LIKE JOGGING,
     OR RUNNING, PLAYING HANDBALL OR TENNIS, VIGOROUS
     SWIMMING, CLIMBING, HIKING, OR DOING HEAVY WORK AROUND
     THE HOUSE. OTHER PEOPLE DON'T ENGAGE IN THIS KIND OF
     STRENUOUS ACTIVITY AT ALL.

     ABOUT <u>HOW MANY HOURS</u> DO YOU SPEND, <u>IN AN AVERAGE WEEK</u>,
     IN <u>STRENUOUS</u> LEISURE TIME ACTIVITIES LIKE THESE?
                                              (Circle one)

     None, don't do strenuous activity 1
     1 hour or less 2
     2 to 3 hours a week 3
     4 to 5 hours a week 4
     6 to 10 hours a week 5
     More than 10 hours a week 6

33. **THEN THERE ARE LEISURE ACTIVITIES THAT REQUIRE A <u>MEDIUM</u> OR <u>MODERATE</u> AMOUNT OF PHYSICAL ACTIVITY — LIKE DANCING, PLAYING GOLF, GARDENING, OR WORKING WITH HOME TOOLS.**

   ABOUT <u>HOW MANY HOURS</u> DO YOU SPEND, <u>IN AN AVERAGE WEEK,</u> IN <u>MEDIUM</u> OR <u>MODERATE</u> LEISURE TIME ACTIVITIES LIKE THESE?

   (Circle one)

None, don't do medium activity	1
2 hours or less	2
3 to 5 hours a week	3
6 to 10 hours a week	4
11 to 15 hours a week	5
More than 15 hours a week	6

34. **WHICH ONE OF THESE STATEMENTS BEST DESCRIBES YOUR PHYSICAL ACTIVITY, IN GENERAL?**

   (Circle one)

Not very active physically, usually just sitting or walking	1
Fairly active physically, moderate or strenuous activity several times a week	2
Quite active physically, at least moderate activity every day	3
Extremely active physically, strenuous activity most days	4

   SAFETY

35. **DURING THE <u>PAST 12 MONTHS,</u> ABOUT HOW MANY MILES DID YOU DRIVE OR RIDE IN A CAR OR TRUCK?**

   (Circle one)

None	1
2,000 miles or less	2
More than 2,000 to 5,000	3
More than 5,000 to 10,000	4
More than 10,000 to 15,000	5
More than 15,000 to 20,000	6
More than 20,000 miles	7

36. **WHEN YOU RIDE IN A CAR OR TRUCK, HOW MUCH OF THE TIME DO YOU USE A SEAT BELT?**

   (Circle one)

All of the time	1
Most of the time	2
Some of the time	3
A little of the time	4
None of the time	5
Never ride in car or truck	6

| SMOKING |

37.   DO YOU SMOKE CIGARS OR A PIPE NOW?

Yes 1

No 2

38.   DO YOU SMOKE CIGARETTES NOW?

Yes .... 1 —Answer 38-A-B-C

No .... 2 —Go to 39,
next page

**38-A. DURING HOW MANY YEARS HAVE YOU SMOKED CIGARETTES
REGULARLY?**

(Circle one)

Less than 2 years 1

2 - 5 years 2

6 - 10 years 3

11 - 15 years 4

16 - 20 years 5

21 - 25 years 6

26 - 30 years 7

31 - 35 years 8

36 - 40 years 9

More than 40 years 0

**38-B. ON THE AVERAGE, ABOUT HOW MANY <u>PACKS</u> A DAY DO YOU
SMOKE NOW?**

(Circle one)

Less than 1 pack a day 1

About 1 pack a day 2

About 2 packs a day 3

More than 2 packs a day 4

**38-C. HAS A DOCTOR EVER TOLD YOU TO STOP OR CUT DOWN ON
YOUR SMOKING?**

Yes .... 1 —Go to 40,

No 2   page 19

39. HAVE YOU EVER SMOKED CIGARETTES FAIRLY REGULARLY?

Yes 1   *—Answer 39-*
                                                         A-B-C-D
No 2   *—Go to 40,*
                                                         next page

39-A. DURING HOW MANY YEARS DID YOU SMOKE CIGARETTES REGULARLY?

(Circle one)

Less than 2 years 1
2 - 5 years 2
6 - 10 years 3
11 - 15 years 4
16 - 20 years 5
21 - 25 years 6
26 - 30 years 7
31 - 35 years 8
36 - 40 years 9
More than 40 years 0

39-B. ON THE AVERAGE, ABOUT HOW MANY PACKS A DAY DID YOU USED TO SMOKE?

(Circle one)

Less than 1 pack a day 1
About 1 pack a day 2
About 2 packs a day 3
More than 2 packs a day 4

39-C. HOW LONG HAS IT BEEN SINCE YOU SMOKED CIGARETTES REGULARLY?

(Circle one)

6 months or less 1
7 months to 1 year 2
More than 1 year to 2 years 3
More than 2 years to 5 years 4
More than 5 years 5

39-D. DID A DOCTOR EVER TELL YOU TO STOP OR CUT DOWN ON YOUR SMOKING?

Yes 1
No 2

DRINKING

40.   HAVE YOU **EVER** HAD A DRINK OF BEER, WINE, OR LIQUOR?

Yes .... 1 —Answer 40-A
No .... 2 —Go to 53,
                                                          page 24

40-A.   DURING THE **12 MONTHS** OF YOUR LIFE WHEN YOU DRANK **THE MOST**, ABOUT HOW **OFTEN** DID YOU DRINK BEER, WINE, OR LIQUOR?

                                                        (Circle one)

Every day 1
Almost every day 2
3 or 4 days a week 3
1 or 2 days a week .... 4 —Answer 41
1, 2 or 3 days a month 5
Less than once a month,
  but more than 3 times a year.................... 6
3 times a year or less .... 7 —Go to 53,
                                                          page 24

41.   DURING THE **PAST 12 MONTHS**, ABOUT HOW OFTEN DID YOU DRINK BEER, WINE, OR LIQUOR?

                                                        (Circle one)

Every day 1
Almost every day 2
3 or 4 days a week 3
1 or 2 days a week .... 4 —Answer 42,
1, 2 or 3 days a month 5   next page
Less than once a month,
  but more than 3 times........................... 6
1, 2 or 3 times .... 7 —Go to 49,
Haven't had a drink in past 12 months 8   page 22

42. ABOUT HOW OFTEN DO YOU <u>CURRENTLY</u> DRINK BEER?

(Circle one)

Every day 1

Almost every day 2

3 or 4 days a week 3

1 or 2 days a week .... 4 —*Answer 42-A*

1, 2, or 3 days a month 5

Less than once a month,
but more than 3 times a year.................... 6

3 times a year or less 7

Don't drink beer at all .... 8 —*Go to 43*

42-A. WHEN YOU DRINK BEER, ABOUT HOW MUCH DO YOU USUALLY DRINK IN A <u>DAY</u>?

(Circle one)

6 quarts or more (18 glasses, bottles or cans) ... 1

4 - 5 quarts (12 - 15 glasses, bottles or cans) .. 2

2 - 3 quarts (6 - 9 glasses, bottles or cans) 3

1 quart (about 3 glasses, bottles or cans) 5

2 glasses, bottles or cans 5

1 glass, bottle or can (or less) 6

---

43. ABOUT HOW OFTEN DO YOU CURRENTLY DRINK WINE?

(Circle one)

Every day 1

Almost every day 2

3 or 4 days a week 3

1 or 2 days a week .... 4 —*Answer 43-A*

1, 2 or 3 days a month 5

Less than once a month,
but more than 3 times a year.................... 6

3 times a year or less 7

Don't drink wine at all .... 8 —*Go to 44,*
next page

43-A. WHEN YOU DRINK WINE, ABOUT HOW MUCH DO YOU USUALLY DRINK IN A <u>DAY</u>?

(Circle one)

3 or more bottles 1

2 bottles 2

About 1 bottle (6 - 7 wine glasses) 3

5 - 6 wine glasses (3 water glasses) 4

3 - 4 wine glasses (2 water glasses) 5

1 - 2 wine glasses (1 water glass) 6

44.   **ABOUT HOW OFTEN DO YOU <u>CURRENTLY</u> DRINK HARD LIQUOR — LIKE WHISKEY, VODKA, OR GIN?**

(Circle one)

Every day 1
Almost every day 2
3 or 4 days a week 3
1 or 2 days a week 4   *—Answer 44-A*
1, 2 or 3 days a month 5
Less than once a month
  but more than 3 times a year.................... 6
3 times a year or less 7
Don't drink hard liquor at all 8   *—Go to 45*

44-A.   **WHEN YOU DRINK HARD LIQUOR, ABOUT HOW MUCH DO YOU USUALLY DRINK IN A <u>DAY</u>?**

(Circle one)

More than 1 quart or fifth 1
About 1 quart or fifth 2
More than 1 pint but less than 1 quart 3
About 1 pint 4
11 - 15 ounces or shots 5
7 - 10 ounces or shots 6
4 - 6 ounces or shots 7
1 - 3 ounces or shots 8

45.   **DURING THE <u>PAST 3 MONTHS</u>, HOW MUCH HAS YOUR DRINKING WORRIED OR CONCERNED YOU?**

(Circle one)

A great deal 1
Somewhat 2
A little 3
Not at all 4

46.   **DURING THE <u>PAST 3 MONTHS</u>, HOW MUCH OF THE TIME HAS YOUR DRINKING KEPT YOU FROM DOING THE KINDS OF THINGS OTHER PEOPLE YOUR AGE DO?**

(Circle one)

All of the time 1
Most of the time 2
Some of the time 3
A little of the time 4
None of the time 5

47. DURING THE <u>PAST 30 DAYS</u>, HOW MANY DAYS HAS YOUR DRINKING KEPT YOU IN BED ALL DAY OR MOST OF THE DAY? (If none, write in "0")

_____ days in bed last month

48. ARE YOU <u>CURRENTLY</u> DOING ANYTHING TO CUT DOWN OR TO STOP YOUR DRINKING?

Yes .... 1 —Answer 48-A
No .... 2 —Go to 49

48-A. WHAT ARE YOU DOING TO CUT DOWN OR STOP YOUR DRINKING? (Circle one number on each line.)

	Yes	No
Going to AA (Alcoholics Anonymous)	1	2
Seeing a psychologist or psychiatrist	1	2
Seeing a doctor	1	2
Talking to a social worker or counselor	1	2
Taking medication (Antabuse, etc.)	1	2
Using will power, saying No	1	2
Other	1	2

What? _____

49. A. HAS A DOCTOR EVER TOLD YOU TO STOP OR CUT DOWN ON YOUR DRINKING?

Yes 1
No 2

B. HAS A DOCTOR EVER SAID YOU HAD CIRRHOSIS (seer-ROE-sis) OF THE LIVER, ALCOHOLIC LIVER DISEASE, OR "FATTY LIVER"?

Yes 1
No 2

C. HAVE YOU EVER HAD D.T.'S, DELIRIUM TREMENS (dil-LEER-ee-um-TREM-ens)?

Yes 1
No 2

50. HAVE YOU EVER HAD AN ACCIDENT, WHICH REQUIRED MEDICAL ATTENTION, WHILE UNDER THE INFLUENCE OF LIQUOR, LIKE FALLING DOWN STAIRS OR BEING HIT BY A CAR?

Yes 1

No 2

51. HAVE YOU EVER HAD A TRAFFIC ACCIDENT, OR BEEN STOPPED BY POLICE, WHILE DRIVING UNDER THE INFLUENCE OF LIQUOR?

Yes 1

No 2

52. HAVE YOU EVER STOPPED DRINKING COMPLETELY?

Yes 1   —*Answer 52-A*

No 2   —*Go to 53,*
next page

52-A. HOW LONG DID YOU STOP COMPLETELY, THE LAST TIME YOU STOPPED?

(Circle one)

Less than 2 weeks 1

2 weeks but less than 1 month 2

1 month but less than 3 months 3

3 months but less than 6 months 4

6 months but less than 1 year 5

1 year or more 6

Statistical Methods

We used analysis of variance (ANOVA) techniques (that is, direct age and sex adjustment) as well as a negative binomial regression model to estimate the effect of poor health habits on the use of medical services (outpatient visits, outpatient episodes of treatment, and inpatient admissions) and on work loss. With direct age and sex adjustment we derived sample means for these outcomes to provide simple contrasts purged of the known association between age, sex, and habits. We augmented these results with estimates based on the negative binomial model. Three characteristics of the distribution of medical expenses and work loss caused us to choose this estimation technique. First, a large proportion of the participants use no medical services or have no work loss during the year. Second, the distribution of outpatient and inpatient services among users and work loss among workers is very skewed. Third, the distribution of medical use is quite different for individuals with only outpatient use than for individuals with inpatient use; thus we separated inpatient from outpatient use.

Because of these characteristics, techniques like ANOVA (including direct age and sex adjustment) and the analysis of covariance (ANOCOVA) yield imprecise though consistent estimates of the effects of health habits on the use of medical services and work loss, even with a sample as large as the NHIS 1983 habits supplement. A model that exploits the characteristics of the medical use and work-loss distributions yields more precise and robust estimates.

We used a model based on the negative binomial distribution to estimate the response to poor health habits of admissions, outpatient episodes of treatment, and work loss. The model is appealing because it can yield a large proportion of zeros and a skewed distribution of positive outcomes. It is also attractive because of its ability to adjust the estimates for different time frames for different individuals—that is, its convolution properties with respect to time observed. The negative binomial regression model is more appealing than a Poisson regression because it allows for unmeasured characteristics to generate over dispersion. In our case the outcomes have variances larger than their means.

The convolution property of the negative binomial model is especially desirable for our application. We have counts on episodes of treatment, admissions, and work loss that cover varying periods of time at risk—from one day to five years. The negative binomial technique can effectively "annualize" all of our estimates, while controlling for age, sex, and other confounding variables.

The negative binomial can be formulated as a mixture of Poisson variates. Let the ith individual's admissions (or episodes) be drawn independently from a Poisson distribution with rate λ_i:

$$p(\text{admits} = n|\lambda_i, T_i) = (\lambda_i T_i)^n \exp(-\lambda_i T_i)/n!$$

where T_i is the period observed for individual i.

If different individuals have different rates that are sampled from a (type III) gamma distribution,

$$f_{\alpha,\beta}(\lambda) = [\beta^\alpha \Gamma(\alpha)]^{-1} \lambda^{\alpha-1} \exp(-\lambda/\beta),$$

where λ, α, and β are all greater than zero, then the observed number of admissions follows a negative binomial distribution (Johnson and Kotz, 1969, pp. 122–142) where

$$\text{prob}(\text{admits} = n) = \binom{\alpha + n - 1}{\alpha - 1} \left(\frac{\beta}{T_i + \beta}\right)^n \left(\frac{T_i}{T_i + \beta}\right)^\alpha.$$

In the results below, we specify the parameters α and β in terms of linear combinations of observed individual characteristics. For admissions and work loss, the log of the parameter α is a constant. For outpatient episodes, it is a linear function of sex, income, and insurance coverage. The log of the parameter β is a linear combination of all characteristics mentioned in the text such as insurance plan, health status, age, sex, education, and income:

$$\ln\beta = -x_i\delta,$$

where x_i is a row vector of given individual characteristics, including an intercept, and δ is a column vector to be estimated.

The model is estimated by maximum likelihood.

Inpatient Use

The estimated model provides a good fit to the actual distribution of admissions over the three- to five-year period; Table D–1 compares the actual and predicted density function for those who stayed until the end of the HIE; the $\chi^2(7) = 3.94$. There is similar agreement between predicted and observed if we break the sample by length of enrollment.

APPENDIX TABLE D-1.   Predicted and observed HIE admissions

Number of Admissions	Predicted Percentage	Observed Percentage
0	74.60	74.32
1	15.46	16.22
2	5.33	5.31
3	2.23	1.92
4	1.05	1.03
5	0.54	0.40
6–10	0.69	0.66
11+	0.10	0.13

NOTE: Adults aged 20–59. Adjusted for time on the study.

Outpatient Use

We conducted a similar analysis for the use of outpatient care.[1] The estimated model provides a good fit to the actual distribution of the outpatient episodes. Table D–2 compares the actual and predicted distributions; the $\chi^2(8) = 8.42$.

Work-Loss Days

The estimated model for work-loss days does not fit the data as well as the corresponding outpatient episode and admission equations did. Table D–3 presents the results for HIE adult males, aged 20 to 59 years. The observed data have fewer cases with many work-loss days (11 +) than do the predicted data. The observed distribution is more peaked than the predicted one. These

APPENDIX TABLE D-2.   Predicted and observed HIE outpatient episodes of treatment

Number of Episodes	Predicted Percentage	Observed Percentage
0	9.8	10.2
1–3	25.4	24.2
4–6	19.3	19.8
7–9	13.9	13.3
10–12	9.8	10.6
13–15	6.8	6.7
16–18	4.7	4.8
19–30	8.0	8.4
31+	2.4	1.9

NOTE: Adults aged 20–59. Adjusted for time on the study.

APPENDIX TABLE D-3.   Predicted and observed HIE work loss, adult males

Number of Days	Predicted Percentage	Observed Percentage
0	41.06	39.95
1	12.34	12.13
2	7.55	8.19
3	5.41	5.76
4	4.17	5.72
5	3.35	4.90
6	2.76	3.16
7	2.33	2.25
8	1.99	1.95
9	1.72	2.21
10	1.50	1.69
11+	15.81	12.09

NOTE: Aged 20–59. Data cover periods of varying length.

differences in the predicted and observed distributions are statistically significant: $\chi^2(11) = 57.78$. Because the absolute differences seem relatively small, and for reasons of convolution and simplicity, we have used a negative binomial model.

Correlation in the Error Terms

Although we have observations on nearly twenty thousand person-years of HIE data and over twenty thousand persons in the NHIS, we do not have the same number of *independent* observations, because of substantial positive correlations in the error terms among family members and over time among observations on the same person. These correlations exist in all of our outcome measures. Failure to account for them in the analysis yields inefficient estimates of the coefficients and statistically inconsistent estimates of the standard errors. As a result, the inference statistics (t, F, and χ^2) calculated in the usual way (without adjusting for these correlations) can be too large.

In the results presented herein, we corrected the inference statistics for this positive intrafamily correlation using a nonparametric approach. The correction is similar to that for the random effects least-squares model, or equivalently the intracluster correlation model (Searle, 1971). It is described in Rogers (1983) and Brook et al. (1984), based on prior work by Huber (1967) on the variance of a robust regression.

Comparability of HIE and NHIS

We compared the HIE and NHIS data for three reasons. First, we wanted to verify the generalizability to the nonaged (those under age 60) of the response at the six HIE sites. The HIE sample is representative of the six sites studied, but these sites could differ from the United States as a whole. Second, we wanted to estimate possible changes in habits and their effects for data collected at two different points in time. And most important, when results are based on small or moderate sample sizes, it is important to replicate the study on other data. If the results agree, we can be more confident of their reliability.

To assess the comparability of the two data sources, we examined the prevalence of poor health habits, the average amount of medical use and work loss, and the similarity in the response of utilization and work loss to poor health habits. The comparability is limited to those under 60 years of age.

Prevalence of Poor Health Habits

Tables E–1 to E–3 present the prevalence of poor health habits in the two samples. The distribution of never, former, and current cigarette smokers is roughly similar between the two data sets; but the differences are statistically significant ($p < 0.0001$). The lower proportion of current smokers in the NHIS may be due to shifts in smoking between 1974–1978, when the HIE data were collected, and 1983, when the NHIS data were collected; or it may result from differences between the HIE sites and a national probability sample.

The HIE has more moderate to heavy drinkers than the NHIS. Again, the differences are statistically significant ($p^\cdot < 0.0001$). Although similar, the batteries are not identical; this discrepancy may account for some of the differences between the two data sets.

The exercise responses are substantially different in the two studies ($p < 0.0001$). Thirteen percent of HIE respondents get heavy exercise, while thirty-seven percent of NHIS respondents get more exercise than the average person their age. These variations are probably due to differences in the

APPENDIX TABLE E-1.   Smoking status (percentages)

Survey	Never Smoker	Former Smoker	Current Smoker
Health Insurance Experiment, ages 20–59	41.3	16.9	41.8
National Health Interview Survey			
Ages 20–59	44.7	19.8	35.5
Ages 60+	50.2	31.0	18.8

APPENDIX TABLE E-2.   Drinking status (percentages)

Survey	Abstainer	Former Drinker	Current Drinkers			
			0.01–0.21 Ounce/Day	0.22–0.99 Ounce/Day	1.0–2.99 Ounces/Day	3.0 or More Ounces/Day
Health Insurance Experiment, ages 20–59	35.9	2.8	25.6	25.2	8.5	2.0
National Health Interview Survey						
ages 20–59	47.4	10.1	23.1	12.2	7.2	None
ages 60+	29.8	5.5	32.1	22.8	8.2	1.7

APPENDIX TABLE E-3.   Exercise status (percentages)

Survey	Level of Exercise		
	Light	Moderate	Heavy
Health Insurance Experiment, ages 20–59	24.0	63.4	12.6
National Health Interview Survey, ages 20–59	13.2	49.6	37.2

wording of the two questionnaires. The HIE asks about frequency and level of activity, whereas the NHIS asks each respondent to assess his exercise level relative to others in his age group.

Rates of Use and Work Loss

Table E–4 presents the overall outpatient visit, admission, and work-loss rates for the two data sets. The admission rates are virtually identical for the two studies. The HIE visit rates are higher than those for the NHIS, a

APPENDIX TABLE E-4.   Annual measures of morbidity, Health Insurance
Experiment and National Health Interview Survey

Measure	HIE		NHIS	
	Mean	S.D.	Mean	S.D.
Hospitalization	0.15	0.46	0.14	0.46
Visits	4.08	7.27	3.59	8.22
Work-loss days (males only)	6.18	19.25	3.07	21.85

NOTE: Ages 20–59. All rates are annual. In the case of NHIS work loss, the two-week reported values were multiplied by 26. HIE visits exclude psychotherapy, which averages 0.66 visit per person per year (S.D. = 4.29).

discrepancy that could reflect differences in insurance coverage or reporting methods. Although most people in the United States have relatively complete inpatient coverage, their outpatient coverage is less generous than that of typical HIE participants. If the insurance coverage were equal, we would expect lower visit rates for the HIE than for the NHIS, because the HIE rates are based on claims data, whereas those for the NHIS are based on twelve-month recall. Claims data tend to generate fewer visits, in that doctors do not bill separately for visits associated with maternity and certain inpatient surgical procedures. Instead, they bill for these services on a lump-sum basis at the time of hospitalization.

The average annual number of work-loss days for adult males is substantially higher in the HIE than in the NHIS, probably because the definition of work loss differed in the two studies. In the HIE time lost due to doctor office visits is counted as work loss; in the NHIS those days may not be so counted unless a whole day was missed.

Effects of Poor Health Habits

We also compared the magnitude of the estimated effects of the three poor health habits on visit, admission, and work-loss rates. Given the observed differences in levels of use and work loss, we might expect that the response to habits would differ as well. We are interested in proportional effects—do smokers have x percent more visits than those who never smoked?

We used negative binomial regression methods to adjust admission, visit, and work-loss rates for age, sex, and education in estimating the effects of the three poor health habits; see Appendix D for further details. The negative binomial model's convolution properties allowed us to adjust for different time frames for the measures in the two data sets. Although admission and visit numbers are annual in both studies, HIE work-loss data cover periods that vary from person to person, while NHIS work-loss data are biweekly.

APPENDIX TABLE E-5. Test statistics (χ^2) for habit response, Health Insurance Experiment and National Health Interview Survey

Habit	df	Visits	Hospitalizations	Work Loss
Cigarette smoking	2	1.90	2.55	1.39
Exercise	2	2.10	1.25	3.34
Drinking	4	11.61[a]	1.99	4.31
All	8	17.81[a]	5.98	8.94

NOTE: Visits and hospitalizations are annual measures. Work-loss days are for all adults and are not conditioned on employment status. NHIS work-loss rates have been annualized through the negative binomial regression. Ages 20–59; df = degrees of freedom.

a. Significant at 5 percent level.

Despite the problem of fit for work loss, we felt that it was important to find a model that avoided the time frame problem, controlled for covariates, and yielded a proportional test.

Over all habits, we found statistically significant differences between the NHIS and HIE only for outpatient visits. Table E–5 presents the chi-square statistics for the Wald test for equality of the habit coefficients between the two data sources. The estimated model includes covariates for all three health habits—age, sex, and education level. As the table indicates, the estimated responses were not significantly different for either admissions or work loss. For smoking and exercise, there were no significant differences between the two studies for any of the three rates. For drinking, only outpatient visits showed a significantly different response.

Although most of the responses were not statistically significantly different from one another, there were appreciable differences in some of the estimated coefficients. Table E–6 presents the habit coefficients for each of the three outcomes—admissions, visits, and work loss; the coefficients should be exponentiated to obtain proportional effects.

Habit response of persons 20 through 59 years of age, Health Insurance Experiment and National Health Interview Survey

Outcome	Variable	HIE		NHIS	
		β	t	β	t
Visits					
	Former smoker	0.065	0.78	0.119	2.61
	Current smoker	−0.092	−1.39	0.019	0.41
	Abstainer	0.019	0.20	−0.220	3.43
	Former drinker	−0.041	−0.26	−0.018	−0.21
	Log monthly volume	0.074	0.96	−0.188	−3.46
	$(\text{Log} \ldots)^2$	−0.025	−1.45	0.039	3.08
	Moderate exercise or average	0.045	0.50	−0.055	−1.37
	Little exercise or less than average	0.189	1.82	0.203	3.43
Hospitalizations					
	Former smoker	0.074	0.62	0.287	4.15
	Current smoker	0.120	2.25	0.201	3.36
	Abstainer	0.063	0.43	−0.011	−0.13
	Former drinker	0.226	0.90	0.301	2.56
	Log monthly volume	−0.139	−1.16	−0.200	−2.61
	$(\text{Log} \ldots)^2$	0.035	1.48	0.035	2.00
	Moderate exercise or average	0.125	0.93	−0.039	−0.63
	Little exercise or less than average	0.311	2.08	0.169	1.79
Work loss					
	Former smoker	−0.045	−0.42	0.053	0.35
	Current smoker	0.066	0.67	0.260	1.98
	Abstainer	0.242	−1.71	0.064	0.33
	Former drinker	0.549	1.29	0.581	1.99
	Log monthly volume	−0.163	−1.28	0.212	1.50
	$(\text{Log} \ldots)^2$	0.030	1.06	−0.043	−1.55
	Moderate exercise or average	0.207	1.51	−0.135	−1.02
	Little exercise or less than average	0.268	1.74	0.091	0.52

NOTE: Coefficients are on the log scale. Exponentiate to obtain *proportional* differences.

Excise Taxes and Demand

The adverse health effects associated with cigarette smoking and excessive alcohol consumption are well known. In addition, smokers and heavy drinkers may impose costs on society in the form of collectively financed health expenditures, diminished job productivity financed through employer-covered sick leave, property damage due to cigarette-caused fires, highway accidents and deaths attributable to drunk driving, and even criminal activity caused by drunkenness. As the various health effects and social costs of smoking and drinking have been identified, federal and state legislators and other public officials have considered, and at times enacted, measures aimed at curtailing consumption of these goods.

The purpose of this appendix is to examine one promising policy instrument available for reducing smoking and alcohol consumption: an increase in excise taxes. In addition to assessing how excise taxes influence the demand for cigarettes and alcohol, we will look at other economic forces that are present in the markets for these goods, including tobacco production quotas and price supports. Alternative policies for reducing cigarette and alcohol consumption such as advertising restrictions, antismoking or anti-drinking publicity campaigns, and smoking and drinking prevention programs may be used in place of or in conjunction with taxation. We will not attempt a detailed exploration of these policies.

Historically, excise taxes on cigarettes and alcoholic beverages have served to finance war efforts. As early as 1791 a tax was imposed on distilled spirits to pay Revolutionary War debts. Later repealed by Jefferson, the tax was reimposed after the War of 1812. Alcoholic beverage taxes also helped to finance the Civil War and World War I and were raised substantially to assist in covering the costs of World War II and the Korean conflict (Mosher and Beauchamp, 1983). Enacted in 1864, the cigarette excise tax too was an important source of revenue for covering war debts.

Prior to the advent of the income tax just before World War I, excise taxes were the federal government's principal source of revenue. Clark (1984) has noted: "At the turn of the century, taxes on alcoholic beverages supplied 62 percent of Treasury receipts and levies on tobacco, 20 percent. But as progressivity became an important objective of the tax system and, more recently, as social insurance payroll taxes assumed an increasingly important role in supplying revenues, excise taxes have diminished in importance." Presently, excise taxes on tobacco and alcoholic beverages account for only 0.4 and 0.8 percent of federal tax revenues, respectively (U.S. Department of Commerce, 1984).

While cigarette and alcohol taxes have been an important means of generating revenue for federal and state governments (tobacco taxes generate 1.2 percent and alcohol taxes 0.82 percent of overall state revenues), several other rationales for taxing these goods have surfaced. For instance, as the health consequences of cigarette smoking and heavy drinking have become apparent, taxes have been viewed as a potential vehicle for limiting consumption and improving the public's health by reducing smoking-induced and drinking-induced diseases and premature deaths. Related to this approach is the notion that there are significant externalities associated with smoking and drinking. Lewit et al. (1981), for example, suggested that the case for government intervention in the cigarette market is derived in part from the presumed existence of both externalities in consumption (the health of some persons enters the utility function of others) and externalities of production (smoking by some may harm the health of others). Similarly, concerning alcohol, Mosher and Beauchamp (1983) observed that "alcohol taxes are often justified because they help control the social costs of alcohol use, which are extensive."

By levying appropriate taxes on these goods, the government can in principle drive consumption of these goods toward socially optimal levels (that is, to the point where the marginal cost to smokers or drinkers equals the marginal social cost). The tax revenues received could potentially provide compensation to those harmed (financially or otherwise) by smokers and drinkers, although the transaction costs associated with directly compensating the "victims" of smokers and heavy drinkers may prove to be prohibitively high. Instead, tax revenues from cigarettes and alcohol could be used to finance a social program, the costs of which are partially determined by the amounts of these goods we collectively consume. For example, Munnell (1985) has argued that cigarette and alcohol tax revenues should be used to help finance the Medicare program:

> Two alternative lines of reasoning can be used to justify increasing the excise taxes on alcohol and tobacco as a means of financing Medicare. On the one hand, consumption of these items affects health and health status and determines the usage of Medicare services. The relationship between heavy smoking and increased lung and heart disease is well established, as is the relationship between excessive use of alcohol and cirrhosis of the liver, certain cancers, and highway injuries. Increasing excise taxes on alcohol and tobacco could be viewed as advance payment by those who smoke and drink for the higher medical costs that they,

as a group, will inevitably incur. Alternatively, higher excise taxes can be viewed as desirable insofar as they will raise the price of alcohol and tobacco relative to other goods, thereby discouraging their consumption and improving the general level of health in the nation.

It should be noted, with respect to Munnell's last point, that if higher excise taxes are indeed successful in reducing alcohol and cigarette consumption, then increases in these taxes may have the effect of raising the cost of the Medicare program (Wright, 1986), because taxes would lengthen the lives of smokers and heavy drinkers.

Finally, our current excise taxes on alcoholic beverages and cigarettes have not been set in a manner that suggests that the federal and state legislators who imposed them had any particular economic rationale in mind, other than allowing them to meet the exigencies of the relevant budgets.

Excise Taxes and the Demand for Cigarettes

TAX RATES AND REVENUE

Excise taxes on cigarettes are imposed at the federal, state, and local levels. Between 1951 and 1982 the federal excise tax stood at 8 cents per pack; it was raised to 16 cents in 1983, where it remains today. Because the tax did not change in a period of marked inflation, the real tax has declined dramatically over the last thirty-five years. As Table F–1 indicates, in 1951 the tax represented 42.3 percent of the purchase price of a package of cigarettes. In contrast, in 1982 the tax rate as a percentage of the purchase price fell to 10.7 percent; it increased to 17.8 percent in 1983 when the 16-cents-per-pack tax took effect and then fell off somewhat in 1984.

State excise taxes, shown in Table F–2, vary considerably, ranging from a low of 2 cents per pack in the tobacco-producing state of North Carolina to a high of 38 cents per pack in Minnesota. Additionally, 392 cities, towns, and counties in 6 states (Alabama, Illinois, Missouri, New York, Tennessee, and Virginia) impose cigarette taxes. These local taxes range between 1 and 15 cents per pack.

For the fiscal year ending June 30, 1987, federal, state, and local cigarette excise taxes generated over $9.6 billion in revenue. The federal and state shares of the total were nearly equivalent, with each realizing approximately $4.7 billion in revenue; combined local revenues amounted to $197 million, a negligible 0.06 percent of all local tax revenues (Tobacco Institute, 1987). Given that just under 30 billion packages of cigarettes were sold in 1987, this implies an average tax burden of over 30 cents per pack.

PRICE AND INCOME ELASTICITIES OF DEMAND

Apart from their revenue-generating potential, excise taxes have an influence on the quantity of cigarettes demanded, with higher taxes causing a lower level of consumption. The ability of excise tax increases actually to reduce

APPENDIX TABLE F-1.   Federal cigarette excise taxes, 1951–1984

Year	Tax Rate Current $ (cents/pack)	Tax Rate 1984 $ (cents/pack)	Average Price[a] Current $ (cents/pack)	Tax Rate (percent)
1951	8.0	32.0	18.9	42.3
1952	8.0	31.3	19.9	40.2
1953	8.0	31.1	20.9	38.3
1954	8.0	30.9	21.2	37.7
1955	8.0	31.0	21.3	37.6
1956	8.0	30.6	21.8	36.7
1957	8.0	29.5	22.4	35.7
1958	8.0	28.7	23.2	34.5
1959	8.0	28.5	24.2	33.1
1960	8.0	28.1	24.9	32.1
1961	8.0	27.8	25.1	31.9
1962	8.0	27.5	25.4	31.5
1963	8.0	27.1	25.9	30.9
1964	8.0	26.8	26.4	30.3
1965	8.0	26.3	27.7	28.9
1966	8.0	25.6	29.1	27.5
1967	8.0	24.9	30.2	26.5
1968	8.0	23.9	32.1	24.9
1969	8.0	22.7	33.9	23.6
1970	8.0	21.4	37.0	21.6
1971	8.0	20.5	38.7	20.7
1972	8.0	19.9	40.9	19.6
1973	8.0	18.7	42.0	19.0
1974	8.0	16.9	44.1	18.1
1975	8.0	15.4	47.3	16.9
1976	8.0	14.6	49.3	16.2
1977	8.0	13.7	51.6	15.5
1978	8.0	12.7	54.3	14.7
1979	8.0	11.4	57.3	14.0
1980	8.0	10.1	62.0	12.9
1981	8.0	9.1	66.9	12.0
1982	8.0	8.6	74.7	10.7
1983	16.0	16.7	90.1	17.8
1984	16.0	16.0	96.3	16.6

SOURCE: Institute for the Study of Smoking Behavior and Policy, 1985, p. 70.

a. Includes excise taxes.

APPENDIX TABLE F-2. State cigarette excise taxes per pack (as of November 1, 1987)

State	Tax Rate (cents/pack)	State	Tax Rate (cents/pack)
Alabama	16.5	Montana	16.0
Alaska	16.0	Nebraska	27.0
Arizona	15.0	Nevada	20.0
Arkansas	21.0	New Hampshire	17.0
California	10.0	New Jersey	27.0
Colorado	20.0	New Mexico	15.0
Connecticut	26.0	New York	21.0
Delaware	14.0	North Carolina	2.0
Dist. of Columbia	17.0	North Dakota	27.0
Florida	24.0	Ohio	18.0
Georgia	12.0	Oklahoma	23.0
Hawaii	30.0	Oregon	27.0
Idaho	18.1	Pennsylvania	18.0
Illinois	20.0	Rhode Island	25.4
Indiana	15.5	South Carolina	7.0
Iowa	26.0	South Dakota	23.0
Kansas	24.0	Tennessee	13.0
Kentucky	3.0	Texas	26.0
Louisiana	16.0	Utah	23.0
Maine	28.0	Vermont	17.0
Maryland	13.0	Virginia	2.5
Massachusetts	26.0	Washington	31.0
Michigan	21.0	West Virginia	17.0
Minnesota	38.0	Wisconsin	30.0
Mississippi	18.0	Wyoming	8.0
Missouri	13.0		

SOURCE: Tobacco Institute, 1987.

cigarette consumption depends on (1) the extent to which such tax increases are incorporated into the prices consumers face and (2) the degree to which the demand for cigarettes is sensitive, or responsive, to price increases. Empirical evidence suggests that excise tax increases are in fact passed on to smokers. The evidence concerning the response of smokers to increased prices, in terms of the quantity of cigarettes they demand, is somewhat more ambiguous.

One measure of the degree to which smokers are responsive to price changes is the price elasticity of demand—the percentage change in quantity demanded divided by the percentage change in price. Estimates of the price elasticity of demand for cigarettes vary enormously from study to study. In a review of the early work on cigarette price elasticities, Laughhunn and

APPENDIX TABLE F-3.   Price and income elasticities of demand for cigarettes

Study	Price Elasticity	Income Elasticity	Method of Estimation	Comments
Baltagi and Levin (1986)	−0.22	−0.002 to 0.004	Ordinary least squares or Hausman-Taylor efficiency estimation	Pooled cross-sectional and time-series data; U.S.
Fujii (1980)	−0.47	0.22	Ridge regression	Time-series data; U.S.
Hamilton (1972)	−0.51[a]	0.73	Ordinary least squares	Time-series data; U.S.
Laughhunn and Lyon (1971)	−0.81	0.42	Bayesian regression	Pooled cross-sectional and time-series data; U.S.
Leu (1984)	−1.00	0.93	Ordinary least squares	Time-series data; Switzerland
Lewit et al. (1981)	−1.19 −1.44	Not estimated	Ordinary least squares	Smoking participation (teens) Quantity smoked (teens)
Lewit and Coate (1982)	−0.42	0.08	Ordinary least squares	Elasticities by age and sex
Warner (1981)	−0.37	Not estimated	Ordinary least squares	Time-series data; U.S.
Wasserman (1988) Wasserman et al. (1991)	−0.23 to 0.06	−0.023 to 0.002	Generalized linear model	Cross-sectional data; U.S.
Witt and Pass (1983)	−0.31	0.13	Ordinary least squares	Time-series data; UK
Young (1983)	−0.33	0.15	Ridge regression	Alternative specification of Fujii's model

a. Extraneous estimate, taken from Lyon and Simon (1968).

Lyon (1971) found estimates ranging from −0.10 to −1.48. Lewit and Coate (1982), in their review of work completed since 1970 that used data from the United States, reported estimates that had a somewhat narrower range, −0.4 to −1.3. The studies summarized in Table F–3 show a similar amount of variation. The rather disparate estimates are attributable to differences in data and estimation techniques applied. The data and methodology used in each of the studies, along with any interesting or unusual findings, are described briefly below.

Estimates of the income elasticity of demand for cigarettes are also shown in Table F–3. Apparently the demand for cigarettes is income inelastic, with the estimates ranging from a low of −0.002 to a high of 0.93. This suggests that cigarettes may in fact be considered a necessity (at least among smokers), probably because of the addictive nature of smoking.

Baltagi and Levin (1986) pooled cross-sectional and time-series data from forty-six states between 1963 and 1980 to estimate their cigarette demand model. The results of their log-linear model indicated an own-price elasticity of −0.22 and a neighboring-state price elasticity of 0.08.[1] This finding implies that if prices were increased by 10 percent in all states, per capita consumption would fall by 1.4 percent, a rather small overall effect that prompted

Baltagi and Levin to conclude that, "as an antismoking tool, cigarette taxation may not be as effective in reducing cigarette consumption as previously thought." Their reported income elasticities, which ranged between −0.002 and 0.004, were not statistically different from zero.

Fujii (1980), in an effort to circumvent multicollinearity problems (among the price, income, and advertising variables) that he asserts were present in several previous studies of cigarette demand, used ridge regression techniques to estimate demand equations for cigarettes. He used time-series data from the United States from 1929 to 1973, and specified equations in both linear and double-log forms. Independent variables used to explain cigarette consumption per capita included price, real income per capita, advertising expenditures, lagged consumption, and a set of dummy variables to capture the effects of various "health scares" (Surgeon General and other reports on the health effects of smoking). The linear equations were found to provide better fits than the double-log equations. Price and income elasticities, calculated at the sample means in the linear specification, were −0.47 and 0.22, respectively.

In his attempt to deal with the price-income collinearity problem Hamilton (1972)—who was primarily interested in examining how cigarette consumption has been affected by both advertising and the health scares—used extraneous estimates for the price and income parameters. The price elasticity figure of −0.51 was taken from Lyon and Simon (1968), who used a quasi-experimental technique which compared changes in consumption in states that experienced a tax increase with adjoining states where there was no such increase. Using the Lyon-Simon price elasticity estimate, Hamilton estimated an income elasticity of 0.73.

Using Bayesian regression methods, Laughhunn and Lyon (1971) estimated per capita cigarette consumption as a function of price, personal consumption expenditures (income), and region of the country (West, North Central, Northeast, and South). While they estimated the overall price and income elasticities to be −0.81 and 0.42, they found a substantial amount of variation in their estimates of these elasticities at the regional level. For example, price elasticities ranged from a quite inelastic −0.40 in the West to an elastic −1.14 in the Northeast; income elasticities reached a high of 0.79 in the West and a low of 0.21 in the Northeast.

Leu (1984), in his study of antismoking publicity and taxation in Switzerland, estimated the nominal cigarette price elasticity of demand to be −1.00 and calculated the income elasticity as 0.93. After noting that the real cigarette price failed to be significant once the nominal cigarette price was included in the estimating equation, Leu rejected the explanation that this result can be accounted for by smokers' money illusion because of the addictive nature of smoking. Rather, he posits that the observed responsiveness of cigarette consumption to nominal price is due to the indirect effects of antismoking publicity. According to his line of reasoning, tax-related price increases act as a "final trigger" for smokers who are displeased with their habit and wish to quit.

Lewit et al. (1981) used data from the Health Examination Survey to estimate cigarette demand functions for teenagers. The authors examined two measures of smoking behavior: whether or not the teenager smoked and the quantity smoked per day (not conditioned on smoking). The estimated elasticities for both the smoking participation equation (where a dichotomous dependent variable was used to indicate whether a person smoked or not) and the quantity smoked equation are quite large (-1.19 and -1.44) relative to the other estimates presented in Table F–3. Lewit et al. suggest that these large values may incorporate income as well as substitution effects—for while the study held family income constant and included a proxy measure of a youth's discretionary income, without a true measure of his or her real income the estimated price parameter is biased in that it represents more than the pure price effect. Yet this is not a problem from a policy perspective: the total effect is what matters, not the pure price effect. With respect to the quantity smoked equation, the price coefficient need not even be negative because of selection effects (if light smokers quit, cigarettes per smoker could rise). Still, the high price elasticity estimates led the authors to conclude that increasing cigarette excise taxes is a potent way to achieve a reduction in smoking among young people.

In their study of the potential of excise taxes as a means to reduce smoking, Lewit and Coate (1982) used data on individuals from the 1976 Health Interview Survey to estimate the price and income elasticities of demand for cigarettes. The authors offer a cogent argument to support their view that utilizing data on individuals is preferable to using states as the units of observation (as was done in most cross-sectional studies of cigarette demand) because the latter approach produces elasticity estimates that are biased upward. Sales figures based on taxes paid fail to adquately reflect actual consumption, inasmuch as there is considerable smuggling or bootlegging of cigarettes from low-tax to high-tax states. In a further effort to eliminate the potential for producing biased estimates, individuals were dropped from the sample if they lived in areas where the price of cigarettes in their community was greater than another price within a twenty-mile band around their place of residence.

The regression estimates obtained from this "restricted sample" indicated an overall price elasticity of -0.42 and an income elasticity of 0.08 when the elasticities were calculated at the sample means. For the equation in which the dependent variable was smoking participation, the price elasticity was -0.26; when the dependent variable was quantity of cigarettes consumed, the price elasticity was -0.10.

Finally, after estimating demand equations for different age and sex groups, the authors concluded that price has its greatest effect on young people and that it primarily influences the decision to begin smoking rather than determining the quantity smoked. They also found that price effects were stronger for males than females.

Warner (1981) used aggregate time-series data from 1947 to 1978 to estimate an ordinary least-squares linear regression model of cigarette demand. At the means of price and consumption the estimated price elasticity of demand was −0.37. Warner's analysis also included a measure of laws restricting smoking in public places.[2] This measure was strongly correlated with decreases in consumption, climbing from 9 cigarettes per capita in 1964 to 606 in 1978.

Wasserman (1988) and Wasserman et al. (1991) estimated a generalized linear model of cigarette demand using data from National Health Interview Surveys. Separate equations were estimated for adults and teenagers. The adult results indicated that the price elasticity of demand is unstable over time, ranging from 0.06 in 1970 to −0.23 in 1985. The teenage price elasticity of demand was not statistically different from the adult estimates. Furthermore, regulations restricting smoking in public places had a significant effect in reducing both adult and teenage cigarette demand.

Using data from the United Kingdom for the period 1955 to 1975, Witt and Pass (1983) developed a model for explaining cigarette consumption based on price, income, and alternative specifications for the various health scares that occurred in the United States and the United Kingdom throughout the sixties and early seventies. The estimated price and income elasticities were, respectively, −0.32 and 0.13.

Young (1983) provided an alternative specification of Fujii's (1980) demand equation for cigarettes. Because of the addictive nature of smoking, he argued that the cigarette demand curve is kinked in a way that makes the response to a price increase less elastic than the response to a price decrease. The obvious implication is that attempts to reduce smoking through tax increases may be somewhat less successful than the elasticity estimates in other studies lead one to believe.

In order to test his asymmetry hypothesis, Young estimated two ratchet models using ridge regression. He concluded that there is "substantial evidence of asymmetry of consumer response to price and income changes," and that the two models resulted in better overall fits than Fujii's symmetric model. His estimates of the price and income elasticities of demand for cigarettes were −0.33 and 0.15, respectively.

The apparent lack of consensus regarding the elasticity of demand for cigarettes implies that the effects of a tax increase on consumption and government revenues are uncertain. In the absence of a precise estimate of the price elasticity, we cannot gauge exactly the change in demand that will be elicited from a given tax increase. In general, the different estimated elasticities may be high enough to have a substantial impact on consumption (Lewit and Coate, 1982). For example, the range of elasticities shown in Table F–3 implies that a tax-induced price increase of, say, 10 percent would reduce adult cigarette consumption by 2.2 to 10 percent.

Finally, in evaluating the potential of increasing the federal excise tax in order to achieve reductions in cigarette consumption, we need to recognize that a relationship exists between elasticity of demand and the possible trade-off between changes in consumption and changes in government revenues. Specifically, as long as the demand for cigarettes remains inelastic, government revenues will continue to increase as the excise tax is raised. If the demand curve for cigarettes is linear (as opposed to, say, log-linear), the elasticity of demand will increase as smokers cut back on their consumption in response to the higher price resulting from the tax increase. Once the quantity of cigarettes demanded falls within the elastic portion of the demand curve, tax revenues will decline. These forgone revenues might appropriately be viewed as the cost of discouraging consumption through tax-induced price increases (Laughhunn and Lyon, 1971).

QUOTAS, ALLOTMENTS, AND PRICE SUPPORTS

The involvement of the federal government in determining tobacco production and prices dates to the passage of the Agricultural Adjustment Act of 1933. The origin of the current tobacco program, however, can be traced to the second Agricultural Act of 1938 and its amendments of 1939 and 1940. Essentially, the law created a system of price supports and supply controls designed to stabilize the tobacco market. Although the tobacco program is complex (in terms of the institutions involved in its operation, the ways in which actual quotas and support prices are established, and so on) and has undergone many changes since its inception, its basic shape has endured.

As described by Johnson (1984), until 1982 the program functioned as follows. Once tobacco growers agreed by referendum to have a quota program, individual allotments were set for each farm. The allotments (initially based on acreage, later changed to pounds) were distributed to growers in accordance with historical production patterns. Each year the secretary of agriculture determines the overall quota, consistent with the tobacco support price established by a "parity" formula. The national quota for each type of tobacco is set with the intention that on average the market price for that quantity will be slightly above the support price. Additionally, the quota is adjusted so that the support price is not strictly binding and tobacco is generally sold to market buyers in the year it is produced (Sumner and Alston, 1984).

Farmers unable to sell their crops on the open market loaned the excess to one of the two farmer cooperatives, the Burley Tobacco Growers Association or the Flue-Cured Tobacco Cooperative Stabilization Corporation. These cooperatives assumed the role previously held by the Commodity Credit Corporation (CCC) which in the late 1930s and early 1940s acquired tobacco (and other farm products) through nonrecourse loans. The CCC continues to make loans to the farmer cooperatives, typically at below-market rates of interest.

In July of 1982 the Congress, under pressure to reduce the costs of the

tobacco program to the federal government—because of both general budget-
ary distress and widespread criticism that the government should not continue subsidizing the production of a commodity associated with distinctly
adverse health effects—enacted the "No-Net-Cost Tobacco Program." The
new program stipulated that, in order to be eligible for price supports, tobacco producers must contribute to a fund designed to ensure that the tobacco loan program operates at no cost to the government except for general
administrative expenses, which currently run about $15 million a year (Clark,
1985).

While the tobacco program has been quite successful in stabilizing tobacco
prices and farmer incomes, it has certainly not served economic efficiency.
According to Sumner and Alston (1984), deregulation of U.S. tobacco production (including the elimination of rather stringent output restrictions) would
lead to an increase in output of 50 to 100 percent; a reduction of 20 to 30
percent in the price of tobacco; a substitution of domestic tobacco for most
imported tobacco leaf used in cigarette manufacturing; a 3 percent drop in
the price of cigarettes; and a 100 percent increase in tobacco exports.

Nevertheless, the economic inefficiencies in the tobacco program may have
inadvertently improved the public's health. Contrasting the tobacco program
with other agricultural price support programs, Johnson (1984) has noted:

> The program is an income transfer program, whereby income is trans-
> ferred from consumers to producers. Tobacco consumers are the ones
> who are at potential risk from the effects of smoking. Two side effects
> are brought about by raising the price of the program: First, consump-
> tion is reduced and there is less smoking. Second, by paying the higher
> price the smokers are paying for the transfer to producers, in effect
> taxing themselves. These bits of irony seem lost on certain antismoking
> individuals and groups.

If this view and the empirical estimates of the tobacco program's effects
(lower output and higher prices) generated by Sumner and Alston are correct, then society may on the whole be better off maintaining, and perhaps
even strengthening, the tobacco program rather than seeking its abolition on
the grounds that it provides a prima facie subsidy to producers.

Excise Taxes and the Demand for Alcoholic Beverages

TAX RATES AND REVENUE

Excise taxes on alcoholic beverages (distilled spirits, wine, and beer) are
imposed by all three levels of government: federal, state, and local. Between
1951 and 1985 the federal excise tax on distilled spirits stood at $10.50 per
proof gallon (defined as a standard U.S. gallon containing 50 percent ethyl
alcohol by volume). On October 1, 1985, the tax was increased to $12.50 per
proof gallon. Federal excise taxes on wine and beer have remained constant

since 1951, amounting to 17 cents for a gallon of wine having alcohol content of 14 percent or less and 29 cents per gallon of beer (Distilled Spirits Council of the United States, 1985). Measured on the basis of alcohol content, the respective taxes on wine and beer are roughly 5 percent and 30 percent of the tax on distilled spirits. Because nominal taxes on these beverages have remained unchanged for almost thirty-five years, the real tax has declined substantially, as the purchasing power of the dollar has fallen by 75 percent since 1951 (U.S. Department of Commerce, 1984).

Determining state excise taxes on alcoholic beverages is complicated by the fact that eighteen states (referred to as the control states) have state-run monopolies in liquor sales. It is extremely difficult—if not impossible—to determine effective excise tax rates since, as Mosher and Beauchamp (1983) have noted, "in control states the 'tax' is a function of official excise taxes, and also of commodity prices and rates of profit."

Table F–4 contains tax rates by beverage type for the remaining states and the District of Columbia, known collectively as the "license" states (because they grant licenses to sell alcoholic beverages at the wholesale and retail levels). Tax rates in 1985 on distilled spirits in the license states ranged from a low of $1.50 per gallon in Maryland and the District of Columbia to a high of $6.50 per gallon in Florida, with an average tax of $3.06. State excise taxes on wine and beer are considerably less than the taxes on distilled spirits, on both an alcohol content and per gallon basis. For instance, the state tax levied on wine varies from 1 cent per gallon in California to $2.25 in Florida, with a mean of 56 cents. Beer taxes range from 3 cents per gallon in New Jersey to 77 cents per gallon in South Carolina, an average of 18 cents. In addition to the state taxes, local excise taxes are imposed on alcoholic beverages in six license states.

In 1984 federal excise taxes on alcoholic beverages generated over $5.7 billion in revenue. State and local taxes in the license states alone resulted in an additional $2 billion in revenue (Distilled Spirits Council of the United States, 1985).

PRICE AND INCOME ELASTICITIES OF DEMAND

The results from models of the demand for alcoholic beverages vary widely. The problems encountered in estimating such models are even more complex than those associated with demand models of cigarettes. In general, the divergent results can be explained by differences: in the data analyzed, the estimation techniques, and by the fact that some studies have attempted to estimate demand for each type of beverage (distilled spirits, wine, and beer), whereas others have aggregated the different types and produced estimates of the overall demand for alcohol. Efforts to estimate the price elasticities for the different kinds of beverages are further complicated by the fact that spirits, wine, and beer may be substitutes for one another. Thus, cross-elasticities of demand must be considered as well.

APPENDIX TABLE F-4. Excise taxes in license states, by type of beverage (as of May 1985)

State	Distilled Spirits Tax Rate ($ per gallon)	Wine Tax Rate[a] ($ per gallon)	Beer Tax Rate ($ per gallon)
Alaska	5.60	0.85	0.35
Arizona	3.00	0.84	0.16
Arkansas	2.50	0.75	0.23
California	2.00	0.01	0.04
Colorado	2.28	0.277	0.08
Connecticut	3.00	0.30	0.097
Delaware	2.25	0.40	0.06
Dist. of Columbia	1.50	0.15	0.07
Florida	6.50	2.25	0.48
Georgia	3.79	1.51	0.48
Illinois	2.00	0.23	0.07
Indiana	2.68	0.47	0.12
Kansas	2.50	0.30	0.18
Kentucky	1.92	0.50	0.08
Louisiana	2.50	0.11	0.32
Maryland	1.50	0.40	0.09
Massachusetts	4.05	0.55	0.11
Minnesota	4.39	0.27	0.13
Missouri	2.00	0.34	0.06
Nebraska	2.75	0.65	0.14
Nevada	2.05	0.40	0.09
New Jersey	2.80	0.30	0.03
New Mexico	3.94	0.95	0.18
New York	4.09	0.12	0.055
North Dakota	2.50	0.50	0.16
Oklahoma	5.00	0.63	0.40
Rhode Island	2.50	0.40	0.06
South Carolina	2.72	1.08	0.77
South Dakota	3.80	0.90	0.27
Tennessee	4.00	1.10	0.13
Texas	2.40	0.204	0.198
Wisconsin	3.25	0.25	0.06

SOURCE: Distilled Spirits Council of the United States, 1985.

NOTE: To convert the figures in the table to dollars per gallon of ethanol, divide the spirits, wine, and beer taxes by 0.45, 0.15, and 0.04, respectively. This table excludes Hawaii, which levies a 20 percent tax on spirits, wine, and beer.

a. Less than 14 percent alcohol.

APPENDIX TABLE F-5. Price and income elasticities of demand for alcoholic beverages

Study	Price Elasticity	Income Elasticity	Method of Estimation	Comments
Cook (1981)				
All types	−1.6	Not estimated	Quasi-experimental	State tax changes occurring between 1960 and 1975
Cook and Tauchen (1982)				
Spirits	−1.8	0.43	Generalized least squares	Pooled cross-sectional and time-series data; U.S
Duffy (1983)				
Spirits	−0.80 to −1.00	1.61 to 1.83	Ordinary least squares; two-staged least squares	Time-series data; U.K.
Wine	−0.64 to −0.99	2.20 to 2.50		
Beer	0.20 to 0.24	0.66 to 1.10		
Hogarty and Elzinga (1972)				
Beer	−0.9	0.4	Ordinary least squares	Pooled cross-sectional and time-series data; U.S.
Johnson and Oksanen (1977)				
Spirits	−1.13 to −1.14	0.10 to 0.11	Ordinary least squares; generalized least squares; least-squares dummy variables	Time-series data; Canadian provinces
Wine	−0.67 to −0.68	0.01 to 0.04		
Beer	−0.25 to −0.27	−0.02 to 0.002		
Levy and Sheflin (1985)				
All types	−0.5	0.4	Weighted least squares	Time-series data; U.S.
McGuinness (1980)				
All types	−0.22 to −0.26	0.18 to 0.51	Ordinary least squares	Time-series data; UK
Niskanen (1962)				
Spirits	−2.0	0.4	Three-stage least squares	Time-series data; U.S.
Wine	−0.7	1.0		
Beer	−0.6	−0.3		
Ornstein and Levy (1983)				
Spirits	−1.5	Not summarized	Literature review	
Wine	−1.0			
Beer	−0.3			

The studies of the demand for alcoholic drinks are consistent, however, in that, for the most part, the equations used in the analyses comprise the following independent or explanatory variables: own-price, prices of substitute goods, personal disposable income, a time-trend variable to account for changes in consumer tastes and other changes correlated with time, and in some instances an advertising variable (Ornstein and Levy, 1983).

The ranges of the price elasticity estimates presented in Table F–5 are between −0.80 and −2.0 for spirits; −0.64 and −1.0 for wine; −0.25 and 0.24 for beer; and −0.5 and −1.6 for all types of beverages.

The estimates of income elasticities of alcoholic beverages, shown in Table F–5, also cover a broad range. In the studies that computed separate elasticities for each beverage type, beer was consistently found to be the most income inelastic. In fact, the income elasticity estimate for beer provided by Niskanen (1962) is negative, indicating that beer is an inferior good (that is, the level of consumption declines as income increases). Johnson and

Oksanen (1977) also had a negative income elasticity estimate for beer, but it was not statistically significant.

Cook (1981) estimated the price elasticity of demand for distilled spirits using a quasi-experimental technique which was applied to data on state tax changes that occurred between 1960 and 1975. His analysis yielded a point estimate of −1.6 for the price elasticity of demand; no attempt was made to estimate the income elasticity.

Cook and Tauchen (1982), in their study of chronic drinkers' consumption in response to liquor price changes, found measured liquor consumption to be quite responsive to changes in state liquor taxes. Since state tax rather than price was included in their model, the estimated price elasticity of demand of −1.8 had to be inferred from their regression results. The authors believe that this point estimate probably exaggerates the true responsiveness of per capita liquor consumption to changes in state excise taxes; measured consumption is held to be below actual consumption owing to moonshining, possible underreporting of sales by dealers, and out-of-state purchases by consumers.

Duffy (1983) investigated consumption of spirits, wine, and beer in the United Kingdom using quarterly data from 1963 to 1978. To account for possible feedback of sales on advertising, he estimated a simultaneous-equation model, in addition to his ordinary least-squares model. The results obtained from these two approaches, with respect to price and income elasticities for each beverage type, were roughly equivalent. The demands for spirits and wine were fairly responsive to price changes, whereas the beer price coefficients were not statistically different from zero under both approaches (and in fact had the "wrong" sign).

Hogarty and Elzinga (1972) estimated annual beer consumption per adult as a function of price, per capita income, and percent of each state's population that was foreign born. This last variable, which was statistically significant, was included "on the presumption that immigrants were more prone to beer drinking than native Anglo-Saxons." The authors offer no empirical evidence to support this assertion, or even an explanation of why they believe it is so. The obtained price and income elasticity estimates of −0.9 and 0.4 resulted from applying ordinary least squares to data from forty-eight states and the District of Columbia for the period 1956 to 1959.

Johnson and Oksanen (1977) employed a basic linear model to explain the quantities of spirits, wine, and beer consumed in Canada, using province-level data over a fifteen-year period. The model included price, personal disposable income, lagged consumption, and vectors of ethnic, religion, and education variables as regressors. Different estimation procedures (ordinary least squares, generalized least squares, and least-squares dummy variables) produced remarkably similar results with respect to the price and income elasticities for all three beverages. Their findings suggest that direct price effects are highly significant in explaining consumption of the three beverages. Income had a significant effect only on the demand for distilled spirits.

The Johnson and Oksanen analysis is regarded by Cook (1981), Ornstein and Levy (1983), and others as the best of the studies that have been completed in this area. While the applicability of their results to the United States may be problematic, one could argue persuasively that the two cultures are sufficiently similar to allow use of the Johnson and Oksanen results to develop at least a first approximation of the impact that a tax-induced price increase would have on consumption in this country.

Levy and Sheflin (1985) studied the total demand for alcoholic beverages in the United States. The overall estimated price elasticity of demand was −0.5, and the income elasticity was 0.4. They estimated their model, which included only price and income as regressors, using two measures of consumption. In the first instance quantity of pure alcohol consumed served as the dependent variable, while the second equation used real expenditures. The two approaches yielded similar estimates of the price and income elasticities.

By choosing to estimate the total demand for alcoholic beverages, rather than estimating the demand for spirits, wine, and beer separately, Levy and Shiflin avoided the problems encountered in earlier attempts to estimate cross-price effects—which, as they accurately noted, "have produced inconsistent and improbable cross-elasticity estimates" (that is, in several studies, the different beverages were found to be complements of one another). The main limitation of this approach, apart from the aggregation problems posed by different state and local tax rates, is that the results are only useful for assessing the effects of applying a uniform percentage tax increase across all beverages, a policy option that may prove politically infeasible.

McGuinness (1980) examined the demand for alcoholic drinks in the United Kingdom, using data from 1956 to 1975 and ordinary least squares. Price and income elasticities, estimated at 1975 values for price and income, ranged from −0.22 to −0.26 and from 0.18 to 0.51, respectively. McGuinness also found a strong positive relationship between alcohol consumption and the number of licensed premises. Although he acknowledged that more must be learned about the nature of the relationship, he concluded that "the observed relationship is so strong, compared to that between demand and other variables, that any policy designed to curb alcohol consumption would be advised to give high priority to further investigation of its nature."

In an early study of the demand for alcoholic beverages, Niskanen (1962) used three-stage least squares to estimate price and income elasticities of demand for spirits, wine, and beer from a sample of annual observations from the periods 1934 to 1941 and 1947 to 1960 (the years 1942 through 1946 were excluded because of government controls on production, consumption, and prices throughout the period). The author found the price elasticities for spirits, wine, and beer to be approximately −2.0, −0.7, and −0.6, respectively. Income elasticities for the three beverages were on the order of 0.4 for spirits, 1.0 for wine, and −0.3 for beer. With respect to cross-price effects, Niskanen concluded: "Consumption of each beverage is primarily determined by conditions within each separate market. Spirits and beer appear to be weak substitutes, but the relations between the spirits and wine markets and the beer and wine markets are highly unstable."

Finally, based on their comprehensive review of the literature, Ornstein and Levy (1983) developed the following summary estimates of beverage price elasticities: −1.5 for spirits, −1.0 for wine, and −0.3 for beer. The authors are quick to point out that these estimates are "crude at best, particularly for wine, but seem the best available."

Distributional Effects of Increasing Excise Taxes

Excise taxes on cigarettes and alcoholic beverages have similar, though not identical, distributional effects—mainly because the two goods have in many respects the same nature. Both are consumed by large numbers of people in all income groups. Both are habit forming, making it difficult to characterize them as being either luxuries or necessities in the usual sense. And both generate significant external costs, a fact that in turn makes consumers of these goods prime candidates for assuming the burden of these costs.

The first concern that must be addressed in assessing the distributional effects of cigarette and alcoholic beverage excise taxes is the extent to which such taxes are passed on to consumers of these goods, as opposed to being borne by producers. With respect to cigarettes, Barzel (1976) found that cigarette prices increase by more than 100 percent of the tax increase. Specifically, for each 1 cent increase in the tax the retail price is raised by 1.065 cents. His explanation for this rather surprising result was that excise taxes, in contrast to ad valorem taxes, tend to cause firms to upgrade the quality of their products.

> Commodities as transacted in the market are complex, and the margins with respect to which optimization takes place are numerous. Because commodity tax statues will not generally cover all of these margins, any tax will induce multiple changes not only in resource allocation away from the taxed commodity and into others but also in the "quality" of the commodity and how it is transacted, a substitution away from the taxed attributes and into the others.

Barzel's empirical work is supported by Johnson (1978) who, after respecifying Barzel's model to include a separate dummy variable for each state, found the tax coefficient to be even larger than reported by Barzel (1.101 versus 1.065). Both Barzel's and Johnson's results have been challenged by Sumner and Ward (1981), who argue that tax increases are not solely responsible for the larger retail price increases found in the Barzel and Johnson analyses. After accounting for changes in the wholesale price of cigarettes, Sumner and Ward concluded that "the diffused sources of price changes represented by general inflation enter both directly and in conjunction with tax changes; and that once allowance is made for the indirect influence of tax changes in effecting backlogged price increases, the coefficient on tax change itself becomes significantly less than unity." In other words, in place of Barzel's quality hypothesis, Sumner and Ward hold that tax increases give retailers the opportunity to incorporate in their costs minor increases that had previously accrued but were not large enough to justify a price increase.

Disagreement persists over precisely how much of the tax increase is passed along to smokers. But based on the existing body of empirical work that addresses this issue, as well as studies indicating that the demand for cigarettes is relatively inelastic, most if not all of the cigarette excise tax is paid by smokers.

Considerably less is known regarding the degree to which taxes on alcoholic drinks are passed on to consumers. On the basis of the price elasticity estimates contained in Table F–5, it is possible that a smaller fraction of these taxes are borne by consumers than is the case with cigarettes. Still, if the long-run supply of alcoholic beverages is perfectly elastic—and there is little reason to believe that it is not in the relevant range—then all excise taxes will be transmitted to consumers.

Having established that cigarette and alcoholic beverage taxes are for the most part passed along to consumers, the next issue is the incidence of these taxes. It is generally believed that per unit excise taxes on goods are regressive. Toder (1985), using data from the Consumer Expenditure Survey by the Bureau of Labor Statistics, shows that taxes on cigarettes and alcoholic drinks are highly regressive. Households in the lowest-income quintile spend over 2 percent of their incomes on tobacco products, while households in the highest-income quintile spend less than 0.005 percent. A similar but somewhat less dramatic pattern emerges with alcoholic beverages. People in the lowest-income group devote roughly 3 percent of their incomes to alcohol, while individuals in the highest-income group spend approximately 1 percent. (Here a case can be made that income is endogenous—that is, income falls for individuals who are alcoholics.)

The regressivity issue has prompted a substantial amount of controversy, especially in the literature on smoking. Rock (1983), using a measure of tax progressivity known as the S-Index, found the cigarette excise tax to be among the most regressive of all taxes typically imposed on individuals or households. Harris (1982) and Warner (1984), by contrast, discount the regressivity of cigarette taxes because (1) the very poorest groups in the United States have lower smoking rates than middle-income groups; (2) among women there is a positive relationship between smoking rate and income, which does not hold for men; (3) many low-income smokers are teenagers and young adults who may be only temporarily low-income and who are most likely to respond to a tax-related price increase by either quitting or not starting at all; and (4) there is some evidence that lower-income groups have a greater elasticity of demand than higher-income groups.

Proponents of increasing the cigarette and alcoholic beverage taxes cite an additional reason for alleviating concern over the regressive nature of the taxes: the benefits to be realized from diminished consumption. But attempts to realize health and possibly other benefits through increased taxation may yield highly undesirable results, particularly in cases where there is a strong addiction to the taxed good. As O'Hagan (1983) has written:

> If misuse of alcohol is but a symptom and not the cause of the problem, it could be argued that attacking the source (e.g., home background, unemployment) is the more appropriate solution for alcohol abuse. A high tax policy for control purposes could also have alarming distributional effects—resulting simply, perhaps, in a massive transfer of resources from the families of heavy drinkers, thereby worsening the problems it was supposed to have counteracted.

In short, although raising cigarette and alcohol excise taxes may lead to social benefits including health care cost savings (and ultimately improved health—assuming that the tax does not cause people to pursue other unhealthful habits such as illicit drugs), the potential distributional effects of increasing taxes cannot be ignored.

Conclusions

There is no doubt that public policy toward cigarettes and alcoholic beverages has been confusing and contradictory. Over the last thirty-five years or so, real federal taxes on these goods have declined sharply, despite mounting evidence that their consumption (cigarettes, in particular) has adverse health effects and imposes substantial external costs on society. As these consequences have become increasingly apparent, pressure on federal legislators to curtail consumption and require smokers and drinkers to assume financial responsibility for the social costs of their habits has mounted and will continue to do so. We have already witnessed examples of such action at the state level; ultimately the federal government will be forced to intervene, since the potential for state action is limited (it will simply encourage the growth of illegal activities such as bootlegging).

While federal legislative initiatives to reduce cigarette and alcoholic beverage consumption and to compel smokers and drinkers to bear the full costs of these activities may be inevitable, there is a good deal of uncertainty about the relative effectiveness of the means available for achieving these ends. Estimates of the impact on consumption of the different policy measures (tax-induced price increases, advertising restrictions, antismoking publicity campaigns, and the like) vary widely.

Several authors of studies on the demand for cigarettes and alcoholic drinks recognize that the quality of their work, and hence the precision of their estimates, is constrained by both a lack of data and the typical problems associated with using standard analytical techniques. Levy and Sheflin (1985), acknowledging the limitations of their own research, identify a set of econometric problems that afflict many, if not most, of the studies in this area. These factors include a simultaneity bias in instances where supply is treated as an exogenous variable (as it is in almost all of the studies reviewed in this appendix), a bias from omitting relevant and possibly important explanatory variables, errors in the measurement of variables (for instance, actual consumption of both cigarettes and alcoholic beverages is often underestimated), and a bias from aggregating over individuals and/or products.

The gravity of these problems is such that some observers are extremely skeptical of the work to date on factors influencing the demand for cigarettes and alcoholic drinks. Ornstein and Levy (1983), for instance, characterized the studies they reviewed as having produced "a bewildering set of results." Cook (1981) took an even dimmer view: "My conclusion from reviewing the econometric studies of alcoholic beverages is that there are no reliable estimates for the price elasticities of demand based on U.S. data." Similarly, Johnson (1985) wrote, "Our major conclusion from this is that econometric estimation of demand functions is a tricky business and that conclusions drawn from any one study should be cautiously considered before they are used."

Although it may not be possible to draw precise quantitative conclusions about the individual effects on demand of price, income, advertising, and other variables, it is obvious that at least some of these factors can be manipulated in order to achieve policy objectives. While price elasticity estimates for cigarettes and alcoholic beverages vary across studies, all of the researchers found price effects that are highly significant. And unlike income and, to an even greater extent, different sociological variables (which were found to influence demand in at least one study of alcoholic drinks), price can be easily increased or decreased through tax changes. The degree to which advertising—perhaps the second-best "policy variable"—affects the demand for cigarettes and alcohol is much less certain and, as indicated by congressional hearings on the proposed cigarette advertising ban, a highly controversial subject.

Should policy makers decide to increase excise taxes on cigarettes, alcoholic drinks, or both, for whatever reason (to increase revenues, to cover the social costs of smoking and drinking, and so on), alternative elasticity estimates could be applied to determine the approximate effect of a specific contemplated tax rate change. Based on the results of this analysis, the tax rate could be adjusted to reflect the effect of the good's price elasticity on whatever the tax change was designed to achieve (say, raising a certain amount of money to cover the social costs of smoking). Initially one could use Ornstein and Levy's summary estimates of -1.5, -1.0, and -0.3 for considering potential changes in the spirits, wine, and beer excise taxes, respectively. According to the figures reported in Table F–3, -0.4 might be an appropriate starting point for analyzing a change in the cigarette excise tax. Sensitivity analyses could then be conducted to determine the magnitudes of change in variables of interest if the true elasticity differed from the initial estimate.

APPENDIX G

Parameters Used in the Cost Model

The abridged life table is based on five-year periods. Deaths within each period are assumed to occur after 2.5 years, except for 85-year-olds. Men of this age are assumed to live 5 additional years; women, 6.4 more years.

The columns headed Five-Year Survival in Tables G–1 and G–3 give the probability that those with bad habits will live to the next period. The Survival Ratio columns in Tables G–2 and G–4 give the ratio of "survival with bad habit" to "survival with bad habit corrected." Thus, the probability that

APPENDIX TABLE G-1.   Pooled smokers (units explained in text)

Age	Five-Year Survival	Covered Outpatient	Covered Inpatient	Covered Work Loss	Estimated Packs	Reported Pension Income	Total Wages
Males							
20	0.9891	43.49	113.65	105.53	1.0615	102	8,922
25	0.9891	76.27	188.85	155.47	1.0087	93	17,603
30	0.9896	101.17	260.65	222.79	1.0706	207	21,381
35	0.9852	103.22	339.80	381.90	1.0722	190	24,592
40	0.9789	98.07	476.39	272.89	1.0902	420	25,361
45	0.9664	120.36	581.41	295.27	1.0224	574	24,847
50	0.9425	175.51	596.68	289.13	0.9370	1,096	23,549
55	0.9217	184.98	691.73	314.99	0.8077	1,880	20,617
60	0.8805	57.52	1,293.29	36.40	0.6169	4,768	15,158
65	0.8241	94.31	1,617.21	11.73	0.5458	8,769	5,723
70	0.7418	89.87	1,769.74	3.71	0.4092	8,978	2,344
75	0.6646	96.61	1,915.54	0.77	0.2181	8,027	1,445
80	0.5417	107.36	2,042.21	0.04	0.1641	7,314	1,144
85	0.0000	104.46	2,343.58	0.00	0.0465	6,630	655
Females							
20	0.9972	125.35	187.02	58.43	0.9233	75	5,350
25	0.9966	128.51	226.97	51.79	0.9493	121	8,031
30	0.9955	166.12	313.76	69.70	0.9402	152	8,865
35	0.9928	159.96	320.93	64.93	0.9752	209	8,753
40	0.9862	185.94	608.57	54.29	1.0666	228	9,858
45	0.9807	163.63	515.94	52.61	0.9830	309	7,978
50	0.9718	224.64	576.97	56.52	0.9150	436	8,080
55	0.9600	225.46	508.83	47.49	0.8286	676	5,887
60	0.9310	67.26	1,203.48	18.25	0.7190	2,178	4,598
65	0.9092	104.10	1,527.03	7.72	0.5466	4,880	1,297
70	0.8568	101.01	1,837.66	3.99	0.3963	5,280	666
75	0.7794	105.17	2,000.76	0.42	0.4197	5,462	202
80	0.6658	118.44	1,948.51	0.14	0.2534	5,848	104
85	0.0000	113.57	2,245.27	0.00	0.4393	5,273	27

APPENDIX TABLE G-2.   Pooled nonsmoking smokers (units explained in text)

		Annual Dollars		
Age	Survival Ratio	Covered Outpatient	Covered Inpatient	Covered Work Loss
Males				
20	0.9998	42.93	84.95	107.25
25	0.9994	73.85	143.98	160.74
30	0.9981	98.18	199.61	232.18
35	0.9954	98.87	262.12	395.34
40	0.9907	94.28	367.63	289.95
45	0.9841	115.34	452.60	313.62
50	0.9761	166.52	472.28	309.27
55	0.9631	173.45	549.85	338.51
60	0.9424	54.42	959.17	26.65
65	0.8953	89.23	1,199.51	8.67
70	0.8573	84.90	1,307.13	2.76
75	0.8853	90.71	1,391.16	0.58
80	0.9111	100.64	1,472.43	0.03
85	NA	97.75	1,683.39	0.00
Females				
20	0.9999	122.46	141.14	40.349
25	0.9996	125.42	171.39	35.366
30	0.9990	161.91	237.12	47.258
35	0.9980	154.80	244.72	45.472
40	0.9959	182.69	452.99	36.928
45	0.9925	159.11	392.27	36.035
50	0.9882	215.32	444.33	38.962
55	0.9843	215.95	393.88	33.252
60	0.9744	63.95	905.68	13.143
65	0.9571	98.94	1,149.19	5.609
70	0.9324	95.39	1,355.76	2.849
75	0.9080	99.40	1,481.05	0.319
80	0.9200	111.53	1,429.56	0.109
85	NA	107.03	1,649.18	0.000

a male nonsmoking smoker will survive from age 60 to age 65 is 0.8805 (from Table G–1) divided by 0.9424 (from Table G–2).

In addition to heavy drinkers, ex-drinkers are categorized as light drinkers. In some cases the risk in the HRA programs may thereby be increased. Among 50- and 55-year-old women there are many more former drinkers than heavy drinkers, so there is an anomalous slight fall in survival for controlled drinkers. All of the survival ratios for women in the drinker's

APPENDIX TABLE G-3. Pooled heavy drinkers (units explained in text)

Age	Five-Year Survival	Covered Outpatient	Covered Inpatient	Covered Work Loss	Reported Excess Ounces	Reported Pension Income	Total Wages
Males							
20	0.9844	38.22	101.64	93.91	29.43	91	9,325
25	0.9861	74.25	195.92	159.53	22.42	88	18,210
30	0.9840	99.65	287.83	470.50	34.33	212	21,342
35	0.9798	94.28	376.03	659.06	50.82	196	24,308
40	0.9648	94.23	466.23	332.48	48.91	408	25,923
45	0.9516	114.22	669.19	344.67	38.35	531	24,457
50	0.9231	173.53	649.75	401.43	28.60	1,123	21,359
55	0.9090	216.31	1,003.93	500.63	24.62	1,898	20,585
60	0.8807	63.00	1,434.71	39.99	22.79	4,828	16,027
65	0.8159	102.02	1,789.20	12.71	21.90	8,698	5,749
70	0.7823	97.23	1,871.70	7.37	19.04	9,078	2,429
75	0.6666	100.51	1,982.17	0.68	9.91	8,270	1,573
80	0.5854	109.35	2,088.49	0.03	21.97	7,381	1,190
85	0.0000	111.42	2,391.85	0.00	10.28	6,714	662
Females							
20	0.9958	97.84	173.44	26.35	14.57	74	5,340
25	0.9944	71.73	108.14	40.32	26.47	111	9,763
30	0.9932	144.44	326.67	29.36	9.93	192	7,480
35	0.9823	123.74	312.11	41.83	22.89	226	7,699
40	0.9810	176.05	723.17	39.77	32.57	194	11,601
45	0.9648	165.45	786.00	75.42	18.92	298	8,293
50	0.9686	260.64	757.97	75.53	5.50	402	9,737
55	0.9683	180.03	431.27	56.69	3.84	705	7,283
60	0.9308	73.56	1,300.42	22.15	10.76	2,197	5,193
65	0.9084	113.14	1,640.75	4.63	18.84	5,028	1,406
70	0.8583	111.29	1,993.90	6.36	4.29	5,553	694
75	0.8085	112.97	2,042.32	0.00	9.35	5,639	230
80	0.7047	110.60	1,476.18	0.00	19.54	5,707	115
85	0.0000	123.28	2,323.75	0.00	0.17	4,998	26

tables are very close to one, reflecting the fact that drinking on average has little effect on women's longevity.

The Covered Outpatient, Covered Inpatient, and Covered Work Loss columns give external annual costs. To get the five-year period costs, we multiply costs for each survivor by 5 (years) and costs for each decedent by 2.5. For inpatient costs, decedents get an additional sixfold increase, as explained in the text.

Reported Pension Income is the annual sum of Social Security, Supplemental Security Income (SSI), public assistance, veterans' compensation, and private pension incomes. To correct for underreporting of pension income we divide by 0.79.

Total Wages are the annual sum of earnings and self-employment income. These are also multiplied by 5 for survivors and 2.5 for decedents to get period sums.

Estimated Packs in Table G-1 are reported numbers per day for current and former smokers (who report 0 packs) multiplied by 1.5 to correct for underreporting. Reported Excess Ounces of alcohol in Table G-3 are those in excess of twenty-eight drinks per month and are given by month for current and former drinkers. We are less sure of the underreporting factor here, so have not built it into the parameters.

APPENDIX TABLE G-4. Pooled heavy nondrinking drinkers (units explained in text)

Age	Survival Ratio	Covered Outpatient	Covered Inpatient	Covered Work Loss
Males				
20	0.9960	38.06	90.47	82.21
25	0.9974	73.65	172.86	127.00
30	0.9954	97.03	239.55	399.98
35	0.9917	93.93	317.54	564.26
40	0.9883	92.69	386.53	244.82
45	0.9913	109.98	499.90	245.19
50	0.9923	169.00	514.30	222.08
55	0.9857	205.49	750.93	342.99
60	0.9912	55.55	1,078.13	37.07
65	0.9906	89.82	1,309.33	11.34
70	0.9908	86.15	1,378.01	6.95
75	0.9993	90.02	1,458.45	0.67
80	0.9885	95.34	1,486.79	0.03
85	NA	99.25	1,752.46	0.00
Females				
20	0.9996	94.59	142.14	26.92
25	0.9991	70.56	84.93	40.71
30	0.9993	136.86	241.48	27.34
35	0.9965	122.27	258.77	38.57
40	0.9941	170.07	581.30	41.09
45	0.9961	161.34	605.99	68.55
50	1.0007	247.01	564.80	74.52
55	1.0017	165.29	281.09	52.34
60	0.9989	65.54	958.33	20.46
65	0.9986	99.10	1,180.62	4.07
70	0.9997	98.89	1,409.83	5.44
75	0.9969	100.26	1,471.65	0.00
80	0.9919	101.78	1,270.67	0.00
85	NA	107.36	1,521.12	0.00

APPENDIX H

A Note on the Alcohol Tax

Unlike smoking, where the external costs are roughly proportional to the amount smoked, the external costs of drinking vary by the amount drunk *and* circumstance. It is difficult to distinguish problem from nonproblem drinkers at the point of sale; as a result, there is some cross-subsidy of problem drinkers by nonproblem drinkers.

Although a tax such as the one we propose (total external cost divided by total drinking) is imperfect, it is still preferable to no tax or to a tax that does not cover the full cost of drinking.[1] In the text we argued that penalizing light drinkers for damage they did not cause, so that we can penalize heavy drinkers, is in fact better than not raising the tax on alcohol at all. Here we elaborate on that point.

From an economic point of view, we are trading the losses from overtaxing nonabusive drinkers against the gains from making abusive drinkers pay more appropriate prices. As long as the gains from providing incentives to heavy drinkers to face the full consequences of their actions are greater than the losses to light drinkers, society will benefit from a tax increase.

To illustrate this point, let us consider a simplification of a tax model that Pogue and Sgontz (1989) used to make a similar point. Assume that there are only two classes of drinkers, heavy (H) and light (L) drinking groups. For the sake of argument we assume that light drinkers impose no external costs, whereas heavy drinkers impose external costs that sum to E. Let both groups of drinkers have linear demand curves:

$$Q_i = a_i + b_i(p + t_i), \quad i = H, L$$

where Q is the quantity of alcohol, p is the before-tax price, t is the tax, and a and b are constants that differ for heavy and light drinkers.

If we could distinguish light and heavy drinkers at the points of sale and consumption, then the best tax would be zero for light drinkers and (E/Q_H) for heavy drinkers. Only the heavy drinkers would have to pay a tax to offset the external costs they impose. But we must settle for a common tax (T) on drinking, rather than separate taxes, because of the difficulty of identifying heavy drinkers at the point of sale.

To answer the question of whether an average tax is more efficient than no tax, we will determine whether the increase in welfare from raising the price to heavy drinkers is greater than the loss in welfare from taxing light or nonproblem drinkers. To do so, we will use the usual Harberger measure of the welfare loss from less than optimal pricing.[2] It is $0.5\,(\Delta p)(\Delta Q)$, where the Δ indicates the change in price or quantity. In this instance we examine the loss from using the average tax $T_A = E/(Q_H + Q_L)$, rather than $t_H = (E/Q_H)$ and $t_L = 0$. The welfare loss from the average tax is

$$0.5[b_L\,(T_A/2)^2 + b_H\,(T_A/2)^2]$$

while the welfare loss from no alcohol tax would be

$$0.5[0 + b_H\,(2\,T_A/2)^2].$$

To compare the two welfare losses, we need to know the price response of the two groups and the relative magnitudes of Q_H and Q_L. We know that heavy drinking is about one-half of the total, but we do not know the relative magnitude of the price responses of the two groups. The demand for alcohol is price responsive (see Appendix F), and we can infer that problem drinking is price responsive because fatal auto accidents are negatively related to alcohol taxes (Cook and Tauchen, 1982). If the two groups have the same price response ($b_H = b_L$), then using the average tax is more efficient than using no tax, because the average tax welfare loss is half what it would be without a tax increase.

Pogue and Sgontz (1989) examined the general case, allowing for differences in the price response across drinking groups. They showed that the single ad valorem tax (τ, stated as a proportion of the before-tax price of alcohol, p) that makes the optimal economic trade-off is proportional to

$$1/[1 + (\eta_H/\eta_L)(\text{total } Q_L/\text{total } Q_H)]$$

where η is the price elasticity of demand.[3]

In their formulation the optimal tax on alcohol need not cover exactly the external costs of heavy drinking or drunk driving for two reasons. First, if the light drinkers are much more responsive to price than are the heavy drinkers, then the optimal alcohol tax may well be less than the average external cost of drinking. To set the tax at the average level would impose too much of a welfare loss on light drinkers. The importance of this possibility is unclear; we are aware of little research in this area.[4] Second, they focus on the incremental or marginal damage that results from drinking, rather than the average. To the extent that the external costs imposed by problem drinking rise more rapidly than volume consumed, then the tax revenues should exceed the external costs of drinking.

The approach by Pogue and Sgontz does not necessarily ensure that revenues from alcohol taxes would just cover costs. To the extent that the external costs are an increasing function of quantity consumed, then their marginal tax approach would generate higher revenues than costs. To the extent that light drinkers are more price responsive, their approach would generate lower revenues than costs. In either case, how the excess revenue or shortfall is financed can have additional welfare implications.

Pogue and Sgontz assume that the difference between revenue and cost can be returned or financed by lump-sum transfers to or from alcohol abusers, without introducing any income effects or altering prices (see their note 4). In a world where choices can be made over time, lump-sum taxes are not as neutral as they appear in simple one-period models (Arnott and Stiglitz, 1982). Suppose that individuals are deciding whether to be light or heavy drinkers by maximizing their lifetime discounted utility. In the absence of an alcohol tax, assume that there is an annual transfer of costs, T, to each abuser from society as a whole. Then the lifetime transfer is approximately T/r, where r is the discount rate. Thus, in the absence of the alcohol tax, the transfer of costs via a lump-sum tax actually lowers the costs of heavy drinking and thereby encourages more of it. If heavy drinkers are 10 percent of the adult population, then the welfare loss from the transfer is approximately $1.11 \ T/2r$.

Further, it is difficult to target the lump-sum transfers to drinkers only. Inability to do so is the source of the external cost associated with health insurance, sick leave, and other collectively financed programs. In the absence of an alcohol tax, the external costs of medical care and other collectively financed services are reimbursed by health insurance, disability, retirement, and other premiums paid ultimately by all workers, whether or not they drink. Shifting the burden of these costs to an alcohol tax reduces the welfare costs from taxing labor, by putting the costs onto drinkers—albeit on all drinkers, not just alcohol abusers. If more revenue is generated, the excess can be used to reduce the welfare burden of taxing labor to finance other burdens. In either case the welfare gain (one-half the change in wages times the change in hours worked) is omitted from the Pogue and Sgontz formula. If the extra term had been included, then the trade-off of overtaxing light drinkers as drinkers, instead of taxing them as workers, would have been clearer. The result would be a higher tax on alcohol than their formula suggests.

A stronger version of the argument we are considering is that moderate drinking has external benefits relative to no drinking or light drinking. This hypothesis seems unlikely to be true, as noted in the text. First, the risk of a fatal traffic accident among youths aged 16 to 21 (data are not available for other age groups) rises with any consumption of alcohol (Phelps, 1988). Because traffic accidents generate more than half of external costs, this fact alone makes it doubtful that there are any overall external benefits from moderate drinking. Second, there is no observed difference in inpatient use between light and moderate drinkers. In the NHIS there is a U-shaped relationship with outpatient use (Table 5–9), but in the HIE there is an insignificant inverted U-shape (Table 5–7). Between abstainers and any drinkers, there is increased inpatient use among abstainers in both data sets, a trend that is consistent with the existence of some external benefits from modest consumption. The problem with this comparison is that abstainers are different from drinkers in many measurable ways (they are notably more female, more black, and less educated; see Tables 5–1 and 5–3), which raises the possibility that they differ in important nonmeasurable ways and that the differential hospital utilization we observe is not causally related to drinking. Moreover, if there were health benefits to moderate use, it seems plausible that moderate drinkers (say, one actual ounce per day) would also show some benefit relative to light drinkers (say, one actual ounce per week), but the data just cited give little support to that thesis.

In sum, the data do not suggest that among light and moderate drinkers any reduction in drinking resulting from higher taxes would lead to a large increase in external costs; it seems more plausible that there would be a reduction in external costs. Thus, our assumption of no external costs or benefits from light and moderate drinking seems tenable.

Notes

1. An Overview

1. These figures are based on average weekly expenditures per household unit of $4.84 and $3.60, respectively (U.S. Department of Commerce, 1989), pp. 438–439).
2. After 1983 the fraction of heavy drinkers decreased.
3. There are more smokers than sedentary people, and lack of exercise does not take the health toll that smoking does.
4. By "taxes on earnings" we mean all the payments into the system that go toward medical care, sick leave, group life insurance, disability, and retirement benefits. These may be made by third parties or individuals, and they may be paid as taxes, premiums, payroll deductions, or employer contributions. Not all payments are taxes on earnings, but we approximate the actual mix of taxes with the assumption of a payroll tax. See Chapter 2 for further discussion.
5. In order to provide conservative estimates of the external costs, we are considering the family as a single decision-making unit and treating costs imposed on other family members as internal. To the extent that smokers and heavy drinkers do not consider the effects of their actions on other family members, however, the costs of those actions should be considered external. Later in the book we indicate how sensitive our results are to this assumption.
6. Not all heavy drinkers are drunk drivers, and vice versa. But when people are drunk enough to cause accidents they are, at least at that time, heavy drinkers. Thus, we include external costs of drunk drivers as a cost of heavy drinking.
7. Rice et al. (1986); Office of Technology Assessment (1985).
8. With the exception of Leu and Schaub (1983, 1985) and Stoddart et al. (1986), all studies have looked at total costs.
9. Some economists consider retirement pensions and taxes as transfer payments and hence not as external costs. We explain in Chapter 2 why they are incorrect.
10. If food poisoning differs systematically between smokers and nonsmokers, it is probably because of other underlying differences between those who smoke and those who do not.

11. As we discuss later, taxation is one means of making drinkers pay the external costs of their habit, but it is not possible to tax only excess ounces.

12. The time given up to exercise occurs long before the life-extending benefits, however. People who care more about time now than time later may need other benefits to be motivated to exercise (such as enjoyment of the exercise or an increased sense of well-being).

13. We also assume for this "lower bound" estimate that the particular habit has no effect on early retirement: that is, the reason people who have retired early drink more is not that drinking caused their retirement but that retirement allows them to drink. Put another way, we assume that if they were to stop excessive drinking, they would still retire early.

14. Although there is general agreement that future costs should be discounted, there is controversy about the appropriate discount rate. We used the common discount rate of 5 percent. If the rate is lower (say, 2 to 3 percent), then the discounted costs are approximately zero. The pensions, Medicare, and nursing home benefits lost because smokers die earlier largely offset their heavier medical costs.

15. Technically, they should be set at a level that covers the marginal external social cost. See Chapter 2.

16. Based on data from Tobacco Institute (1987). The sales tax figures are a weighted average across the states (weighted by dollar volume). Excise taxes account for 32 of the 37 cents.

17. The average excise tax is taken across distilled spirits, wine, and beer, where the excise taxes are 25, 3, and 9 cents per ounce of ethanol, respectively. For state taxes we used the weighted average of license states. Excise and sales tax figures are from Distilled Spirits Council of the United States (1985). Excise taxes comprise about three-quarters of the tax revenue.

18. See Toder (1985) and Rock (1983). For alternative views of regressivity see Hacker (1987), Harris (1982), and Warner (1984).

19. Note, however, that the argument is framed in terms of "the poor" as a group. In actuality, the poor who are heavy smokers and drinkers will be worse off (as will the rich who are heavy smokers and drinkers), but the poor who are not will be better off.

20. Put another way, abstainers, former drinkers, and heavy drinkers constitute less than half the population (see Tables 5–1 and 5–3 in Chapter 5). The moderate drinkers, who make up more than half the population, pay only a third of the alcohol tax. Especially because moderate drinkers are disproportionately college graduates, it is likely that they pay more than half of other taxes (income, sales, payroll), for which alcohol taxes would substitute.

21. Between light and moderate drinkers, there is no observed difference in inpatient use; in one of our two data sets there is a U-shaped relationship with outpatient use (consistent with external benefits from moderate drinking), but in the other data set there is an insignificant inverted

U-shape. Between abstainers and any drinkers, there is increased inpatient use among abstainers, which would be consistent with the existence of some external benefits from modest consumption. The problem with comparing drinkers to abstainers is that the abstainers are different from drinkers in many measurable ways (they are notably more female, more black, and less educated; see Tables 5–1 and 5–3), which raises the possibility that they differ in important nonmeasurable ways and that the differential hospital utilization that we observe is not causally related to drinking. Moreover, if there were health benefits to moderate use, it seems plausible that moderate drinkers (say, 1 actual ounce per day) would also show some benefit relative to light drinkers (say, 1 actual ounce per week), but the data just cited give little support to that thesis.

22. Increasing cigarette or alcohol taxes is not the only strategy for discouraging the initiation of these poor health habits. Banning advertising or promoting negative advertising (against smoking) or regulating smoking in public places may be complementary strategies. See Warner (1986) and Wasserman (1988) for a discussion of these issues.

23. We have not tried to estimate what proportion of external costs stem from alcohol consumed in bars and restaurants relative to that consumed in homes. Even an extra bar tax, however, involves cross-subsidies because not everyone who drinks in a bar drives home.

24. U.S. Department of Commerce (1975b).

25. A proof gallon is defined as a U.S. standard gallon containing 50 percent ethyl alcohol by volume.

26. Determining state excise taxes on alcoholic beverages is complicated by the fact that eighteen states have state-run monopolies. This makes it extremely difficult, if not impossible, to determine effective excise tax rates since in those states the tax reflects official excise taxes as well as commodity prices and rates of profit (Mosher and Beauchamp, 1983). The discussion of taxes here is based on the thirty-two states that license the sale of alcoholic beverages.

27. For discussion of cigarette demand, see Appendix F, as well as Laughhunn and Lyon (1971), Fujii (1980), Lewit and Coate (1982), Leu (1984), and Wasserman (1988). For alcohol, see Johnson and Oksanen (1977), Cook (1981), Cook and Tauchen (1982), Duffy (1983), Ornstein and Levy (1983), and Levy and Sheflin (1985).

28. In the 1983 NHIS survey, 55 percent of the population were current or former smokers; 10 percent were heavy drinkers; and 14 percent were physically inactive for reasons other than their health. Increased health promotion publicity may drive these figures down, but not to near zero. For example, a quarter-century after the Surgeon General's first report on smoking, during which time there has been massive publicity about the dangers of smoking, more than a quarter of all adults in the United States still smoke, including many individuals in their twenties and thirties who started smoking after the Surgeon General's report appeared.

29. Economists will already have noted that one appropriate tax rate (or

subsidy) is the cost imposed on others by the marginal cigarette or drink (or mile walked). Average and marginal costs may be similar for cigarettes, but in the case of drinking the marginal cost is considerably higher than the average cost. The implication here is that we have probably underestimated appropriate alcohol taxes.

2. Conceptual Framework

1. This statement assumes that cigarettes are private goods, sold in competitive markets, with all parties having complete information and tastes that do not change. It also assumes that other, nonrelated people do not care, for instance, if a smoker dies, except for the financial effects of such a death. These assumptions rule out later regret at addiction and altruistic regret of nonrelated people. Economic efficiency requires that each individual pay the marginal social costs of his actions.
2. We can ignore the effects of smoking on a smoker's insurance premium because it is negligible—to a first approximation, $1/n$th the insurer's share of extra costs if there are n members in the group.
3. We are indebted to Jerry Green of Harvard University for this argument.
4. We did not begin before age 20 for two reasons. First, we are interested in established habits; an adolescent who reports smoking may be only experimenting and subsequently quit. Second, we are concerned about underreporting to an even greater degree for teenagers than for adults.
5. Similarly, in estimating external costs of drinking, we treated former drinkers as part of the group who had ever drunk. In estimating the external costs of not exercising, we excluded the physically limited from the group that did not exercise.
6. In policy terms, if we consider only the economic costs of smoking, a program that costs x dollars today to reduce the effects of smoking should be considered efficient only if it saves more than x dollars in the future (discounted back to today). If it does not, we would be better off investing the x dollars to pay for the future costs when they arise. Because the value of life itself (as opposed to the effects on life insurance, pension, and work) is not external to the smoker or his family, it does not enter into our model.
7. We discount life expectancy for similar reasons: the value of the health benefits of not smoking is less if they occur in future years. Benefits in life expectancy are discounted at the same rate as future monetary costs to maintain a common perspective on their value. Analyses that discount future costs but not future survival benefits can lead to peculiar and undesirable recommendations (Keeler and Cretin, 1983). Fortunately, inasmuch as discounting life expectancy is controversial, whether it should be discounted is irrelevant to our tax calculations.
8. For heavy drinking, we assume that the costs of motor-vehicle accidents and criminal justice are immediate.
9. By "covered," we mean covered by a public or private insurance policy whose premiums do not vary with smoking status.

10. In the model we estimate the costs to the average family of these secondary effects and add them to those of the individual with the bad habit. For example, the costs associated with the secondary effects of husbands' smoking on nonsmoking wives are multiplied by the estimated fraction of smoking men who have nonsmoking wives, and added to the medical costs of smoking men.

11. For each habit we used the effect of that habit on *all* diagnoses related to poor health habits in Tables 3–1 to 3–4 in Chapter 3, controlling for age, sex, and socioeconomic status.

12. These data came from the self-administered medical history questionnaire and the physical examination collected at the beginning of the Health Insurance Experiment (HIE). Data from the National Health Interview Survey (NHIS) were prepared for input based on a 1983 interviewer-administered questionnaire. Of the thirty-four variables listed in Table B–1, twenty-five are available from the HIE and eleven from the NHIS.

13. In principle, such costs would include low-birthweight infants born to smoking mothers. In a sample the size of the HIE there was not enough precision to detect such effects. We do use other data, however, to provide an estimate of the costs of such infants.

14. The 38 percent value comes from Price (1986) and is one of our "softest" numbers. But our estimates of total external costs are insensitive to it. Even doubling this number would have only a modest effect on our results.

15. The HIE data include snapshots of employment status, and a continuous history of work loss. To estimate the work-loss model conditional on being employed, we assumed stability in employment status between snapshots. For men there was little problem, given the high employment rates and stability of employment for prime-aged males. For women such an approximation was inadequate, given the turnover in their labor force status. In contrast, the NHIS provides labor force status and work loss for the same two-week period, which makes it possible to condition work-loss estimates on labor force status.

16. The $19,300 figure was derived by taking 45 percent (insurance that is group coverage) of $60,000 (the amount of insurance of the average household) to get an estimate of the group coverage per household, and dividing it by 1.4 workers (average per household) to obtain the group coverage per worker. (Inflated by the Consumer Price Index, from data in U.S. Department of Commerce, 1982.)

17. Because we used an average pension for women in our calculation that already includes this bonus, adding in the bonus leads to a slight double count. We did so to distinguish smokers from nonsmokers; that is, both smoking and nonsmoking women who are themselves alive were imputed an average pension, but only widows get the Social Security bonus. For our purposes it was more important to estimate the differential impact of smoking correctly than to estimate exactly the overall level of pensions.

18. Waldo and Lazenby (1984) give $443 per person over 65 not paid out of pocket, and $443/4.79 percent = $9,247. (From the National Nursing Home Survey—Van Nostrand et al., 1979—4.79 percent of those over age 65 are in nursing homes.)

19. Although lower-income people pay a higher percentage of earnings than higher-income people for private health insurance, they pay a lower percentage of earnings for nursing home care and they collect proportionately more in Social Security payments, so the error in assuming that overall financing is proportional to earnings should be small (Pechman, 1977). We assume that costs of fires, motor vehicle accidents, and criminal justice are immediate and calculate them as the annual cost divided by annual packs of cigarettes smoked. Even though a portion of their costs is financed by fire and auto insurance, because the cost of these factors is immediate we do not need to account for them in our tax figure.

20. Our use of average wages (standardized for age, sex, and education) to estimate smokers' wages involved a slight double count of wages, but the averaging was necessary to get the smoking differential right.

21. If there actually were such a spillover effect on the medical, labor, and insurance markets, then our estimates would be too high. Less smoking would reduce the demand for medical services, which would lower the cost of medical services, which would lower the external costs of smoking. As a result, the lower the level of smoking, the lower the external costs, and hence the lower the corrective tax.

22. Market imperfections in other markets could also lead to a modification of our results. This traditional second-best concern is beyond the scope of the present book.

23. In the absence of corrective taxes, it would be better to have a profit-maximizing monopoly on cigarette production. Monopolies reduce output from the competitive level to increase their profits. The exercise of such monopoly behavior here would have the beneficial effect of reducing consumption.

24. For example, if the monopolist faces a straight-line demand for cigarettes, and if the unit costs of production are constant, then an increase in the excise tax of 10 cents per pack will result in an increase in the price per pack (including the tax) of 5 cents. The remaining 5 cents is absorbed by the monopolist in lower prices, net of tax. On the other hand, if the market is competitive, the price to the smoker will go up the full 10 cents. If the market is imperfectly competitive, we would have an intermediate result, with some of the tax being shifted to producers.

25. The reported standard errors are 1.1 and and 1.3 percent, respectively.

3. Data and Statistical Methods

1. Newhouse (1974) and Brook et al. (1979) provide fuller descriptions of the design. Newhouse et al. (1979) discuss the measurement issues for the second generation of social experiments, to which the HIE belongs.

Ware et al. (1980a) discuss many aspects of data collection and measurement for health status. For our analysis of the effects of health habits, the HIE was not a randomized trial but an observational study.

2. This study does not use data from participants enrolled in a prepaid group practice.

3. We excluded dental care on the grounds that most dental care is not causally related to poor health habits. To the degree that it *is* related (for example, if smokers were to get their teeth cleaned more frequently), any effect would be modest because only 36 percent of dental care is collectively financed (unpublished data made available by the Health Care Financing Administration).

4. In subsequent chapters, for ease of exposition, we sometimes fail to note the qualification about well-care and maternity and simply use the term "all medical care."

5. As Table 3–3 shows, many of the drinking-related conditions also relate to cigarette smoking.

6. For the Seattle and Massachusetts sites these were the first two years of the HIE, while for the Dayton and South Carolina sites these were the second and third years.

7. A pipe or cigar smoker who smoked or had smoked cigarettes was classified as a current or former cigarette smoker, respectively. A former pipe or cigar smoker who had never smoked cigarettes was classified as a never smoker.

8. We selected these definitions because they conform as closely as possible to the drinking status measure of the NHIS.

9. In all but the last plan, there was a maximum out-of-pocket limit per year of $1,000 or a percentage of family income, whichever was lower. The percentage was 5, 10, or 15 percent, depending on which plan the family was assigned. In the last plan, the limit was $150 per person or $450 per family per year.

10. The average rates were 16, 24, and 31 percent respectively for the 25, 50, and 95 percent plans.

11. The average coinsurance rate for the preexperimental plans was defined using the service mix on the 25 percent coinsurance plan.

12. This questionnaire was self-administered for people 14 years or older. Parents responded for children 13 or younger.

13. Family income data are from 1975 in Dayton, 1978 for the three-year group in South Carolina, and 1976 for all other participants. The first year of participation for the Dayton participants was 1975 (about a quarter participated for two months in 1974, and another quarter participated for one month in 1974); the South Carolina three-year group began participating beginning in late 1978 (about a quarter participated for two months and another quarter for one month). The remainder of the HIE sample enrolled in 1976 or January 1977. We used income data from the first year of the study, which were collected on forms keyed to income tax returns.

4. The External Costs of Smoking

1. Unlike the rest of our analysis, Table 4–1 contains a column for current pipe or cigar smokers *that does not depend on cigarette smoking status.* Elsewhere, we define pipe or cigar smokers as such if, and only if, they have never been cigarette smokers. The reason for the discrepancy is that here we are describing the prevalence of the habits. Elsewhere we are interested in the effects of cigarette smoking, but do not want to confuse never smokers with never cigarette smokers.

2. Pack-years are the product of the number of packs smoked per day times the number of years smoked. They are a commonly used measure of cumulative cigarette exposure.

3. One possible explanation for this pattern is that smokers may stop smoking at home if a member of their household is sensitive to cigarette smoke.

4. That is, in Table 4–8 outpatient use excluding well-care (in column 1) for the former smoker (row 3) is 112.4 percent of the same use by the never smoker (row 1, which is set at the index level of 100).

5. Owing to lack of data on other sources of secondhand smoke, we limited ourselves to the effects from smoking by household members.

6. For the work-loss analysis, we were interested in workers only. We assumed that poor health habits such as smoking do not causally affect labor force participation, although both labor force participation and smoking may be related to some third factor. Further, with the HIE data we examined the effect of smoking on work loss for men only. We knew that most men were working at any point in time; we did not know the employment status of women except at certain periods when we collected data.

7. Poor health habits, as a group, are significant at $p < 0.01$, if we adjust for age, sex, and education.

8. This figure is based on the number of packs smoked in the 1983 NHIS supplement, by age and sex, and the HRA life table.

9. The tax on earnings shown in Table 4–13 is the amount that will collectively finance the costs of the insurance programs shown, the most important components of which are pensions and medical care. Each discount rate has its own earnings tax rate.

10. This trend reflects differential survival—smokers who live longer are a hardy group except for their smoking habits, so older nonsmoking smokers have a greater life expectancy than older never smokers. The difference in survival pattern is reflected in life expectancy; undiscounted life expectancy places relatively greater emphasis on survival in later years and is larger for nonsmoking smokers than for never smokers, but discounted life expectancy is larger for never smokers. (For more on the effects of differential survival, see Shepard and Zeckhauser, 1984.)

11. This figure includes a value of zero for wages of nonworkers, including the retired.

12. In the absence of a market in human lives, it is necessary to infer a value for the loss of a life from people's actions. One method is to determine how much more must be paid to workers to undertake more hazardous jobs. The implied value of a life is then the difference in income divided by the difference in the risk of dying. Similarly, one can infer the valuation of life by whether people are willing to pay for or use safety equipment (seat belts, for example).

Our estimate of $1.66 million is based on a review of the literature by Shepard and Zeckhauser (1984) and is in the lower part of their range. For more recent reviews see Rice et al. (1989, pp. 101–104) and Miller (1989). They find an average value of $2 million (in 1985 after-tax dollars) across twenty-nine studies. For a theoretical discussion see Mishan (1988) or Rosen (1988).

5. The External Costs of Heavy Drinking

1. One ounce of pure ethanol is the equivalent of approximately 2.2 mixed drinks, 2.2 glasses of wine (4 ounces), or 2.2 cans of beer (12 ounces).
2. As noted earlier, actual consumption is 2.5 times reported consumption. We categorized the sample and established prevalence according to reported consumption; our cost analyses are based on actual consumption.
3. Eight percent switched from abstainer to drinker and another 8 percent went from drinker to abstainer. The switch from drinker to abstainer probably resulted from our definition of an abstainer as one who rarely, if ever, drinks. In contrast, for smoking the question is whether the individual ever smoked cigarettes. "Ever" is more crisply defined than "rarely."
4. An "episode" has at least one visit, but may have more. Because we could not construct episodes for the NHIS sample, we used "visits" as our unit for analysis.
5. Actually, in the NHIS former drinkers had the second highest rates of outpatient visits and the very highest rates of inpatient admissions. For the sake of comparability, however, we did not include former drinkers in Table 5–5.
6. We use the natural logarithm of ethanol consumption as an explanatory variable to make the results more robust, that is, to reduce the influence of the extremely heavy drinkers.
7. These figures are based on the exponentiated value of the coefficient for the former drinkers in Table 5–7.
8. Again, these figures are based on the exponentiated value of the coefficient for the former drinkers in Table 5–7.
9. We assumed that underreporting is proportional to consumption; we could find no evidence for differential reporting at varying levels of consumption. Our category of heavy drinkers comprises about 20 percent of men and 5 percent of women.

10. There are a substantial number of nondrinking years. The percentage of former male drinkers increases with age from 2 to 7. We used the data on the percentage of heavy drinkers at each age interval to estimate lifetime consumption.

11. We do not have an estimate of the direct health costs and lost productivity of nondrinking victims in alcohol-related accidents (either for those who died or those who survived).

12. In contrast, the external costs of smoking are quite sensitive to the definition of relevant medical costs, which raises a question about the causal connection for the broader definition for smoking effects.

13. In our data the association of heavy drinking with early retirement is strong, but the effect of drinking on retirement payments is uncertain.

6. The External Costs of Sedentary Life-Styles

1. Although exercise levels were more stable among people enrolled for three than for five years, the differences were not great—65 and 61 percent, respectively.

2. In principle, one should allow for feedback between health and exercise; lack of exercise reduces health status, and those who are ill do not exercise as much as those who are well. Unfortunately, our data do not allow us to estimate such a model.

3. Specifically, we adjusted the HRA model's predictions so that the relative risk of exercising was set to be the HRA model's relative risk to the 0.136 power. Accordingly, the male exercisers were estimated to live 1.5 years longer than the nonexercisers. This figure was the gain in life expectancy reported in Paffenbarger et al., (1986) for those exercising more than 2,000 kilocalories per week, compared to those exercising less after adjustment for blood pressure, cigarette smoking, weight gain, and age of parental death.

4. Recall that the costs for drinkers include more than the collectively financed costs for smokers and sedentary people. Drinkers also impose costs related to drunk driving and other crimes.

5. We computed according to the HRA model that men who switch from a sedentary life-style to exercise will live 9 years longer, almost double the computed effects of not smoking!

6. By contrast with exercise, doctors may advise sick people to stop smoking, which would diminish our estimate of the link between smoking and health.

7. In the Paffenbarger study of Harvard alumni, the adjusted relative risk of death of current smokers was 1.76 as opposed to 1.31 for exercisers. Similarly, after adjusting for other factors Wiley (1981) found exercise about half as important as smoking and less important than nondrinking or heavy drinking in Alameda County (California) data.

8. If we were fitting a logit-type model, the multiplier for the probabilities of dying at older ages would be quite different from the multiplier at younger ages. The difference between 6 and 8 percent (Paffenbarger

et al., 1986) is 0.31 logit. Adding 0.31 logit to 60 percent brings us to only 67 percent, and even doubling risk at 6 percent (0.69 logit to go from 6 to 12 percent) only brings a 60 percent chance of death to 75 percent. See Breslow et al. (1983) and the Spasoff and McDowell (1987) study for more discussion of modeling issues.

9. For example, by age 75 the less healthy half of the sedentary group may have died, but only the least healthy 10 percent of the exerciser group may have died.

10. Suppose that the risk ratio of very active to sedentary is 3.0, instead of sedentary's having a heart disease mortality multiplier of 2.0 (two times average risk) and very active's having a multiplier of 0.7. With a change in underlying proportions, the multipliers should be about 1.2 and 0.4, respectively. Because 40 percent of the deaths of older males are due to heart disease, doubling this percentage in the current HRA gets to 140 percent of total risk: (100) [2(0.4) + 0.6]. Very actives at 0.7 end up at 88 percent of average total risk: (100) [0.7(0.4) + 0.6]. (The 0.6 is the fraction of deaths from other than heart disease.) Thus, the ratio of mortality due to all causes for sedentary as opposed to active persons is 140/88 = 1.59. A multiplier of 1.2 for sedentary persons leads to a total mortality ratio of 1.08, and a multiplier for very actives of 0.4 leads to a total mortality ratio of 0.76; the ratio between the two groups is then 1.08/0.76 = 1.42. In fact, Paffenbarger et al. (1986) had an adjusted ratio of 1.31, and Wiley had an adjusted ratio of 1.18.

11. To the extent that present exercise is a poor proxy for future exercise, the present gains (lower use of services) will not persist. Thus, our estimates could overstate the benefits. To the extent that there is an extra advantage from consistent exercise, our estimates understate the benefits of exercise.

12. The sedentary group is assumed to be 64 percent women. We have compared them to the same blend of exercising men and women, to avoid a confounding of the effects of gender with exercise. Both sedentary and exercising groups are shown in the table to cost the rest of society money (at a 5 percent discount rate), because women as a whole get more payments out of the system than they put in. This effect is mitigated somewhat by our excluding the physically limited from the exercise calculations (the sedentary are supposed to be those who could exercise but do not).

13. Most of these costs occur after retirement, so that on average only $700 of wage taxes is lost. But surveys have shown that most people are willing to pay many times their expected increase in earnings for safety, and most retired people do want to live. This component of costs may well be as much as $3,000 (Howard, 1978).

7. Conclusions, Limitations, and Implications

1. For a discussion of this issue see Shoven et al. (1989).
2. There are two main reasons why our results are so much lower than, for

example, the Office of Technology Assessment (OTA) estimate of $2.17 per pack. First, OTA estimated total costs including the costs of a shorter life, which we do not count because for the most part they are not external costs. Second, OTA compared this year's costs of dying, due presumably to past cigarette consumption, with this year's cigarette purchases—a comparison that avoids discounting the latency period.

3. The cost of innocent lives is 23 cents per actual ounce in our analyses.
4. If the underreporting is due to the systematic exclusion of skid row alcoholics and the homeless, as Polich and Orvis (1979) suggest, then there may be no bias in our estimates from using the reported consumption for the general population. We are unable to generalize our estimates to these highly relevant groups, however. They were effectively excluded by the HIE and NHIS sampling frames, both of which are based on a sample of dwelling units.
5. In principle, this issue could be settled by a randomized experiment on the results of an effective *exercise promotion* program.
6. We have only accounted for differential taxes to finance the costs that we consider, such as health insurance and social security.

Appendix A. Literature Review of the Costs of Smoking and Drinking

1. For more on this idea see Gori and Richter (1978).
2. If Berry and Boland had included the costs of lost production that they estimated were associated with these activities, approximately $12 billion would have been added to the $40 billion figure.
3. It is quite clear that there are costs at the margin associated with the crimes that these studies have characterized as "transfers." For example, many of us incur substantial costs in our efforts to protect ourselves and our property from burglars.

Appendix D. Statistical Methods

1. The data cover the first three years of the study. In the case of the group enrolled for five years in South Carolina, we used the last three years and ignored attrition during the first two years.

Appendix F. Excise Taxes and Demand

1. The neighboring-state price elasticity was estimated by including a variable in the model for the minimum real price of cigarettes in any neighboring state.
2. The variable used by Warner in his equation was the percentage of the adult population who resided in states that restrict smoking in public places. Interestingly, he refers to the measure as an index of the success of the nonsmokers' rights movement, reasoning that laws and regula-

tions limiting smoking in public places may "reflect opinion and coincident behavior change" rather than shape opinion and behavior.

Appendix H. A Note on the Alcohol Tax

1. We do not mean to imply that other actions that are more selective against problem drinking, such as stronger enforcement of drunk-driving laws, should not be undertaken. But we feel that any such actions, themselves likely to entail collective costs (such as higher taxes for more law enforcement), are unlikely to have the effect of lowering external costs enough to change our conclusion that the tax on alcohol should be raised.
2. In this case, we focus only on the losses from incorrect prices. In the case of no alcohol tax, we ignore the burden of external costs borne by society at large.
3. Pogue and Sgontz refer to light and heavy drinkers as nonabusers and abusers, respectively.
4. Work by Grossman and his colleagues suggests that beer consumption by young adults, a group prone to drink and drive, is price responsive. Phelps (1988) used their estimates to gauge the impact of a change in beer prices on driving fatalities.

Bibliography

Arnott, R., and J. Stiglitz. "Moral Hazard and Optimal Commodity Taxation." *Journal of Public Economics* 29 (1986): 1–24.

——— "Equilibrium in Competitive Insurance Markets—The Welfare Economics of Moral Hazard. I. Basic Analytics." Discussion Paper 465, Queens University, Kingston, Ontario. 1982.

Atkinson, A. B., and J. L. Townsend. "Economic Aspects of Reduced Smoking." *Lancet* (September 3, 1977): 492–494.

Baltagi, B. H., and D. Levin. "Estimating Dynamic Demand for Cigarettes Using Panel Data: The Effects of Bootlegging, Taxation and Advertising Reconsidered." *Review of Economics and Statistics* 68 (1986): 148–155.

Barzel, Y. "An Alternative Approach to the Analysis of Taxation." *Journal of Political Economy* 84 (1976): 1177–97.

Baumol, W. J., and D. F. Bradford. "Optimal Departures from Marginal Cost Pricing." *American Economic Review* 60 (1970): 265–283.

Berkow, R., ed. *The Merck Manual of Diagnosis and Therapy*. 14th ed. Rahway, N.J.: Merck, Sharp, and Dohme Research Laboratories, 1982.

Berry, R. E., and J. P. Boland. *The Economic Cost of Alcohol Abuse*. New York: Free Press, 1977.

Breslow, L., J. Fielding, A. A. Afifi, et al. "Risk Factor Update Project." Atlanta: Centers for Disease Control, 1985.

Brook, R. H., J. E. Ware, A. Davies-Avery, et al. "Overview of Adult Health Status Measures Fielded in RAND's Health Insurance Study." *Medical Care* (suppl.) 17 (1979): 1–131.

Brook, R. H., J. E. Ware, W. H. Rogers, et al. "Does Free Care Improve Adults' Health? Results from a Randomized Controlled Trial." *New England Journal of Medicine* 309 (1983): 1426–34.

Brook, R. H., J. E. Ware, W. H. Rogers, et al. *The Effect of Coinsurance on the Health of Adults*. Santa Monica: RAND Corporation, R-3055-HHS, 1984.

Brown, K. S., and W. Nabert. "Evaluation of the Existing Method for Calculating Health Hazard Appraisal Age." Final report on service contract between Non-Medical Use of Drugs; Directorate, Health Protection Branch, Health and Welfare, Canada; and University of Waterloo, Ontario. August 31, 1977.

Burdette, M. E., and M. Mohr. "Characteristics of Social Security Disability." Social Security Administration Publication No. 13-11947, Department of Health, Education and Welfare. December 1979.

Centers for Disease Control. *CDC Health Risk Appraisal User Manual.* Atlanta: CDC, 1984.

Chave, S. P. W., J. N. Morris, S. Moss, and A. M. Semmence. "Vigorous Exercise in Leisure Time and the Death Rate: A Study of Male Civil Servants." *Journal of Epidemiology and Community Health* 32 (1978): 239–243.

Clark, T. B. " 'Sin' Taxes Won't Be Spared by Capitol Hill Revenue Raisers." *National Journal* 16 (1984): 869–872.

———— "Tax and Price Support Issues Causing Tobacco Interests' Solidarity to Crack." *National Journal* 17 (1985): 2423–27.

Clasquin, L. A. *Mental Health, Dental Services, and Other Coverage in the Health Insurance Study.* Santa Monica: RAND Corporation, R-1216-OEO, 1973.

Clasquin, L. A., and M. E. Brown. *Rules of Operation for the Rand Health Insurance Study.* Santa Monica: RAND Corporation, R-1602-HEW, 1977.

Commission on Professional and Hospital Activities. *Hospital Adaptation of ICDA.* 2nd ed. Ann Arbor: Commission on Professional and Hospital Activities, 1973.

Conceptualization and Measurement of Physiologic Health for Adults (series). Santa Monica: RAND Corporation, R-2262-HHS, various dates.

Cook, P. J. "The Effect of Liquor Taxes on Drinking, Cirrhosis, and Auto Accidents." In M. H. Moore and D. R. Gerstein, eds. *Alcohol and Public Policy: Beyond the Shadow of Prohibition,* pp. 255–285. Washington, D.C.: National Academy Press, 1981.

Cook, P. J., and G. Tauchen. "The Effect of Liquor Taxes on Heavy Drinking." *Bell Journal of Economics* 13 (1982): 379–390.

Cruze, A. M., H. J. Harwood, P. L. Kristiansen, et al. *Economic Costs to Society of Alcohol and Drug Abuse and Mental Illness.* Research Triangle Park, N.C.: Research Triangle Institute, 1981.

Davies, A. R., and J. E. Ware. *Measuring Health Perception in the Health Insurance Experiment.* Santa Monica: RAND Corporation, R-2711-HHS, 1981.

Distilled Spirits Council of the United States. *Public Revenues from Alcohol Beverages.* Washington, D.C.: Distilled Spirits Council, 1985.

Duffy, M. "The Demand for Alcoholic Drink in the United Kingdom, 1963–1978." *Applied Economics* (1983): 125–140.

Eisen, M., C. A. Donald, J. E. Ware, and R. H. Brook. *Conceptualization and Measurement of Health for Children in the Health Insurance Study.* Santa Monica: RAND Corporation, R-2313-HEW, 1980.

Farrell, P., and V. R. Fuchs. "Schooling and Health: The Cigarette Connection." *Journal of Health Economics* 1 (1982): 217–230.

Forbes, W. F., and M. E. Thompson. "Estimating the Health Care Costs of Smokers." *Canadian Journal of Public Health* 74 (1983): 181–190.

Fuchs, V. R. "Time Preference and Health: An Explanatory Study." In V. R. Fuchs, ed., *Economic Aspects of Health,* pp. 93–120. Chicago: National Bureau of Economic Research, 1982.

Fujii, E. T. "The Demand for Cigarettes: Further Empirical Evidence and Its Implications for Public Policy." *Applied Economics* 12 (1980): 479–489.

Gori, G. B., and B. J. Richter. "Macroeconomics of Disease Prevention in the United States." *Science* 200 (1978): 1124–30.

Grossman, M. "Government and Health Outcomes." *American Economic Review* 72 (1982): 191–195.

Grossman, M., D. Coate, and G. M. Arluck. *Advances in Substance Abuse.* suppl. 1, p. 169, 1987.

Hacker, G. A. "Taxing Booze for Health and Wealth." *Journal of Policy Analysis and Management* 6 (1987): 701–708.

Hamilton, J. L. "The Demand for Cigarettes: Advertising, the Health Scare, and the Cigarette Advertising Ban." *Review of Economics and Statistics* 54 (1972): 401–411.

Harris, J. E. "Increasing the Federal Excise Tax on Cigarettes." *Journal of Health Economics* 1 (1982): 117–120.

Harwood, H. J., D. M. Napolitano, P. L. Kristiansen, et al. *Economic Costs to Society of Alcohol and Drug Abuse and Mental Illness.* Research Triangle Park, N.C.: Research Triangle Institute, 1984.

Haskell, W. L. "Exercise-Induced Changes in Plasma Lipids and Lipoproteins." *Preventive Medicine* 13 (1984): 23–26.

Hogarty, T. F., and K. G. Elzinga. "The Demand for Beer." *Review of Economics and Statistics* 54 (1972): 195–198.

Howard, R. A. "Life and Death Decision Analysis." In *Proceedings: Second Lawrence Symposium on Systems and Decision Analysis.* Berkeley: University of California, 1978.

Huber, P. J. "The Behavior of Maximum Likelihood Estimates under Nonstandard Conditions." *Proceedings of the Fifth Berkeley Symposium on Mathematical Statistics and Probability.* Vol. 1, pp. 221–233, 1967.

Institute for the Study of Smoking Behavior and Policy. *The Cigarette Excise Tax.* Cambridge, Mass.: Harvard University, 1985.

Johnson, J. A., and E. H. Oksanen. "Estimation of Demand for Alcoholic Beverages in Canada from Pooled Time Series and Cross Sections." *Review of Economics and Statistics* 59 (1977): 113–118.

Johnson, L. W. "Alternative Econometric Estimates of the Effect of Advertising on the Demand for Alcoholic Beverages in the United Kingdom." *International Journal of Advertising* 4 (1985): 19–25.

Johnson, N. L., and S. Kotz. *Discrete Distribution.* Boston: Houghton Mifflin, 1969.

Johnson, P. R. *The Economics of the Tobacco Industry.* New York: Praeger, 1984.

Johnson, T. R. "Additional Evidence on the Effects of Alternative Taxes on Cigarette Prices." *Journal of Political Economy* 86 (1978): 325–328.

Keeler, E. B., and S. Cretin. "Discounting of Life-Saving and Nonmonetary Effects." *Management Science* 29 (1983): 300–306.

Keeler, E. B., J. P. Newhouse, and C. E. Phelps. "Deductibles and the Demand for Medical Care Services: The Theory of a Consumer Facing a Variable Price Schedule under Uncertainty." *Econometrica* 45 (1977): 641–656.

Keeler, E. B., J. E. Rolph, N. Duan, et al. *The Demand for Episodes of Medical Services: Interim Results from the Health Insurance Experiment*. Santa Monica: RAND Corporation, R-2829-HHS, 1982.

Keeler, E. B., J. L. Buchanan, J. E. Rolph, et al. *The Demand for Episodes of Medical Treatment in the Health Insurance Experiment*. Santa Monica: RAND Corporation, R-3454-HHS, 1988.

Keeler, E. B., W. G. Manning, J. P. Newhouse, et al. "The External Costs of a Sedentary Life-Style." *American Journal of Public Health* 79 (1989): 975–980.

Keesey, J., E. B. Keeler, and W. Fowler. *The Episodes-of-Illness Processing System*. Santa Monica: RAND Corporation, N-1745-1-HHS, 1985.

Koplan, J. P., D. S. Siscovick, and G. M. Goldbaum. "The Risks of Exercise: A Public Health View of Injuries and Hazards." *Public Health Reports* 100 (1985): 189–195.

Kottke, T. E., C. J. Caspersen, and C. S. Hill. "Exercise in the Management and Rehabilitation of Selected Chronic Diseases." *Preventive Medicine* 13 (1984): 47–65.

Kristein, M. M. "How Much Can Business Expect to Profit from Smoking Cessation?" *Preventive Medicine* 12 (1983): 358–381.

Laughhunn, D. J., and H. L. Lyon. "The Feasibility of Tax Induced Price Increases as a Deterrent to Cigarette Consumption." *Journal of Business Administration* 3 (1971): 27–35.

Leu, R. E. "Anti-Smoking Publicity, Taxation, and the Demand for Cigarettes." *Journal of Health Economics* 3 (1984): 101–116.

Leu, R. E., and T. Schaub. "Does Smoking Increase Medical Care Expenditure?" *Social Science and Medicine* 17 (1983): 1907–14.

——— "More on the Impact of Smoking on Medical Care Expenditures." *Social Science and Medicine* 21 (1985): 825–827.

Levit, K. R., H. Lazenby, D. R. Waldo, and L. M. Davidoff. "National Health Expenditures, 1984." *Health Care Financing Review* 7 (1985): 1–35.

Levy, D., and N. Sheflin. "The Demand for Alcoholic Beverages: An Aggregate Time-Series Analysis." *Journal of Public Policy and Marketing* 4 (1985): 47–54.

Lewit, E. M., and D. Coate. "The Potential for Using Excise Taxes to Reduce Smoking." *Journal of Health Economics* 1 (1982): 121–145.

Lewit, E. M., D. Coate, and M. Grossman. "The Effects of Government Regulation on Teenage Smoking." *Journal of Law and Economics* 24 (1981): 545–570.

Luce, B. R., and S. O. Schweitzer. "Smoking and Alcohol Abuse: A Comparison of Their Economic Consequences." *New England Journal of Medicine* 198 (1978): 569–571.

Lyon, H. L., and J. L. Simon. "Price Elasticity of Demand for Cigarettes in the United States." *American Journal of Agricultural Economics* 50 (1968): 881–893.

Manning, W. G., J. P. Newhouse, and J. E. Ware. *The Status of Health in Demand Estimation: Beyond Excellent, Good, Fair, and Poor*. Santa Monica: RAND Corporation, R-2696-1-HHS, 1981.

Manning, W. G., A. Leibowitz, G. A. Goldberg, et al. "A Controlled Trial of the Effect of a Prepaid Group Practice on Use of Services." *New England Journal of Medicine* 310 (1984): 1505–10.

Manning, W. G., J. P. Newhouse, N. Duan, et al. *Health Insurance and the Demand for Medical Care: Evidence from a Randomized Experiment*. Santa Monica: RAND Corporation, R-3476-HHS, 1986. A shorter version is available in *American Economic Review* 77 (1987): 251–257.

Manning, W. G., E. B. Keeler, J. P. Newhouse, et al. "The Taxes of Sin: Do Smokers and Drinkers Pay Their Way?" *Journal of the American Medical Association* 261 (1989): 1604–9.

Marquis, M. S. *Characteristics of Health Insurance Coverage: Descriptive and Methodological Findings from the Health Insurance Experiment*. Santa Monica: RAND Corporation, N-2503-HHS, 1986.

McGuinness, T. "An Econometric Analysis of Total Demand for Alcoholic Beverages in the U.K., 1956–1975." *Journal of Industrial Economics* 29 (1980): 85–109.

Miller, T. R. *Narrowing the Plausible Range around the Value of Life*. Washington, D.C.: Urban Institute, 1989.

Mishan, E. J. "Evaluation of Life and Limb: A Theoretical Approach." *Journal of Political Economy* 79 (1971): 687–705.

────── *Cost-Benefit Analysis*. 4th ed., Winchester, Mass.: Unwin Hyman, 1988.

Morris, C. N. "A Finite Selection Model for Experimental Design of the Health Insurance Study." *Journal of Econometrics* 11 (1979): 43–61.

Mosher, J. F., and D. E. Beauchamp. "Justifying Alcohol Taxes to Public Officials." *Journal of Public Health Policy* (December 1983): 422–439.

Munnell, A. H. "Paying for the Medicare Program." *Journal of Health Politics, Policy, and Law* 10 (1985): 489–511.

National Research Council. *Environmental Tobacco Smoke: Measuring Exposures and Assessing Health Effects*. Washington, D.C.: National Academy Press, 1986.

Newhouse, J. P. "A Design for a Health Insurance Experiment." *Inquiry* 11 (1974): 5–27.

Newhouse, J. P., et al. "Measurement Issues in the Second Generation of Social Experiments: The Health Insurance Study." *Journal of Econometrics* 11 (1979): pp. 117–130.

Niskanen, W. A. *The Demand for Alcoholic Beverages*. Santa Monica: RAND Corporation, P-2583, 1962.

Oakes, T. W., G. D. Friedman, C. S. Seltzer, et al. "Health Service Utilization by Smokers and Non-smokers." *Medical Care* 12 (1974): 958–966.

Office of Technology Assessment, U.S. Congress. "Smoking-Related Deaths and Financial Costs," OTA Staff Memorandum. 1985.

────── *Neonatal Intensive Care for Low Birthweight Infants: Costs and Effectiveness*. Washington, D.C.: OTA, HCS-38, 1987.

O'Hagan, J. W. "The Rationale for Special Taxes on Alcohol: A Critique." *British Tax Review* 6 (1983): 370–380.

Ornstein, S. I., and D. Levy. "Price and Income Elasticities of Demand for

Alcoholic Beverages." In M. Galanter, ed., *Recent Developments in Alcoholism*, vol. 1, pp. 303–345. New York: Plenum Press, 1983.

Oster, G., G. A. Colditz, and N. L. Kelly. *The Economic Costs of Smoking and Benefits of Quitting*. Lexington, Mass.: D.C. Heath, 1984.

Paffenbarger, R. S., and R. T. Hyde. "Exercise in the Prevention of Coronary Heart Disease." *Preventive Medicine* 13 (1984): 3–22.

—— Letter. *New England Journal of Medicine* 325 (1986): 400–401.

Paffenbarger, R. S., R. T. Hyde, A. L. Wing, and C. C. Hsieh. "Physical Activity, All-Cause Mortality, and Longevity of College Alumni." *New England Journal of Medicine* 314 (1986): 605–613.

Pauly, M. V. "The Economics of Moral Hazard." *American Economic Review* 58 (1968): 231–237.

—— *Medical Care at Public Expense*. New York: Praeger, 1971.

Pechman, J. A. *Federal Tax Policy*. 3rd ed. Washington, D.C.: Brookings Institution, 1977.

Pernanen, K. "Validity of Survey Data on Alcohol Use." In R. J. Gibbins et al., eds., *Research Advances in Alcohol and Drug Problems*, vol. 1, pp. 335–374. New York: John Wiley and Sons, 1974.

Phelps, C. E. "Death and Taxes: An Opportunity for Substitution." *Journal of Health Economics* 7 (1988): 1–24.

Pogue, T. F., and L. G. Sgontz. "Taxing to Control Social Cost: The Case of Alcohol." *American Economic Review* 79 (1989): 235–243.

Polich, J. M., and B. R. Orvis. *Alcohol Problems: Patterns and Prevalence in the U.S. Air Force*. Santa Monica: RAND Corporation, R-2308-AF, 1979.

Powell, K. E., P. D. Thompson, C. J. Caspersen, and J. S. Kendrick. "Physical Activity and the Incidence of Coronary Heart Disease." *Annual Review of Public Health* 8 (1987): 253–287.

Price, D. N. "Cash Benefits for Short-Term Sickness: Thirty-Five Years of Data, 1948–1983." *Social Security Bulletin* 49 (1986): 5–38.

Ramsey, F. "A Contribution to the Theory of Taxation." *Economic Journal* 37 (1927): 47–61.

Rice, D. P., and T. A. Hodgson. "Economic Costs of Smoking: An Analysis of Data for the United States." Paper presented at the Allied Social Science Association annual meeting, San Francisco, 1983.

Rice, D. P., T. A. Hodgson, et al. "The Economic Costs of the Health Effects of Smoking, 1984." *Milbank Memorial Quarterly* 64 (1986): 489–548.

Rice, D. P., E. J. MacKenzie, et al. *Cost of Injury in the United States: A Report to Congress*. San Francisco: Institute for Health and Aging, University of California, 1989.

Richter, E. A., and S. H. Schneider. "Diabetes and Exercise." *American Journal of Medicine* 70 (1981): 201–209.

Robbins, L. C., and J. H. Hall. *How to Practice Prospective Medicine*. Indianapolis: Methodist Hospital of Indiana, 1970.

Rock, S. M. "Measurement of Tax Progressivity: Application." *Public Finance Quarterly* 11 (1983): 109–120.

Rogers, W. H. "Analyzing Complex Survey Data." Unpublished. RAND Corporation, Santa Monica, 1983.

Rogers, W. H., and J. P. Newhouse. "Measuring Unfiled Claims in the Health Insurance Experiment." In L. Burstein, H. E. Freeman, and P. H. Rossi, eds., *Collecting Evaluation Data: Problems and Solutions*, pp. 121–133. Beverly Hills: Sage, 1985.

Rosen, S. "The Value of Changes in Life Expectancy." *Journal of Risk and Uncertainty* 1 (1988): 285–304.

Schelling, T. C. "The Life You Save May Be Your Own." In S. B. Chase, ed., *Problems in Public Expenditure Analysis*. Washington, D.C.: Brookings Institution, 1968.

Schoenbach, V. J., E. H. Wagner, and J. M. Karon. "The Use of Epidemiologic Data for Personal Risk Assessment in Health Hazard/Health Risk Appraisal Programs." *Journal of Chronic Diseases* 36 (1983): 625–638.

Schoenborn, C. A., and B. H. Cohen. "Trends in Smoking, Alcohol Consumption, and Other Health Practices among U.S. Adults, 1977 and 1983." *Advance Data*, USDHHS no. 118, 1986.

Searle, S. R. *Linear Models*. New York: John Wiley and Sons, 1971.

Shepard, D. S., and R. J. Zeckhauser. "Survival Versus Consumption." *Management Science* 30 (1984): 423–439.

Shoven, J. B., J. O. Sundberg, and J. P. Bunker. "The Social Security Cost of Smoking." In D. A. Wise, ed., *The Economics of Aging*. Chicago: University of Chicago Press, 1989.

Simon, H. B. "The Immunology of Exercise." *Journal of the American Medical Association* 252 (1984): 2735–38.

Siscovick, D. S., R. E. LaPorte, and J. M. Newman. "The Disease-Specific Benefits and Risks of Physical Activity and Exercise." *Public Health Reports* 100 (1985): 180–188.

Smith, K. W., S. M. McKinlay, and B. D. Thorington. "The Validity of Health Appraisal Instruments for Assessing Coronary Heart Disease Risk." *American Journal of Public Health* 77 (1987): 419–424.

Spasoff, R. A., and I. W. McDowell. "Potential Limitations of Data and Methods in Health Risk Appraisal: Risk Factor Selection and Measurement." *Health Services Research* 22 (1987): 467–498.

Stewart, A., J. E. Ware, Jr., and R. H. Brook. "The Meaning of Health: Understanding Functional Limitations." *Medical Care* 15 (1977): 939–952.

—— *Construction and Scoring of Aggregate Functional Status Indexes*. Vol. 1. Santa Monica: RAND Corporation, R-2551-HHS, 1981a.

—— "Advances in the Measurement of Function Status: Construction of Aggregate Indexes." *Medical Care* 19 (1981b): 473–488.

Stewart, A. L., J. E. Ware, Jr., R. H. Brook, and A. Davies-Avery. *Conceptualization and Measurement of Health for Adults in the Health Insurance Study*. Vol. 2, *Physical Health in Terms of Functioning*. Santa Monica: RAND Corporation, R-1987/2-HEW, 1978.

Stoddart, G. L., R. J. Labelle, M. L. Barer, and R. G. Evans. "Tobacco Taxes and Health Care Costs: Do Canadian Smokers Pay Their Way?" *Journal of Health Economics* 5 (1986): 63–80.

Sumner, D. A., and J. M. Alston. "The Impact of Removal of Price Supports and Supply Controls for Tobacco in the United States." *Research in Domestic and International Agribusiness Management* 5 (1984): 107–164.

Sumner, M. T., and R. Ward. "Tax Changes and Cigarette Prices." *Journal of Political Economy* 89 (1981): 1261–65.

Taylor, L. D. "The Demand for Electricity: A Survey." *Bell Journal of Economics* 6 (1975): 74–110.

Tobacco Institute. *The Tax Burden on Tobacco*, vol. 22, Washington, D.C.: Tobacco Institute, 1987.

Toder, E. J. "Issues in the Taxation of Cigarettes." In Institute for the Study of Smoking Behavior and Policy, *The Cigarette Excise Tax*, pp. 65–87. Cambridge, Mass.: Harvard University, 1985.

U.S. Department of Commerce. *Historical Statistics of the United States, Colonial Times to 1970.* Bicentennial ed., pt. 1. Washington, D.C.: Bureau of the Census, 1975a.

―――― *Historical Statistics of the United States, 1975.* Series Y567-589. Washington, D.C.: Bureau of the Census, 1975b.

―――― *Statistical Abstract of the United States: 1982–83.* 103rd ed. Washington, D.C.: Bureau of the Census, 1982.

―――― *Statistical Abstract of the United States: 1985.* 105th ed. Washington, D.C.: Bureau of the Census, 1984.

―――― "Money Income of Households, Families, and Persons in the United States: 1984." In *Current Population Reports, Consumer Income.* Series P.60, no. 151, pp. 165–170. Washington, D.C.: Bureau of the Census, 1986.

―――― *Statistical Abstract of the United States: 1988.* 108th ed. Washington, D.C.: Bureau of the Census, 1988.

―――― *Statistical Abstract of the United States: 1989.* 109th ed. Washington, D.C.: Bureau of the Census, 1989.

U.S. Department of Health, Education and Welfare. *Smoking and Health: A Report of the Surgeon General.* DHEW Publication no. (PHS)79-50066. Washington, D.C.: Public Health Service, 1979.

U.S. Department of Health and Human Services. *Fourth Special Report to the U.S. Congress on Alcohol and Health from the Secretary of Health and Human Services.* Washington, D.C.: Public Health Service, 1981.

―――― *The Health Consequences of Smoking, Cancer: A Report of the Surgeon General.* DHHS Publication no. (PHS)82-50179. Washington, D.C.: Public Health Service, 1982.

―――― *Fifth Special Report to the U.S. Congress on Alcohol and Health from the Secretary of Health and Human Services.* Washington, D.C.: Public Health Service, 1983a.

―――― *The Health Consequences of Smoking, Cardiovascular Disease: A Report of the Surgeon General.* DHHS Publication no. (PHS)84-50204. Washington, D.C.: Public Health Service, 1983b.

―――― *Vital Statistics of the United States, 1980.* Hyattsville, Md.: National Center for Health Statistics, 1984a.

―――― *The Health Consequences of Smoking, Chronic Obstructive Lung Disease: A Report of the Surgeon General.* Washington, D.C.: Public Health Service, 1984b.

——— *The Health Consequences of Involuntary Smoking: A Report of the Surgeon General*. Washington, D.C.: Public Health Service, 1986.

——— *Sixth Special Report to the U.S. Congress on Alcohol and Health from the Secretary of Health and Human Services*. DHHS Publication no. (ADM)87-1519. Washington, D.C.: Public Health Service, 1987.

——— *Surgeon General's Workshop on Drunk Driving: Proceedings*. Washington, D.C.: Public Health Service, 1989.

U.S. Department of Labor, Bureau of Labor Statistics. "Employee Benefits in Medium and Large Firms." *BLS Bulletin* 2237 (1985).

U.S. Department of Transportation. "Drunk Driving Facts." Washington, D.C.: National Highway Traffic Safety Administration, 1986. Mimeographed.

Van Nostrand, J. F. V., A. Zappolo, E. Hing, et al. *The National Nursing Home Survey, 1977*. DHEW Publication no. (PHS)79-1794. Hyattsville, Md.: Department of Health, Education and Welfare, 1979.

Veit, C. T., and J. E. Ware. "The Structure of Psychological Distress and Well-Being in General Populations." *Journal of Consulting and Clinical Psychology* 51 (1983): 703–742.

Vogt, T. M., and S. O. Schweitzer. "Medical Costs of Cigarette Smoking in a Health Maintenance Organization." *American Journal of Epidemiology* 122 (1985): 1060–66.

Waldo, D., and H. C. Lazenby. "Demographic Characteristics and Health Care Use and Expenditures by the Aged in the United States, 1977–1984." *Health Care Financing Review* 6 (1984): 1–29.

Ware, J. E. "Scales for Measuring General Health Perceptions." *Health Services Research* 11 (1976): 596–619.

Ware, J. E., S. A. Johnston, A. Davies-Avery, and R. H. Brook. *Conceptualization and Measurement of Health for Adults in the Health Insurance Study*. Vol. 3, *Mental Health*. R-1987/3-HEW. Santa Monica: RAND Corporation, 1979.

Ware, J. E., S. A. Johnston, A. Davies-Avery, and R. H. Brook. *Conceptualization and Measurement of Health for Adults in the Health Insurance Study*. Vol. 3, *Mental Health*. R-1987/3-HEW. Santa Monica: RAND Corporation, 1979.

Ware, J. E., A. Davies-Avery, and R. H. Brook. *Conceptualization and Measurement of Health for Adults in the Health Insurance Study*. Vol. 6, *Analysis of Relationships among Health Status Measures*. R-1987/6-HEW. Santa Monica: RAND Corporation, 1980b.

Ware, J. E., C. T. Veit, and C. A. Donald. *Refinements in the Measurement of Mental Health for Adults in the Health Insurance Study*. Santa Monica: RAND Corporation, forthcoming.

Warner, K. E. "Possible Increases in the Underreporting of Cigarette Consumption." *Journal of the American Statistical Association* 73 (1978): 314–318.

——— "Cigarette Smoking in the 1970's: The Impact of the Antismoking Campaigns on Consumption." *Science* 211 (1981): 729–731.

——— "Cigarette Taxation: Doing Good by Doing Well." *Journal of Public Health Policy* 5 (1984): 312–319.

———— *Selling Smoke: Cigarette Advertising and Public Health.* Washington, D.C.: American Public Health Association, 1986.

Wasserman, J. *Excise Taxes, Regulation, and the Demand for Cigarettes.* Santa Monica: RAND Corporation, P-7498-RGS, 1988.

Wasserman, J., W. G. Manning, J. P. Newhouse, and J. D. Winkler. "The Effects of Excise Taxes and Regulations on Cigarette Smoking." *Journal of Health Economics* 10 (1991): 43–64.

Wiley, J. A. "Predictive Risk Factors Do Predict Life Events." In L. A. Miller, ed., *Proceedings of the Sixteenth Annual Meeting of the Society of Prospective Medicine*, pp. 75–79. Bethesda, Md., 1981.

Williams, A. W., J. E. Ware, and C. A. Donald. "A Model of Mental Health, Life Events, and Social Supports Applicable to General Populations." *Journal of Health and Social Behavior* 22 (1981): 324–336.

Witt, S. F., and C. L. Pass. "Forecasting Cigarette Consumption: The Causal Model Approach." *International Journal of Social Economics* 10 (1983): 18–33.

Wright, V. B. "Will Quitting Smoking Help Medicare Solve Its Financial Problems?" *Inquiry* 23 (1986): 76–82.

Young, T. "The Demand for Cigarettes: Alternative Specifications of Fujii's Model." *Applied Economics* 15 (1983): 203–211.

Index

Selected RAND Books

Alexiev, Alexander R., and S. Enders Wimbush, eds. *Ethnic Minorities in the Red Army: Asset or Liability?* Boulder, Colo.: Westview Press, 1988.

Builder, Carl H. *The Masks of War: American Military Styles in Strategy and Analysis.* Baltimore: Johns Hopkins University Press, 1989.

Chassin, Mark R., et al. *The Appropriateness of Selected Medical and Surgical Procedures: Relationship to Geographical Variations.* Ann Arbor, Mich.: Health Administration Press, 1989.

Dorfman, Robert, Paul A. Samuelson, and Robert M. Solow. *Linear Programming and Economic Analysis.* New York: McGraw-Hill Book Company, 1958. Reprinted New York: Dover Publications, 1987.

Fainsod, Merle. *Smolensk under Soviet Rule.* Cambridge, Mass.: Harvard University Press, 1958. Reprinted Boston: Unwin Hyman, 1989.

Gale, David. *The Theory of Linear Economic Models.* New York: McGraw-Hill Book Company, 1960. Reprinted Chicago: University of Chicago Press, 1989.

Gustafson, Thane. *Crisis amid Plenty: The Politics of Oil and Gas and the Evolution of Energy Policy in the Soviet Union since 1917.* Princeton, N.J.: Princeton University Press, 1989.

Hosmer, Stephen T. *Constraints on U.S. Strategy in Third World Conflicts.* New York: Taylor & Francis, 1987.

Kanouse, David E., et al. *Changing Medical Practice through Technology Assessment: An Evaluation of the NIH Consensus Development Program.* Ann Arbor, Mich.: Health Administration Press, 1989.

Korbonski, Andrzej, and Francis Fukuyama, eds. *The Soviet Union and the Third World: The Last Three Decades.* Ithaca, N.Y.: Cornell University Press, 1987.

Levine, Robert A. *Still the Arms Debate.* Brookfield, Vt., and Oldershot, England: Gower Publishing Co., 1990.

Morrison, Peter A., ed. *A Taste of the Country: A Collection of Calvin Beale's Writings.* University Park: Pennsylvania State University Press, 1990.

Nerlich, Uwe, and James A. Thomson, eds. *Conventional Arms Control and the Security of Europe.* Boulder, Colo.: Westview Press, 1988.

Quade, Edward S., rev. Grace M. Carter. *Analysis for Public Decisions,* 3rd ed. New York: Elsevier Science Publishing Company, 1989.

Ross, Randy L. *Government and the Private Sector: Who Should Do What?* New York: Taylor & Francis, 1988.

Wolf, Charles, Jr. *Markets or Governments: Choosing between Imperfect Alternatives.* Cambridge, Mass.: MIT Press, 1988.